*Marginality and Dissent in
Twentieth-Century American Sociology*

SUNY Series in Deviance and Social Control
Ronald A. Farrell, editor

Marginality and Dissent in Twentieth-Century American Sociology

The Case of Elizabeth Briant Lee and Alfred McClung Lee

John F. Galliher
University of Missouri-Columbia

James M. Galliher
University of Missouri-Kansas City

STATE UNIVERSITY OF NEW YORK PRESS

Published by
State University of New York Press, Albany

© 1995 State University of New York

For information address State University of New York Press, State University Plaza, Albany, NY 12246

Production by Laura Starrett
Marketing by Fran Keneston

Library of Congress Cataloging in Publication Date

10 9 8 7 6 5 4 3 2 1

Galliher, John F.
    Marginality and dissent in the twentieth century : the case of
Elizabeth Briant Lee and Alfred McClung Lee / John F. Galliher,
James M. Galliher.
        p. cm.—(SUNY series in deviance and social control)
    Includes bibliographical references and index.
    ISBN 0-7914-2483-9 : $54.50.—ISBN 0-7914-2484-7
(pbk.) : $17.95
    1. Lee, Elizabeth Briant.   2. Lee, Alfred Mcclung, 1906–
3. Sociologists—United States—Biography.   4. Clinical sociology—
M., 1946–   .   III. Title.   IV. Series.
HM22.U6L424   1995
301'.092'2—dc20   94-29612
                                                                      CIP

Contents

To Tommy

Alfred McClung Lee

Elizabeth Briant Lee

Introduction

A fundamental axiom among sociologists is that all human enterprise is influenced by its environment. And there is no doubt that this generalization applies to the activities of sociologists themselves. Buxton and Turner have noted that the environments or "audiences" available for academic sociologists include both the educated public and the foundations, both public and private, that make funds available for sociological research.[1] Earlier in this century, and during the last, the educated public could be counted on both for large-scale purchase of social science books, but also frequently for paid attendance at public lectures. Early twentieth-century sociologists including Charles Elwood, Pitirim Sorokin, Harry Elmer Barnes, Robert Lynd, David Riesman, and C. Wright Mills wrote books that by intention or accident had genuine public appeal. Arguably, *The Lonely Crowd*[2] by Riesman, and *Middletown*[3] by Robert and Helen Lynd, are the best known examples of such widely popular social science. Recent illustrations of such mass appeal are more difficult to locate. *Habits of the Heart*[4] by Bellah *et al.* is the only clear recent example Buxton and Turner cite of such an appeal. After WWII a campaign was waged against all "popular" sociological writing. This campaign was aided by sociologists who were themselves foundation officials. They argued that those appealing to a popular audience were given too much credit and that a better gauge of merit was a solely "professional" audience. This transition was in turn made possible by the availability of alternative sources of financial support from foundations.[5]

The careers of Betty and Al Lee began in the 1930s and thus span the decades during which this shift in audience has taken place. Caught in a profession undergoing such changes, the Lees are noteworthy for their attempts to find a means to preserve the legacy of direct appeals to an educated public and at the same time to recognize that some type of professional audience was assuming greater importance in the discipline and thus could not be ignored. The Lees were not content to address existing audiences; they attempted also to mobilize audiences both among the general public and among social science professionals. Throughout this book we will see the ways in which their activities have blurred the distinction between a public and professional social science. In doing so the Lees were for nearly five decades at the center of a maelstrom of professional controversy, often working at tremendous odds at the margins of the profession representing the political left in American social science.

We will demonstrate how the careers of the Lees served at the least as an implicit and sometimes as an explicit critique of contemporary sociology. In the chapters that follow we will explore the nature of their impact upon the substance, methods, goals and organization of mainstream sociology. While the Lees' careers were marked by shortcomings and failures, and while in only a very few instances can it be demonstrated that they altered standard practice in academic culture, we will demonstrate that contemporary sociology is hard to imagine without their efforts. The primary significance of their contribution is that the questions they raised survive as alternatives to dominant themes in sociology. This biography aims to move beyond description to intellectual history and thereby provide a sociology of sociology, with analysis of the organization, operation and change of both the discipline and the profession.

In writing this biography we soon discovered that it was much easier to uncover existing documents concerning Al Lee, his life, and his career than it was to do the same for his wife Betty. Al Lee was always a public person. Over a period of approximately 35 years he held full-time faculty positions at six different American universities. Many of his ideas found their way into print in the numerous books and articles he published. On the other hand, Betty Lee only rarely held a full-time faculty position and expressed herself in print less frequently. After collecting reams of existing materials in the preparation of this joint biography we discovered that the great majority of the information dealt exclusively with Al Lee—making a truly joint biography based on these materials impossible. Speaking of Betty Lee and other professional women of her generation, Deutscher has expressed doubts that "one will ever know the extent of their influence on their more prominent husbands. . . . [T]he hope [is] that those with better memories or better documentation will really set the record straight."[6] Thus, for the joint biography to achieve some balance and to "set the record straight," we necessarily resorted to a different methodology by supplementing existing documentation to learn about most details of Betty's life and career.

For not totally dissimilar reasons, the British writer Henry Mayhew (1812–1887) found that the English lower classes were ignored by British history.[7] To remedy this situation Mayhew produced oral histories by approaching the poor themselves for information.

Mayhew was a chronicler of the lives of the anonymous, using their "ordinary language"[8] to place their behaviors in the proper social and economic context to "save them from oblivion."[9] Mayhew believed that the statements of these relatively powerless people were worthy of publishing, and that such oral histories would "demonstrate the hidden virtues of the lower classes."[10] Like the poor, women traditionally have been ignored by those studying the history of ideas. Dye writes: "Until recently, women have been neither the subjects nor the objects of historical inquiry: they have not been treated as historical actors in their own right nor have their lives been the objects of historical scrutiny. Most historians have written history as if women did not exist or, at best, as if they were some form of rare creature who very occasionally appeared in the background of the historical landscape."[11] Therefore, like Mayhew's use of oral histories to understand the lives of the poor, this joint biography will use the oral history technique to further our understanding of Betty Lee.

Added to this technique of data collection is the analytic approach referred to as revisionist history. Revisionist history typically takes as its primary goal a new and increased understanding of power and oppression.[12] As any grade or high-school student knows, the history of the world typically is the history of people important in their day, including generals, kings, and presidents. The lives of the less powerful and important typically are not grist for the mill of history, for no records of their works and accomplishments are compiled and stored to be gone over by future generations of historians. Given the long history of sexual inequality, it should not be surprising that examples of those ignored by history show a decided bias toward males and against females. Thus Rowbotham advises: "The problem of uncovering this hidden experience can be approached in more recent periods simply by talking to older people. . . . Oral history could be an important means of discovering what women thought and felt in the immediate past."[13] The use of oral history is an essential element in this revisionist history—to understand more about one woman's experiences. To this end, Betty Lee was asked to serve as a narrator of many of the events described in the following chapters.

Biographies are important undertakings for several reasons. Turner argues: "The history of sociology is important *for* sociology. Exposing and questioning current assumptions and practices is one contribution history makes to sociology. But there is another crucial matter: the perceptions of the educated *public* of sociology and of its significance. American sociologists have had an important historical role in many aspects of American life and throughout the world."[14] But to the extent that this history is not documented, the legacy will be lost. A special advantage in tracing the lives and careers of scholars such as the Lees, who have practiced their profession through six decades, is that in following their careers we also can increase our understanding of the historical development of modern sociology and thereby move beyond personal biography to intellectual history. Our history of the lives and careers of the Lees is intentionally revisionist, in that it attempts to evaluate the Lees from their own perspectives as citizens and scholars.

In selecting the subjects for biographies, Horowitz noted that sociology lacks consensus regarding the truly important figures in sociology.[15] Horowitz advised that a first question to ask involves the quality of the subject's ideas.[16] Elsewhere Horowitz has noted that whether scholars merit a book written about their careers depends not only upon the quality of their writing but also upon the quality of their students.[17] The quality of Al and Betty's students involves unusual problems in measurement, because the majority of Al Lee's career was spent at institutions having either no Ph.D. program or at most a weak Ph.D. program. Thus many of his most gifted students were of necessity sent elsewhere to complete their graduate training. Betty never held a full-time, tenure-track position. Just as it is typically men who are remembered in written history, intellectual biographies typically are limited to scholars who have spent the bulk of their careers at elite institutions. Limiting biography to those at elite universities is no less distorting to intellectual history than is limiting such analysis to men. Surely sociologists should know better than most that one gets a different view of the academy from the top down than from the bottom up. Correspondingly, in the chapters that follow it will become clear that Betty and Al Lee attempted to craft what might be called a populist sociology; one with no ties to elite universities or funding agencies, but rather one that would benefit the average man and woman on the street.

Betty and Al Lee were consulted in many phases of the research and have been instrumental in providing massive amounts of existing documentation from their own files. They also recommended many other sources of information, including specific library holdings, possible contacts for interviews, and likely sources for files of their correspondence with their many friends and colleagues. Up until nearly the day of his death on April 19, 1992, Al Lee corresponded with John Galliher and offered assistance. For the Lees' many acts of assistance the authors are profoundly grateful.

For his selfless friendship and gentle prodding the authors are indebted to Gideon Sjoberg. Having spent a few years at the graduate center of CUNY in the late 1960s, he provided us with valuable insights into Al Lee's activities there and elsewhere. We also acknowledge the assistance of James Orcutt, who read the manuscript several times and provided siginficant direction in organization and analysis. In addition, Ronald Farrell, Richard Hall, Stephen Turner, Ted Vaughan, Mary Jo Neitz, and Donald Granberg read early drafts of the manuscript, as did Lorraine and Robert McNamara. Many friends and colleagues provided essential materials and guidance. This list especially includes Kenneth Clark, Judith Blau, Daniel Horowitz, Sylvia Fava, Leo Chall, Ruth and John Useem, Matlida White Riley, James Coleman, Bernard Meltzer, Paul Nyden, Larry Reynolds, Gary Marx, Terry Sullivan, Jan Fritz, Irwin Deutscher, Barrington Moore, Glenn Jacobs, Benjamin Ringer, David Connolly, Fr. Desmond Wilson, Denis Barritt, Victoria Rader, John Leggett, John Malone, Morton Wagenfeld, Harvey Farberman, Mark Hutter, Freda and Samuel Sass, Daniel Claster, John Clark, Frederick Elwood, Irving Louis Horowitz, Stansfield Sargent, Thomas Ford Hoult, Sidney Aronson, Setsuko Nishi, S.M. Miller, Jerome Himelhoch, Ted Goertzel, The Rev. M.C. Van de Workeen, Richard Wells, Stuart Hills, Jon Darling, Gerold Starr, Bruce Grindal, Otto Larson, Alice Myers, Henry Brownstein, and Philip Peek.

PLAN OF THE BOOK

We begin immediately below with a list of all the academic appointments of the Lees. In chapter 1 we will see how the careers of the Lees are consistent with, and depart from, the efforts of sociologists who preceded them in the late nineteenth and early twentieth centuries. Here special attention is given to the role models available to them at the time they were entering the profession. Chapter 2 traces the influence of their families as well as their educational and early career experiences. In chapter 3 the Lees' life-long commitment to clinical sociology is noted, along with their conception of this type of scholarship as a means for addressing social problems. Chapter 4 demonstrates that from the beginning of their careers the Lees recognized the potential of professional associations and sociology departments in social scientists' attacks on social problems. The Lees' enduring concern with teaching and the protection of academic freedom is traced in chapter 5. The final chapter provides a critical assessment of the quality, significance, and impact of the Lees' various activities and the legacy these two lives provide. Here an analysis of the impact of the Lees' ideas and activities on the discipline will be made. A complete bibliography of both Elizabeth Lee and Alfred Lee's writings is included in the appendix.

Professional Appointments: Elizabeth Briant Lee

1944–1946 Lecturer, School of Nursing, Wayne State University

1949–1950 Lecturer, Sociology Department, Brooklyn College

1951–1953 Lecturer, Hartford Theological Seminary Foundation

1953–1954 Visiting Professor and Acting Chair, Department of Sociology and Anthropology, Connecticut College, New London, CT

1957–1958 Research Associate, Center for Sociological Research, Catholic University of the Sacred Heart, Milan Italy

1962–1963; 1965–1966 Lecturer, Department of Sociology and Anthropology, Fairleigh Dickinson University

1965–1980 Associate Director, Irish Culture and Personality Project, Brooklyn College

1966–1967 American Specialist Lecturer, U.S. Department of State, Far East, Middle East, Europe, Iceland

Professional Appointments: Alfred McClung Lee

1934–1937 Assistant to Associate Professor of Journalism University of Kansas (on leave 1937–1939)

1937–1938 Assistant Professor (Research) Yale University

1938–1939 Lecturer, New York University School of Commerce, Accounts and Finance

1939–1942 Assistant Professor, New York University

1940–1942, Executive Director, Institute for Propaganda Analysis

1942–1950 Professor, Wayne State University, Chair 1942–1947, Research Professor 1948–1949

1947–1948 on leave at University of Michigan

1949–1971 Professor Brooklyn College, Chair 1950–1957, 1965–1966, Graduate Center 1961–1971

1957–1958 UNESCO Professor, organizer and director, Center for Sociological Research, Catholic University of the Sacred Heart, Milan, Italy

1960–1961 Senior Fulbright Lecturer, University of Rome

1971–1992 Professor Emeritus, Brooklyn College

1975–1992 Visiting Scholar, Drew University

Notes

1. William Buxton and Stephen P. Turner, "From Edification to Expertise: Sociology as a 'Profession,' " *Sociology and Its Publics: The Forms and Fates of Disciplinary Organization.* Terence C. Halliday and Morris Janowitz, eds. (Chicago: University of Chicago Press, 1992): 373–407.

2. David Riesman (in collaboration with Reuel Denney and Nathan Glazer). *The Lonely Crowd; A Study of the Changing American Character* (New Haven: Yale University Press, 1950).

3. Robert S. Lynd and Helen Merrell Lynd. *Middletown, A Study in Contemporary American Culture* (New York: Harcourt, Brace and Company, 1929).

4. Robert N. Bellah, Richard Madsen, William M. Sullivan, Ann Swidler, Steven M. Tipton. *Habits of the Heart* (New York: Harper and Row, 1985).

5. Buxton and Turner op. cit.

6. Irwin Deutscher, "Revisiting History: Hughes and Lee." *ASA Footnotes* 21 (January 1993): 7.

7. James Bennett. *Oral History and Delinquency: The Rhetoric of Criminology* (Chicago: University of Chicago Press, 1981).

8. Ibid.: 22.

9. Ibid.: 19.

10. Ibid.: 32.

11. Nancy Schrom Dye. "Clio's American Daughters: Male History, Female Reality." *The Prism of Sex: Essays in the Sociology of Knowledge.* Julia A. Sherman and Evelyn Torton Beck, eds. (Madison: University of Wisconsin Press, 1979): 10.

12. William Appleman Williams. *The Contours of American History* (Chicago: Quadrangle Books, 1966); Howard Zinn. *A Peoples' History of the United States* (New York: Harper and Row Publishers, 1980).

13. Sheila Rowbotham. *Hidden from History: Rediscovering Women in History from the 17th Century to the Present* (New York: Pantheon Books, 1974): xxvii.

14. Stephen Turner. "Salvaging Sociology's Past." *ASA Footnotes* 19 (May 1991): 6.

15. Irving Louis Horowitz. *C. Wright Mills: An American Utopian* (New York: The Free Press, 1983).

16. Irving Louis Horowitz. "The Place of the Festschrift." *Scholarly Publishing* 21 (University of Toronto Press, January 1990): 77–83.

17. Irving Louis Horowitz. Letter to John F. Galliher (February 6, 1991).

Chapter 1

The Lees in Historical Context: Moral Reform and the Origins of American Sociology

AWARDS AND ACCOMPLISHMENTS

The Lees were the founders of two professional associations, the Association for Humanist Sociology (AHS) in 1976 and the Society for the Study of Social Problems (SSSP) in 1953; since 1981 this latter association has honored others by giving an annual award in the Lee's name: "Established in 1981, this award is made in recognition of significant achievements, that over a distinguished career, have demonstrated continuing devotion to the ideals of the founders of the Society for the Study of Social Problems and especially to the humanist tradition in sociology, as exemplified in the contributions of Alfred McClung Lee and Elizabeth Briant Lee." The criteria for the award include the following: "These achievements may be in the areas of scholarly research, teaching or service leading to the betterment of human life. Recipients of the award must have demonstrated a commitment to social action programs that promote social justice."[1] This could include study of war and peace, religious conflict, or the mass media and propaganda as related to social problems and inequality including sexism, racism, and poverty. A decade prior to the establishment of this award Al was honored in 1971 for "his years of dedicated service to SSSP."[2]

A long-term friend and colleague of the Lees describes their achievements as follows: "In the history of American sociology, the Lees were among the first to appreciate the importance to the field of the study of social problems and to insist that the sociological perspective be broadened to enlist sociology in the development of social action programs that promote social justice. . . . The basis for the proposed [SSSP] award is not so much the dedication, enthusiasm and commitment of the Lees to the SSSP as it is the well-known fact that they represent its ideals and aspirations and, indeed, did more than anyone else to define them."[3] Betty and Al also were catalysts in the formation of the Clinical Sociological Association in 1978, later renamed the Sociological Practice Association.[4] Al's presidential address to the Eastern Sociological Society, "The Clinical Study of Society," is mentioned frequently in discussions of the founding of this association.

Al was elected president of the American Sociological Association (ASA), the SSSP, the AHS, the Eastern Sociological Society, and the Michigan Sociological Society. Al was the second president of the ASA who was nominated by petition.[5] Betty has also been president of the AHS, vice president of the SSSP, and for many years served as Secretary-Treasurer of the Eastern Sociological Society. In 1975 Betty and Al were made the first two honorary members of the Sociological Association of Ireland in recognition of their longstanding interest and research on the conflict there. "The Eastern Sociological Society recognized their partnership and contributions by awarding them jointly the 1974 Merit Award,"[6] and in 1989 Betty was given an additional award by the ESS for "her many years of service to the Eastern Sociological Society and to a humanistic ideal of knowledge and practice."[7] In 1990 they were jointly given the ASA Distinguished Career Award for the Practice of Sociology.

Even with all of these high offices and distinguished awards, neither of the Lees ever held a permanent position in a major graduate department. As noted earlier, Betty never held a full-time, tenure-track position, and Al held permanent faculty positions only at institutions—the University of Kansas, Wayne State University, Brooklyn College, and the Graduate Center of the City University of New York—all well outside the realm of the nation's most prestigious sociology departments. Being denied institutional support makes their accomplishments even more remarkable. Along with their other achievements, both Betty and Al became accomplished artists. In recent years, Betty has had public exhibitions of her works. In the Lees' dining room hangs a powerful oil painting by Al Lee vividly depicting the environmental ravages of the Pittsburgh steel industry.

Ethical Assumptions

From the beginning Betty and Al Lee's careers have been firmly rooted in an explicit ethical position. The significance of this becomes apparent when we compare the Lees with leading nineteenth and early twentieth-century sociologists who preceded them: "From the beginning social thought in the United States had its roots in Christian religion, especially Protestantism. . . . Nearly all of the major proponents of American sociological thought have hoped that sociology would contribute to the forming of a better world, even a utopia. Frequently they thought of their science as an instrument that would help carry forward the Christian religious promise."[8]

At the turn of the century, if sociology was taught in colleges and universities, it often was in conjunction with courses on charities and social welfare. And not surprisingly, many of the early sociology instructors had backgrounds in the clergy. Their backgrounds combined with the new social science to produce a discipline that had both moral and technical dimensions: "Ultimately, meliorist northern Protestants made their peace with Comtean Positivism, rejecting its agnosticism . . . but adopting its scientific outlook. They perceived the new discipline of sociology as both a social science and a source of moral regeneration."[9]

God and Sociology at Yale

One famous nineteenth-century sociologist, William Graham Sumner, was an Episcopal clergyman who was later on the faculty at Yale. Sumner was of considerable importance to the Lees. A William Graham Sumner Club was founded to promote and honor his ideas. In 1940, Al Lee was named director of the club,[10] and in 1941 and 1942 he served as editor of the club's bulletin. Sumner represents a complex case and thus there is some debate about his legacy. The Lees quote Sumner's comments on the abuses of capitalists that are similar to those of Marx: "Capital, as it grows larger, takes on new increments with greater and greater ease. It acquires a kind of momentum."[11] And in modern plutocracy "the real controlling force is wealth. . . . Modern plutocrats buy their way through elections and legislatures, in the confidence of being able to get powers which will recoup them for all the outlay and yield an ample surplus besides."[12] Sumner is quoted elsewhere by the Lees as saying: "It is inevitable . . . that the classes which constitute the masses should go on to win all the power which is thrown into their hands by the facts of the situation." And: "Industrial war is a sign of vigor in society. It contains a promise of a sound solution." According to the Lees, Sumner held that "militarianism, expansion and imperialism all favor plutocracy" and oppose democracy.[13] In the introduction to a collection of Sumner essays edited by the Lees, they again note Sumner's contention that an "imperial policy" on the part of the American government abroad was inconsistent with, and would destroy, democracy at home, and note also Sumner's contention that the United States is "under no obligation to maintain great armaments."[14] Here the Lees quote Sumner's complaints about American environmental pollution, including this prophetic assessment: "We are . . . cutting down our forests with appalling waste, ruining the land, squandering our resources. The time will come when Americans will pay for all this."[15]

Others have emphasized additional and quite different components of Sumner's work. Sumner argued that workers could not ask the government for much protection or they would risk losing their rights as independent citizens and "throw the republic open to plutocracy."[16] Sumner correspondingly had a firm belief in the capacity of human beings to exercise a free will. Thus no matter how good the intentions, no government controls should be designed to fetter the natural human capacity for free will and individual initiative: "Drawing primarily on Spencer and Darwin and on the Puritan aspect of his Protestant heritage, [he] produced a sociology that emphasized the doctrines of individualism and self-reliance."[17] "[E]spousing the Puritan value of individualism—every man and woman in a personal relationship with God—Sumner denied that the state could act as a surrogate for upholding the utopian ideal of a Kingdom of Heaven on earth."[18] Thus "Sumner's society is lacking in both love and compassion and is always severe in its demands."[19] The fact that all people—the rich and the poor alike—were individuals, alone in their relationship with God, coincided nicely with the requirements of laissez-faire capitalism. Lester Ward was Sumner's chief intellectual opponent during the 1880s, for Ward was a firm believer in liberal social reform: "History, society, and culture were governed by laws, and therefore were subject to human direction."[20] Indeed, Ward called for "social engineering."[21]

For Sumner, monopolies and war represented irrational intrusions into the operation of an unfettered capitalist system, which he saw as most desirable. Given this jaundiced view of developments in capitalist society, not surprisingly Sumner did not want to die for it. The Lees have noted that Sumner apparently was opposed to war, refused to serve in the Union army, and instead pursued his studies abroad.[22] The Lees' view of this Episcopalian sociologist from Yale is of considerable significance, for the strengths the Lees see in Sumner tell us as much about Al and Betty Lee as Sumner himself. This special affinity the Lees have had for Sumner's ideas may attest to the similarity in their backgrounds. Betty and Al, like Sumner, have been associated with both Yale as well as the Episcopal church, and have been unalterably opposed to war. This defense of Sumner also reflects

Al's dogged determination to support and defend those he believed to be politically and morally correct.

In defending his view, Al observed: "There are two W. G. Sumners. One was presented again and again by his student A. G. Keller, who made a career of reinterpreting Sumner's work, and one you can see by looking directly at the works of Sumner. Sumner was actually a radical who was a thorn in the side of Yale." Indeed, by looking at Sumner's *Folkways* we see a much different view of capitalism and classes than that of a Social Darwinist defending laissez-faire capitalism. Sumner speaks plainly: "There is no class which can be trusted to rule society with due justice to all, not abusing its power for its own interest. The task of constitutional government is to devise institutions which shall come into play at the critical periods to prevent the abusive control of the powers of a state by controlling classes in it."[23] Actually, there may be three W. G. Sumners: one as interpreted by Keller, and two very different Sumners seen by looking at different parts of his voluminous writing.

CHRISTIAN SOCIOLOGY AT THE UNIVERSITY OF CHICAGO

The lives and careers of the Lees, we will demonstrate, were much influenced by Christianity and Christian principles. And the early history of American sociology clearly shows how the Lees' predecessors in the discipline were influenced by these ideas. There is no doubt that the University of Chicago was the major American center for graduate training in sociology during the late 19th and early 20th century. And while Christianity seemed to encourage heartlessness among some scholars, in the hands of Albion Small (1854–1926) at Chicago a somewhat different theme was created. Small is known to have closed his sociology course with a prayer asking God to control social and economic activity. Small was the son of a Baptist minister and a clergyman himself.[24] Small's belief that sociology could be used to inform public policy places him much closer to Ward than to Sumner, and certainly close to the Lees. According to Small, "Sociology looks to the equalization of social relations [and was] the ally of any class which was temporarily at a disadvantage against any other class."[25] Elsewhere, he stated: "Indeed, sociology was called into existence by socialism, which has mercilessly exposed social evils, but . . . has not been equally positive in proposal of remedies . . . Socialism is nevertheless a challenge which society cannot ignore."[26] As early as 1895, Small wrote that the ideas of Karl Marx were among the most important of the 19th century, and thus, after the revolution in Russia, he felt these ideas would be greatly feared by the Christian community. To combat Marxism, a Christian moral crusade was required to humanize and Christianize capitalism.[27] Thus, Small's position was conditioned not merely by justice but also by instrumental politics. We will demonstrate below that a similar commitment to equality, as well as a suspicion of Marxism, is also reflected in the lives of the Lees.

In addition to Small, the University of Chicago had several other Christian sociologists on its faculty during the late nineteenth and early twentieth centuries. Charles Henderson was a Christian sociologist who left a pastorate in Detroit to teach sociology at the university. Yet another Christian sociologist in the Chicago department at the turn of the century was George E. Vincent, son of a Methodist bishop.[28] Even during the 19th century, not all social scientists agreed with the religious foundations for sociological reasoning. For example, Franklin Giddings of Columbia University ridiculed Small's Christian socialist sociology.[29] For his part, Small vacillated: his own radical comments made him increasingly uncomfortable, because elites both within and outside the University of Chicago put great pressure on him to conform.

While the reform tradition of Small and Ward did not die, it took on a very different character during the Progressive Era, the first two decades of the twentieth century, when academics became major figures in the progressive movement. On the faculties of several prestigious universities, Edward Allsworth Ross (1866–1951) believed that capitalism would inevitably create inequality; he sought to counter the consequent class conflict with new methods of social control.[30] By this time Chicago sociologists increasingly insisted that building an objective science and not social reform was their top priority.[31] This objectivism represented a rejection of the values of nineteenth-century American Protestantism.[32] Thus, by the early 1900s, a new generation of sociologists was rebelling against the Protestantism of parents and teachers. During the 1920s, private funding agencies spurred the development of scientism and accelerated the movement away from religion. Correspondingly, in 1938, when *The Polish Peasant* was ranked by social scientists as the most influential work since the war, the Social Science Research Council [SSRC], originally funded by Rockefeller money, held a conference to reappraise it. In line with the demands of scientism, the conference severely criticized it for not being sufficiently rigorous and statistical.[33] In the chapters which follow we will see that the impact of research funding on the development of scientism in sociology has long been a complaint of the Lees.

During the first three decades of the twentieth century, the

University of Chicago could claim the top-ranked and most influential American sociology department.[34] In this department the drive toward science did not go unchallenged. Two important strains of thought supporting this challenge developed there, one theoretical, the other empirical. As for theoretical influences, from 1900 onward George Herbert Mead's (1863–1931) significance spread through his social psychology course, where he worked to transform the theory of symbolic interactionism.[35] Another Chicago sociologist, Robert E. Park (1864–1944), had worked as a journalist early in his life, but in 1914 joined the Chicago sociology department. Park became well known for his studies of race relations and was elected the first President of the Chicago Urban League.[36] He was a close associate of Booker T. Washington and the Tuskegee Institute and was also associated with Fisk University. Park has been described as an activist and "wrote a series of muckraking exposés of the Belgian colonial atrocities in the Congo for *Everybody's Magazine*."[37] He had a firm commitment to alleviating the social problems of society and wrote discussions of the Chicago Commission on Race Relations, which was appointed to investigate and report on the causes of the Chicago race riot of 1919. He wrote approvingly that the "Chicago report is unique in one respect: More than any previous study it has succeeded in uncovering the sources of racial friction."[38] Building on this study, he made detailed suggestions for the study of the Asian population in Pacific coast states, including firsthand information on community life through the collection of case studies and life histories. A productive collaborator with Park, Ernest Burgess also emphasized fieldwork and direct observation of urban social problems.[39] Burgess taught in the Chicago department from 1916 to 1951.

The humanist-scientist dispute continued during the 1930s at the University of Chicago, and University President Robert Hutchins claimed that if value-free modern scientists could be faulted, "it is only from the standpoint that rigorous analysis plays too small a role in it."[40] Herbert Blumer, from Chicago's department of sociology, rejected the religious foundations of sociology,[41] but in a lead article in the *American Journal of Sociology* in 1931 singled out statisticians as the archetype for value-free scientists clinging too closely to facts and thus becoming mere "artisans," rather than "scientists," as they claimed to be.[42] "Occasionally, to be sure, in the career of any science there may arise a crop of technicians coincident with the appearance of some new technique. . . . Such individuals may be called scientists because of academic affiliations; actually, they are mere artisans using the technique as a tool to the fulfillment of immediate ends."[43]

Later, Blumer criticized public opinion researchers for the rigidity of their methodology and the "depressing frequency" with which social science methods are equated with the use of quantitative techniques.[44] Blumer became the primary spokesperson for the symbolic interactionist orientation and its emphasis on the use of fieldwork and participant observation, methods also championed by the Lees. Blumer later would become an ally of the Lees in many professional activities. Among these early sociologists there were all varieties of opinion on religion, social reforms, and the scientific method. Nonetheless, as the 20th century wore on, the patterns of beliefs among social scientists began to narrow as a more definite disciplinary normative structure was being developed.

SOME CONSEQUENCES OF CHRISTIAN SOCIOLOGY

After his 1929 appointment at Duke, Charles Elwood indicated he would hire no one who was not "an avowed Christian."[45] There were many Christian sociologists from which he could choose. E. A. Ross "hoped to build a Christian society, using sociology as a major resource. . . . In Ross's evolutionary scheme of things, Christianity was the highest stage of religion in a civilization that had reached the highest stage of development."[46] Ross also judged that for this stage of development: "The right kind of propagators were to be found in only two collectivities: native-born white Americans and Nordic immigrants. Jews, Italians, southeastern Europeans, and Asiatics would have to be disregarded as marriage partners by the favored Anglo-Saxons."[47] Thus the individualism of Sumner is joined by the blatant racism of Ross. Richard T. Ely (1854–1943), at the University of Wisconsin, was another Christian sociologist who, like Small, espoused a type of socialism. Early in their careers the Lees would come to a similar conclusion. But in Ely's view, the "new ecclesiastical welfare state would be exclusively Protestant, admitting to full citizenship only those who exhibited the requisite signs of visible saintliness, and encouraging the unregenerate to emulate them."[48]

In 1893, Ely helped establish the American Institute of Christian Sociology, "a society devoted to applying a distinctly socialist version of Christian teaching to relations between labor and capital."[49] He had earlier been involved with the prolabor Episcopal Christian Social Union. During the late 1890s Ely was involved in founding yet another professional association, the Social Reform Union. Along with other social scientists he was joined by well-known social reformers, including Jane Addams, Clarence Darrow, and Eugene Debs. The goal of this group was nothing less than to influence the policies of both major political parties so that significant progressive reforms could be enacted. These reforms included opposition to imperialism and commitment to public ownership of many monopolies. The efforts of Ely and others caused concern among more conservative social scientists and none of these organizations long endured.[50] The chapters which follow demonstrate the great importance the Lees have attached to the creation of reform-minded professional associations. Unlike these pioneer social science reformers such as Ely, the Lees founded reform-oriented professional associations with considerable durability.

During the late nineteenth century, summary dismissal from a university post was increasingly the object of collective outrage among these social scientists. There was growing support among social scientists for academic freedom for university professors, which produced ironic consequences. The justification for this newfound demand for academic freedom was an increasing claim to objectivity and value neutrality among social scientists whereby these professionals could police themselves.[51] Ely's career is illustrative of these changes. There were considerable pressures on Ely to conform to the demands of his more conservative colleagues. Growing out of his support of liberal reforms and appeals to the general public, Ely was investigated by the administration of his university and ousted by colleagues at other universities from his position as an officer of the American Economic Association. Chastened by these developments, Ely thereafter "relinquished his claim to activism, he exchanged advocacy for acceptability."[52] During much of the twentieth century, the Lees championed the cause of academic freedom much like many of their predecessors, but rejected out of hand the price of value neutrality.

THE GENERATION GAP AND THE BEGINNING CRACKS IN CHRISTIAN SOCIOLOGY

The typical alternative of those rejecting Christian sociology was to adopt a value-free, objective sociology dedicated to precise empirical observation. This growing generation gap can be seen in the careers of two Chicago-trained sociologists who were at the peak of their careers when the Lees entered the profession in the 1930s: Edwin H. Sutherland and Luther L. Bernard. As could be expected at the time when Sutherland and Bernard entered graduate study in sociology in the first two decades of the 20th century, both came from families with the same type of traditional Protestant values. Edwin Sutherland was reared by a father who was a domineering, sober, and religious minister-educator.[53] In 1906, when the younger Sutherland first arrived at the University of Chicago for graduate training in sociology, he studied under Henderson, who as a committed Christian felt that religion should guide all intellectual activities. Bernard was in the same cohort of Chicago graduate students. Bernard's father has been described as a Baptist and a "petty tyrant," which caused his son to lead an adult life opposed to conservatism and religious orthodoxy and hostile to organized religion.[54]

Bernard's first real intellectual stimulation came during his college years from contacts with two Darwinists who were completely opposed by church officials.[55] Unlike Sutherland, from the beginning of his graduate studies at Chicago Bernard disliked Henderson.[56] By the later phases of his graduate training Sutherland also began to reject both the influences of Henderson and that of his own father.[57] Bernard received his Ph.D. from Chicago in 1911. Later he hoped to be hired by the University of Chicago, but in the mid-twenties he was vetoed by Ellsworth Faris, a former missionary who was then department chair.[58] A decade later Sutherland was hired by Chicago, but his contract was not renewed while Faris was still chair.

Yet if Sutherland and Bernard were similar in some ways, in many others they were different. It is instructive to see how each approached the newly accepted canon of objectivity and value neutrality. Describing these two careers provides a comparison with the life and work of Betty and Al Lee. This comparison will further our understanding of the social context in which the Lees began their careers, as well as the role of criticism, conflict, and reward and punishment existing in the academic community. The Lees always strongly rejected this developing value-free perspective, much as had an earlier generation of Christian sociologists.

Sutherland's Alternative to Christian Sociology

Edwin Sutherland clearly thought of himself as diametrically opposed to the Christian role models provided by his father and Charles Henderson. *The Professional Thief,* an often-cited example of value-free analysis and careful empirical description, was published by Sutherland in 1937.[59] This study illustrates Sutherland's famous differential association theory of criminal behavior, which holds that human actors essentially are prisoners of their social environment. This book became the benchmark for the study of criminal careers by making no value judgments, much as one would in studying any other professional career.

Curiously, Sutherland's other research on sexual psychopath laws shows no such dispassionate analysis and reflects many obvious lapses in judgment, suggesting that his reputation for careful empirical observation and measurement has been highly overrated. Sutherland appears to have ignored letters from other scholars warning him that he was on the wrong course in his psychopath legislation research. For example, he neglected to include all the states that had passed such laws, incorrectly blamed psychiatrists for such legislation, and also claimed that serious crimes caused the passage of such laws even though the crimes occurred *after* the laws had been passed.[60] Widely accepted explanations for these lapses included Sutherland's concern that these laws abridged constitutional freedoms and his contempt for the psychiatric ideology they reflected. So it appears that Sutherland's values got the best of him and seriously distorted his analysis. Rejecting Christianity appeared easier for him than avoiding all moral value judgments.

Sutherland passionately rejected out of hand all except social causes of crime. In developing his own theoretical understanding of crime he again demonstrated that he was far from being value-free, for he rejected consideration of both economic and psychiatric theories of crime: "Poverty seldom forces people to steal or become prostitutes in order to escape starvation."[61] In his view economic theories of crime were not even applicable to corporate crime.[62] He even questioned the integrity of Sheldon and Eleanor Glueck, whose research indicated some significance in biological causes of delinquency: "Quite simply, Sutherland went so far as to imply that the Gluecks had fudged their data."[63] Sutherland's intellectual fervor and disciplinary boundary maintenance are clearly reflected in the following passage: "There is no more reason for turning over to the psychiatrist the complete supervision of a criminal who is found to be psychopathic than for turning over to the dentist the complete supervision of a criminal who is found to have dental cavities."[64]

Marshall Clinard recalled that Sutherland became increasingly anti-psychiatric as his career progressed. "The first edition of his textbook in 1924 was a multiple-factor approach which gave the same weight to psychological factors as to others. But if you trace his ideas through the different editions you will see that he became more anti-psychological."[65] Indeed, Sutherland's whole career was devoted, in one way or another, to a political and emotional defense of the discipline of sociology. Sutherland also defended the prerogatives of sociology in the study of crime against those of law, as seen in his famous debate with Paul Tappan. While the lawyer-sociologist Tappan maintained that only offenses that resulted in a criminal conviction could be properly referred to as crime,[66] Sutherland asserted that all harmful behavior of business leaders where any type of penalty existed could be referred to under the general heading of white-collar crime.[67] Sutherland insisted on a behavioral rather than a legalistic definition of white-collar crime and thus all this activity comes under the professional purview of sociologists.

Along with his strident defense of sociology, Sutherland appears to have cared deeply about victims of white-collar crime. He questioned the patriotism of corporate leaders and even compared them with Nazis, for he felt they endangered the capitalist system itself.[68] In 1939, the Lees, with their very new Ph.D.s, were pleased to hear Sutherland's criticisms of the greed and law violation of American corporations, which was the theme of his American Sociological Society (ASS) presidential address. Sutherland's obvious moral passion impressed the Lees much more than his claims of value neutrality. The Lees quote one of Sutherland's prophetic conclusions which envisioned a more just society: "The violations of antitrust law by large business concerns . . . have made our system of free competition and free enterprise unworkable. We no longer have competition as a regulator of economic processes; we have not substituted efficient government regulation. We cannot go back to competition. . . . We must go forward to some new system—perhaps communism, . . . perhaps much more complete government regulation than we have now."[69] On the other hand, Sutherland celebrated the expertise of the professional thief Broadway Jones and gave no consideration to such thieves' victims.[70] Sutherland did no better with violent crime:

> Charges of forcible rape are often made without justification by some females for purposes of blackmail and by others, who have engaged voluntarily in intercourse but have been discovered, in order to protect their reputations. Physicians have testified again and again that forcible rape is practically impossible unless the female has been rendered practically unconscious by drugs or injury; many cases reported as forcible rape have certainly involved nothing more than passive resistance. Finally, statutory rape is frequently a legal technicality, with the female in fact a prostitute and taking the initiative in the intercourse.[71]

While Sutherland attacked women and corporate criminals, he never criticized the discipline and always championed it. Predictably, he was widely respected by his colleagues. Sutherland was elected President of the ASS in 1939 and President of the prestigious Sociological Research Association in 1942, a group that denied Bernard membership. If the Lees were inspired by Sutherland's moral and intellectual passion, they could also easily see that his claims of value neutrality were just that, claims and nothing more.

LUTHER L. BERNARD AND SECULAR HUMANISM

L. L. Bernard was a contemporary of Sutherland's, as well as a classmate and long-time friend. Bernard was an extreme behaviorist, environmentalist, and an outspoken critic of the Chicago sociology department.[72] Bernard demanded a sociology that was more quantitative.[73] He felt sociology should be applied to human values and could provide an "objective standard of social control."[74] For Bernard, "Sociology is in large measure a response to this demand for effective and functional unity in the world under the guidance of science."[75] In other words, science could provide the ethical guidance that religion could not. As an example of this guidance, he criticized the New Deal for not being radical enough for his tastes.[76] In this way, Bernard contrasted his own brand of scientific objectivity with value neutrality, which he rejected.

Bernard was elected president of the ASS in late 1931 and in this role helped to sever the association's ties with the University of Chicago sociology department and its journal the *American Journal of Sociology* (*AJS*). In its place, the *American Sociological Review* (*ASR*) was established as the association's journal. Bernard wanted the ASS constitution revised to make the society more democratic and opposed hiring a paid executive secretary. As ASS president, Bernard proposed 1) open committee meetings, 2) a new constitution, 3) unrestricted membership, 4) more women on the programs and on association committees, and 5) recommended that the association "should provide more guidance to society in a time of crisis."[77] These proposals were much like those of Al Lee when he was elected ASA president over four decades later. In 1933, the association adopted a new constitution, written largely by Bernard which allowed for greater democracy, including regional representation at every level; in addition, nominations were henceforth to be allowed from the floor at the annual meetings, and a new association journal was established that was independent of the University of Chicago: "Behind these questions lay more important ones concerning the nature and control of the discipline."[78] Other sociologists wanted to keep the association free of social activism and the humanistic emphasis of earlier Chicago sociology. Due to such disputes, Bernard ultimately resigned from the association in 1938.

The opposite of Sutherland, Bernard's contributions to sociology are largely forgotten, including his original version of *The American Sociologist* (*TAS*), which he founded in 1938 and continued until 1947. Toward the end of his career, his health failing, he could no longer continue this publication and it folded. The explicit purpose of his *TAS* was to serve as a "medium for discussion of outstanding professional problems in sociology."[79] The journal had few prestigious editorial supporters, although it had many such subscribers. The original *TAS* criticized an American Sociological Society proposal to have active and nonvoting, associate members and argued for representation of regional associations on the ASS executive committee. Indeed, the former plan was never implemented and the latter was. *TAS* editorial statements condemned value-free sociology. Moreover, Bernard obviously considered foreign policy relevant for sociology. In 1945, he complained about the willingness of allied governments to cooperate with Nazis as a way of countering the Soviet Union. When a new *TAS* was begun in 1965, no recognition was given to the earlier version. In fact, Talcott Parsons, the new *TAS* editor, noted that it was "an entirely new venture,"[80] which of course it was not. If others ignored Bernard's *TAS*, the Lees did not. They commented on Bernard's failure to maintain this "rebel" journal, standing alone as it attempted to do without a professional association to give it nurturance and support.[81]

Despite all his efforts, "Bernard left no school, nor a radical tradition."[82] Perhaps Bernard has been forgotten because his career was so filled with contradictions. For example, at various times he appeared to support women, at other times to attack them.[83] While he endorsed the use of statistical techniques, when foundations expressed an interest in such research he rejected their participation out of hand. Bernard rejected the support or, more precisely, the controls exercised by the foundations. In his 1932 ASS presidential address he concluded: "I have little sympathy with research projects that grow out of an institution's or a person's desire to get money from a foundation."[84] As Vidich and Lyman have observed, Bernard seemed trapped between "the bureaucratic mentality of statisticians" and his commitment to creativity.[85] These criticisms of the professional association and of foundations would be echoed a generation later by Betty and Al Lee.

From these two cases we can see that neither Sutherland nor Bernard actually practiced a value-free sociology. While the career of Sutherland might make it appear that a truly value-free sociology is impossible, nonetheless the value-free posture has thrived. Clearly, both Sutherland and Bernard distrusted women and said as much. Perhaps most importantly, one criticized the profession and the other defended it against all outsiders. Both of these early twentieth-century sociologists have something in common with the Lees. For example, Sutherland was a fearless critic of the power of corporations, which the Lees as newcomers to the profession greeted with great enthusiasm. As a reformer with much in common with the Lees, Sutherland's complaints were that the corporations were corrupting and destroying a truly capitalistic economy. For his part, Bernard not only was ready to criticize leaders of business and government, he was just as ready to criticize the profession. As we will see, Betty and Al Lee have been more like Bernard than Sutherland with regard to issues of criticism.

THE WANING OF CHICAGO SOCIOLOGY

By the early 1950s, the influence of Columbia University and Harvard began to surpass that of Chicago. The focus of study of the Chicago department continued to be dictated by urban social problems, including crime, poverty, and the lives of Black Americans.[86] Instead of developing a new tradition, the leaders of the SSSP drew on Chicago sociology and worked against heavy odds to maintain its traditions. Betty and Al and the other early leaders felt that the ASA discouraged social problems research and humanistic ideals and that this bias was well represented at Columbia and Harvard and "personified by Talcott Parsons, Paul Lazarsfeld and George Lundberg."[87] Howard Becker's study of the process of becoming a marihuana user, published in an early issue of the SSSP journal, *Social Problems*, clearly reflects the influence of his Chicago training.[88] It involved fieldwork among marginalized individuals using symbolic interactionism as a guide to both data collection and analysis. A study of the permanent black male underclass by Harold Finestone was written while a graduate student at Chicago. He describes the tastes and preferences of black male drug users, including the value they place on their "kicks" and "hustle."[89] Both are described as a cultural preference, as are tastes for expensive clothing and the use of personal charm, together with a "large, colorful, and discriminating vocabulary." All are portrayed from the drug users' point of view as a "gracious work of art" and one finds no hint of either pity or contempt in this analysis. Finestone's study reflects the fieldwork and race relations tradition of Chicago sociology, as well as analysis based on the symbolic interactionist perspective. By contrast, Harvard and Columbia were never interested in Black Americans.[90] At Harvard, Talcott Parsons became the primary proponent of structural functionalism, carried on by his able student Robert Merton at Columbia. Columbia also could boast Paul Lazarsfeld, a leading proponent of scientific sociology.

Robert S. Lynd, a colleague of Merton and Lazarsfeld at Columbia, is well known for his book *Knowledge for What?*[91] Here Lynd distinguishes between "scholars" working on abstract intellectual riddles aloof from society and its problems as opposed to "technicians" mired in the practical affairs of humankind.[92] Originally trained as a Christian minister, Lynd deplored the reluctance of social scientists to become fully involved in the human enterprise by claiming to be disinterested observers. He noted that this avoidance of "what ought to be" actually assumed that the prevailing order was the most desirable state of affairs.[93] Lynd emphasized the contradictions inherent in American life: poverty is thought to be deplorable yet impossible to erase; total honesty is considered the best policy but in actual business affairs is recognized as naive and impossible; equality is prized even while extremes of inequality are everpresent and growing. Lynd formulated a number of "outrageous hypotheses" dealing with both society and social science, illustrated by the four listed below:

> The chance for the survival of democracy and the prospect of increased human welfare would be enhanced by explicit recognition of the fact that men are unequal; by the discovery and elimination of cultural causes of inequality.[94]
>
> Private capitalism does not operate, and probably cannot be made to operate, to assure the amount of general welfare to which the present stage of our technological skills and intelligence entitle us; and other ways of managing our economy need therefore to be explored.[95]
>
> Current social science plays down the omnipresent fact of class antagonisms and conflicts in the living all about us. . . . The body of fact and theory around the highly dynamic situation of class conflict will have to be much more realistically and centrally considered if social science is to deal adequately with current institutions.[96]
>
> It is possible to build a culture that in all its institutions will play down the need for and the possibility of war.[97]

The work of scholars such as Lynd, Sutherland, and Bernard provide a reflection of the state of the conflict in sociology between the value-neutral and the value-committed positions held at the time the Lees were entering the profession. Lynd's book was published near the beginning of the Lees' careers. With its calls for equality and peace it had a significant impact upon their thinking. In the Lees' hands, Lynd's *Knowledge for What?* was translated into publications with titles such as the question, *Sociology for Whom?*[98] and then answered with *Sociology for People.*[99]

C. WRIGHT MILLS AND ALVIN GOULDNER: A NEW GENERATION OF AMERICAN RADICALS

In the early 1940s, shortly after the Lees began their careers, another prominent sociologist entered the field. He was C. Wright Mills, born in Waco, Texas, to Roman Catholic parents. He attended both parochial and public schools and was equally lonely and unhappy in both.[100] His first real happiness came during his undergraduate years at the University of Texas. Later, during graduate study at the University of Wisconsin, he almost instantly became the department's star student, publishing numerous term papers in major journals. One of the first of these, "The Professional Ideology of Social Pathologists," was a biting critique of the domination of rural Christian ideology in the sociological analysis of social problems.[101] Similar to Giddings, Sutherland, and Bernard before him, Mills had great reservations about the significance of Christianity in the quest for human freedom. Moreover, Mills criticized the clergy for not publicly condemning the military definition of reality.[102] Like the Lees, Mills demanded that social science address social problems with a critical eye.

Mills had no illusions about communism as a political and economic system—a skepticism shared by the Lees. From the beginning Mills dismissed both the leaders of capitalism and communism as domineering autocrats.[103] In addition, Mills opposed WWII, for he saw "little difference between Hitler's Germany and Roosevelt's America."[104] Unlike Marxists, Mills was not a proponent of revolution and argued that economic power is subordinate to legal and social relations, with business, as well as government and military leaders, actually running the nation. Mills demanded freedom for all people and thus the determinism of Marxism was far from his ideal. He rejected the possibility of a value-free science.[105] Often sociologists confined themselves to grand and abstract theory unconnected to the real world, reflected, he argued, in the work of Talcott Parsons, or to microscopic statistical techniques also unconnected to actual human problems.[106] Mills increasingly criticized intellectuals for their failure to help influence society. In *Listen Yankee*[107] and *The Causes of World War III*,[108] Mills directed his message to the general public. He published frequently in nonsociological journals and magazines, which was uncharacteristic of most sociologists who were his contemporaries.[109] Like Bernard, Mills hoped that sociology could provide guidance to a truly democratic state, precisely the goal of the Lees.

After the Holocaust, the pervasive cultural relativism of the allegedly value-free sociology came increasingly under attack. Could one actually study Nazism and the Holocaust without making value judgments regarding these atrocities? And were the practices of the Third Reich merely different than other cultures of the world, but no better and no worse? Surely not. By isolating human values from science, Alvin Gouldner concluded:

I believe that, in the end, this segregation warps reason by tinging it with sadism and leaves feeling smugly sure only of itself and bereft of a sense of common humanity. [Gouldner continues by observing that if students are not apprised of the values of the researcher this would] usher in an era of spiritless technicians who will be no less lacking in understanding than they are in passion, and who will be useful only because they can be used. . . . If sociologists ought not express their personal values in the academic setting, how then are students to be safeguarded against the unwitting influence of these values which shape the sociologist's selection of problems, his preferences for certain hypotheses or conceptual schemes, and his neglect of others. For these are unavoidable and, in this sense, there is and can be no value-free sociology.[110]

Gouldner was a graduate of Columbia University following WWII. He was extremely critical of the work of Talcott Parsons and noted that such work as his with its emphasis on order "can do no other than accept the kind of order in which it finds itself."[111] He also noted that the Parsonians in the ASA had repeatedly nominated Parsons for president even after two defeats and finally pitted him against a likely loser to insure an easy victory.[112] Yet Gouldner was also a critic of Marxism, at least as practiced in the Soviet Union. In Marxism he found essential contradictions stressing both freedom and determinism. He argued that this could be expected since contradictions are an essential part of human existence. His obituary, published in *Transaction* magazine, included his initial editorial statement of purpose for the publication which he helped establish: "*Transaction* attempts to span the communication gap between two communities now poorly connected . . . sociology—and the general public. . . . The main function of social science is to help men understand and solve the problems of modern societies,"[113] including racial segregation. Gouldner was vitally interested in applied sociology that would deal with social problems, including reducing tensions through work in race relations.[114] As we will see below, the parallels between the Lees and Mills, and Gouldner are remarkable. All have been committed to refuting the possibility of a value-free sociology, committed to the use of sociology to solve social problems, and critical of the contributions of Talcott Parsons.

THE ESTABLISHMENT OF VALUE-FREE SOCIOLOGY

For much of his career at Columbia University Lynd felt isolated and unappreciated by his colleagues.[115] For their part Bernard, Mills, and Gouldner were all considered outsiders from the sociological establishment and, thus in spite of all their efforts, allegedly value-free neutrality was spread widely in the profession. In a 1953 recording containing advice from 20 former American Sociological Association (ASA) presidents, only Harry Pratt Fairchild mentioned a concern for social justice.[116] All others emphasized the need for a value-free science. Frank W. Hankins noted the discipline's passage from moral reform to scientific measurement: "Yet we have learned much in fifty years. We now seek understanding rather than reform or uplift. Statistical competence has become a professional necessity."[117] Leonard S. Cottrell mentioned this first requirement, "A thorough grounding in both quantitative and qualitative research methodology and research design. This includes sufficient competence in mathematics."[118] George A. Lundberg agreed and advised new sociologists: "get as soon as possible, a thorough grounding in logic, mathematics, and semantics. . . . [and] if you feel you already know the answers and merely want a pulpit from which to expound them, keep out of the profession of research and teaching in academic institutions."[119] For Lundberg there was a belief that, almost like a secular religion, "science could save us."[120] Al and Betty later would reprint a Lundberg article using this line of reasoning as a foil for their own ideas.

Yet Ernest W. Burgess, who was to become the first president of the Society for the Study of Social Problems started by the Lees, found these new priorities somewhat troubling: "Statistics, has in recent years had a tremendous development. At present it overshadows the other method, that of case study. This imbalance greatly hampers the progress of sociology and should be corrected."[121] And finally only Fairchild noted the anticommunist hysteria and political oppression of the early 1950s: "There will be many temptations and opportunities to relax your standards in the interest of recognition, preferment, or even pecuniary compensation. Just now in this year 1953 there are especially powerful inducements to sacrifice our ideals on the altar of personal tranquility and security. Expediency presses you to trim your sails to the winds of orthodoxy, conformity, and subservience. Betrayal of your profession lies in that quarter."[122]

In stressing their value-free purity, none of these other former ASA presidents seemed to recognize the scourge of McCarthyism sweeping the nation at the time. These comments of the leaders of the profession provide a clear indication of the fate of the perennial conflict between value-neutrality and value-commitment in the discipline. In the chapters which follow we will see how the Lees attempted to address attacks on individual liberty and value-commitment in sociology, again placing them at some distance from the mainstream sociology of the time. During this period Howard P. Becker wrote that "the sociologist is resigned to the fact that the age of prophecy is over. . . . In the scientific role, prophecy has no place; prediction must be our guide."[123]

VALUE-FREE SOCIOLOGY AND INTERNATIONAL CONFLICT

William Ogburn was a prominent University of Chicago sociologist who throughout WWII maintained a "studied silence" regarding Nazism, for to criticize it would have violated his earlier public commitment to an objective, value-free sociology outlined in his 1929 ASS presidential address.[124] Admittedly, he was not alone, for between 1933 and 1947 the *American Journal of Sociology* published only two articles on National Socialism. If Ogburn made no public utterances on Nazism, in more private communications his attitudes became clearer. In a letter to a friend in 1930 concerning possible faculty recruitment Ogburn wrote: "Another possibility is Louis Wirth at Tulane. He has a very keen mind. He is a Jew, however."[125] In his diary his views became even clearer. There he complained that it was not possible to say any "kind words" about Hitler without being condemned.[126] Here he even admitted grudging admiration for the efficiency of the Nazi propaganda machine. In yet another entry he asked himself "why I have to be so damned nice to the Jews if I do not enjoy them."[127] Ogburn's silence, masking an underlying anti-Semitism, illustrates both the heartlessness and deception of the value-free mythology always condemned by the Lees.

In the chapters which follow we will show that there was considerable personal conflict between the Lees and Talcott Parsons. This same conflict involving Parsons is found in the work of both Mills and Gouldner. Just senior to the Lees, Parsons began teaching sociology at Harvard University in 1931. Buxton and Turner report that during WWII Parsons engaged in many activities relating to national defense.[128] We will see that during the 1930s and 1940s the Lees developed a critical interest in propaganda. Parsons did as well. But their methods of approaching this subject could not have been more different. For example, in 1940 and 1941 Parsons was a regular commentator on the news over a radio station and became a contributor to the American war propaganda effort itself. During one of these broadcasts he argued that the Axis alliance with Japan represented " 'an explicit and direct challenge' to the very existence of American democracy."[129] As will be seen in Chapter 2, the Lees were pacifists during all of their adult lives. On the other hand, in a 1940 speech to a rally of Harvard students sympathetic to military intervention, Parsons claimed such noninterventionist positions represented a threat to the United States and benefited the Nazis.[130] We will see that Al Lee worked with several organizations whose goal it was to help Americans resist the efforts of all propagandists, while during the 1940s the Council for Democracy was founded with Parson's help to "help the American public understand the need to fight fascism."[131]

One of Parsons' central wartime concerns was the role of propaganda among an increasingly heterogeneous American public. The question he raised involved how a social scientist could integrate the various divergent tendencies of this population into a single unified social order. Parsons' view was that sociologists could serve as experts in giving advice to national propaganda agencies and by doing so could assist them in maintaining the values and norms essential for the well being of the social system. In 1940, Parsons wrote that given the international crisis, " 'subversive' groups and organizations" would become a serious threat to the nation.[132] Parsons emphasized that Anglo-Saxon Protestant traditions provided a solid foundation for such loyalty, and at the same time he worried that certain minority groups might be vulnerable to Nazi propaganda. These suspect peoples included, but were not limited to, Roman Catholics and Lutherans.[133] Immigrants were a special concern for Parsons because of their political "backwardness" as peasants with little tradition of participation in self governance.[134] With regard to another minority, in a 1942 essay he left the impression that in some way Jews themselves were responsible for anti-Semitism.[135] Jews were allegedly "aggressive" and display "oversensitiveness to criticism"; [t]he " 'chosen people' idea held by Jews is undoubtedly another source of friction. Gentiles usually resent the arrogance of the claim."[136]

Apparently Parsons' unbridled nationalism was not widely recognized as inconsistent with his claims to objectivism and value neutrality. Indeed, Parsons epitomized the value-free sociology so dominant during the 1940s and 1950s. Although the historical record has been subject to differing interpretations, some note that even while Parsons was advocating a value-free sociology, he was working with the U.S. State Department to help certain experts on the Soviet Union, who had assisted the Nazi government during WWII, in obtaining appointments at American universities. The ready justification for such activity was that there was a shortage of reliable information about the Soviet Union and the United States' government felt a great need to know details of the Soviet military capabilities during the Cold War.[137] Some feel that on the advice of such experts the U.S. greatly exaggerated the Soviet threat and thus by "assisting in this process Talcott Parsons contributed to some of the most antidemocratic and anti-intellectual trends in post-war American political life." Thus

Parsons pursued his "self-proclaimed 'value neutrality' in scientific norms, in the name of cold war activism."[138] Indeed, in his own words he was "doing a 'press agent job' for the [Harvard Russian] research center with the American officials, who were needed to run interference among the emigres."[139] Parson's letters document his discussions with U.S. military, political and intelligence officers.[140] It can safely be concluded, then, that "Parsons approved attaching universities to the intelligence apparatus of government—covertly; bringing persons accused of collaboration with the Nazis to the United States—covertly; using Harvard connections to influence government officials to ease their entry to the United States—covertly; breaking down the distinction between research and intelligence".[141]

In defense of Parsons, it could be said that while he may have made an error in judgment, this assessment is based on 40 years of hindsight. At the height of the cold war most Americans would have seen Parsons' activities as both legitimate and necessary. As one observer has noted, "Parsons simply thought of the collaboration with the intelligence community as a natural extension of the struggle for democracy against fascism undertaken during the war. . . . Moreover, fighting the totalitarian regime of Josef Stalin was a morally and politically legitimate task. . . . It was the general feeling that extraordinary things had to be done."[142]

It also could be said that Parsons accepted the value-free stance only in his sociological writing, not in his personal life. But that is precisely the point at which the Lees and Parsons diverge. The Lees claimed that it is impossible to separate one's personal life from one's sociology. Moreover, when such distinctions are attempted it leads the social scientist to an abdication of moral choices, which can be handed over to others such as political leaders, much as Parsons did. In contrast to Parsons, who argued that academic freedom in the university required that the social scientist come to the aid of the nation in time of crisis,[143] Al Lee kept up a constant stream of criticism of the resulting abuses of power by the American government throughout the Cold War years.

George Lundberg was another leading sociologist of approximately the same generation as Parsons, who subscribed to the value-free ideology. Lundberg is probably best remembered for his contributions to scientific methodology. During the McCarthy era, "true to his creed that scientists as scientists should remain politically neutral, he opposed a motion to put the American Sociological Society on record against a California loyalty oath—thus, in a sense, condoning the worst of cold war attitudes."[144] Prior to American entry into WWII, Lundberg consistently opposed taking sides in the war in Europe.[145] Lundberg felt that science had nothing to do with values, for it thrived under quite different regimes, both democratic and totalitarian.

Once the U.S. had entered the war in his 1943 ASS presidential address, he condemned religion for frustrating social science and showed more of his sympathies or values than he dared admit. For an illustration of the interference of religion Lundberg selected Jews. As the true dimensions of the Holocaust were becoming known Lundberg blamed the victims:

> "Large numbers of organized and articulate Jews in their unhappy predicament [are] devoting themselves to legalistic and moralistic conjurings so that their attention is entirely diverted from a realistic approach. They demand legislation prohibiting criticism and they demand international action outlawing anti-Semitism, instead of reckoning with the causes of the antagonism." These "firebrands" would probably attack his remarks as anti-Semitic. . . . But this fact merely showed "how a primitive, moralistic, theological, legalistic attitude obstructs a scientific approach."[146]

With a thinly veiled reference to Nazi Germany Lundberg also concluded of Jews: "They wallow in oratory about inalienable rights. One would think that if recent events had shown anything, they have shown that there is no such thing as inalienable rights."[147] In a letter to a friend he admitted that even with its fascist government he wasn't "at all sure that the Italians aren't as well off as they would have been under any other regime."[148] As for " 'the freedom of speech stuff,' as he termed it: 'how important is it to those who have nothing to say, i.e. about 99%.' "[149] As with Parsons, Lundberg's value-free ideology provided safe haven for a tolerance of fascism.

The disdain of prominent sociologists for the victims of racist oppression survived into the later part of the 20th century, seemingly unhindered by the dominant value-free ideology. Oppenheimer and his colleagues noted that another leading sociologist, Edward Shils, saw the 1960s as a "damaging decade" in which many were lured by the "temptations of spurious ideals."[150] Smugly describing himself as a patriot, Shils contended that the war in Southeast Asia was "justified, and I still regret that it had to be halted without success."[151] Flacks also recalled that Morris Janowitz had frequently expressed the view that "sociologists had no choice but to provide systematic knowledge to elites. . . . Serving as policy researchers and analysts to established elites was, at least, a way to enhance the rationality of the powerful. . . . [He] certainly felt no obligation to share his insights with black leaders and activists."[152] As an example of such policy research Flacks called attention to a pamphlet by Janowitz titled, "The Social Control of Escalated Riots," containing details for successful law enforcement arrest strategies. Janowitz proudly announced that he had mailed the document to every police chief in America. Flacks recalled the ASA meetings of 1968 led by then ASA president Philip Hauser of the University of Chicago: "Hauser's choice for keynote speaker: Wilbur Cohen, Secretary of Health, Education, and Welfare. We found the choice ironic; Hauser, who represented an ASA leadership that had denounced the effort to pass an antiwar resolution, was now inviting a top member of the war administration to be an honored guest of the ASA."[153]

In response to this outrage, immediately following Secretary Cohen's address, a sociology graduate student, Martin Nicolaus, made impassioned remarks to the convention delegates, reproduced in part below:

> This assembly here tonight is a kind of lie. It is not a coming together of those who study and know, or promote study and knowledge of, social reality. . . . The eyes of sociologists, with few but honorable (or: honorable but few) exceptions, have been turned downwards, and their palms upwards. . . . Eyes down, to study the activities of the lower classes, of the *subject* population. . . . Sociology has risen to its present prosperity and eminence on the blood and bones of the poor and oppressed; it owes its prestige in this society to its putative ability to give information and advice to the ruling class of this society about ways and means to keep the people *down*.[154]

In Chapter 3 and 4, we discuss the ways in which the contentions of this graduate student were matched by the Lees three decades earlier when, as new Ph.D.s, they launched attacks on prominent people both within and outside the profession. Yet the tolerance and support of political oppression among those adhering to the value-free mythology is remarkable, and provides a glimpse of certain leaders in the academic environment in which the Lees survived for six decades. Without some notion of the long-term tolerance or denial of political oppression among sociologists in high places, one might be left with the impression that the Lees habitually overreacted to minor disciplinary differences. In the chapters which follow we will see that these strong words of reaction from the student-sociologist Martin Nicolaus nicely express the feelings of Betty and Al Lee. Often nearly alone, the Lees were among the "very few sociologists speaking directly to the issue of responsibility in research."[155]

TYPICAL RESEARCH ASSUMPTIONS: CHRISTIANITY AND
SCIENTIFIC SOCIOLOGY

From the earliest history of what we today call sociology, scholars have made several types of assumptions. First, they have often made assumptions about the nature of human beings. These assumptions have dealt with whether human actors are inherently *equal or unequal* and also whether such actors have the capacity to be *free and self determining* or whether they are of necessity *dominated* by their environment. The second assumption deals with both the nature of people and the nature of government and asks if liberal *reforms of public policy* can really address the problems of human misery. Assumptions also have been made about whether *morality* can play an explicit role in the professional activities of social scientists. Finally, there have been assumptions about social scientists' *methods* used in research and their ability to know, whether through the scientific method or some other means. As we will show, the Lees have made assumptions on all these issues that have guided their careers.

A truly value-free scientific sociology has often been associated with a dismissive attitude toward Christianity, as reflected in the careers of Edwin Sutherland and L. L. Bernard. At the very least, Christianity has typically been considered irrelevant to sociological practice. Modern sociology, by rejecting Christianity, has rejected not just the fundamentalist varieties, but the traditions of liberal Christianity as well. Although there are exceptions such as Peter Berger, who has provided both a sociological analysis and intellectual defense of Christianity,[156] most sociologists undoubtedly fear that by admitting this religion's influence in their professional lives they would run the risk of being seen as biased, unscientific, irrational, and perhaps even untruthful. Yet it has been more acceptable for contemporary sociologists to display religious conviction openly if they are Jewish. Charges of bias against a committed Jew would be quickly seen as evidence of anti-Semitism, something few sociologists would care to risk. But for others, in place of an explicit moral or ethical basis for the profession, there existed a pervasive cultural relativism. And without an explicit moral ethic we find an implicit ethic of utilitarianism where people are seen as means toward ends rather than ends in themselves. For example, early discussions by sociologists of the effects of capital punishment were as much ideological condemnations of this practice as actual empirical demonstrations.[157] More recently sociologists have had a more open mind. Research on the possible deterrent effects of punishment has grown rapidly. These new value-free sociologists are quite different from the earlier generation, who wore their antipunishment ideology proudly. This new generation of researchers could be personally opposed to capital punishment and still feel free to determine the degree to which it is an effective deterrent.[158]

Given their value neutrality, when these researchers find that economic and racial minorities are best deterred by punishment, they feel compelled to report these results,[159] irrespective of their personal feelings about the implications of such results. One social scientist alleged that he found that "an additional execution per year over the period in question may have resulted, on average, in 7 or 8 fewer murders."[160] This researcher describes this as a direct "tradeoff" but later contends "that the efficacy and desirability of capital punishment are separate issues."[161] Yet another deterrence researcher skirts issues in these terms: "In this paper I will be concerned only with the deterrent effect of capital punishment. I will not consider the other important dimensions of this topic, for example, the morality or immorality of capital punishment."[162] Elsewhere he explained this omission: "I have some technical expertise which enables me to discover whether capital punishment has a deterrent effect in some circumstances. I have no moral expertise and consequently my opinion on the morality of capital punishment is worth no more and no less than any one else's."[163] But the late Donald Cressey, clearly a part of the older generation, saw the issue from a moral perspective: "Clearly terror works. . . . There is a humanitarian need for a new rhetoric, one which will again tame the jolly boys who would kill many criminals and chain the rest to the floor."[164] The Lees noted the rapidly rising prison population in the United States and agreed with the American Friends' Service Committee that full employment, rather than imprisonment, is a more just solution.[165] The chapters which follow indicate quite clearly that Betty and Al Lee have spent their lives attempting to supply the "new rhetoric" called for by Cressey.

CONCLUSION: THE SOCIAL CONTEXT OF THE LEES' CAREERS

After World War II, as the Lees matured as scholars, their fellow sociologists "mirrored the optimism and satisfaction found in the broader society."[166] Sociology was increasingly dominated by the value-free orientation, sociological theory as it was reflected in works such as *The Social System*, and also by an increasing dependence upon government funding for research.[167] Sociologists' earlier dissatisfactions with the status quo and the corresponding traditions of moral reform became more and more remote. As Gouldner puts it: "Following World War II there was a tendency in American sociology to return to a more *social* utilitarianism [reflected in] *The Social System*.[168] According to Gouldner, this book, in turn, "placed a relatively great stress on the importance of the gratifying outcome of *individual conformity* (emphasis added) with values."[169] Another part of this trend was the development of a statistical "social accounting system" at the behest of government funding agencies, with the ultimate aim of increasing citizen manipulation and control.[170] Reflective of the great consensus among sociologists, several widely-circulated handbooks were published from the 1940s through the 1960s, presenting what were generally agreed to be the "major developments, issues, and problems in the various subareas of the field."[171]

To be sure, there were other isolated voices of dissent. C. Wright Mills provided caustic criticism of "Grand Theory," such as espoused by Parsons, unrelated to the real world, as well as "Abstract Empiricism" so common in reporting of public opinion research.[172] Yet such criticism was at the time relatively rare. Perhaps dissent was rare and "excitement and enthusiasm" the norm, because at the time the discipline experienced significant numerical growth, as well as increased public recognition.[173] Sociologists' training and research were not only increasingly funded by federal agencies, but sociologists were increasingly consulted in government policy-making. We will examine in Chapters 3–5 how the Lees responded to each of these developing trends in sociology.

Chapter 2 demonstrates that Betty and Al Lee's careers not only were influenced by professional role models but also by their families. And like their families, they have from the beginning gone off in often lonely paths, because unlike most of their contemporaries, they have been deeply involved in religious organizations—first through the Episcopal church and later through the Society of Friends and the Unitarians. We will see also how institutionalized discrimination based on gender had a distorting influence on Betty's career.

NOTES

1. James E. Blackwell. "Call for Nominations, SSSP Founders' Award." *SSSP Newsletter* (Winter 1982).

2. *SSSP Newsletter* (1971–72): 22.

3. *Clinical Sociology Newsletter.* "Introduction," (Fall 1981): 2

4. Ibid.

5. S. M. Miller. "Portrait of our New President." *ASA Footnotes* 3 (August 1975): 1,6.

6. Ibid.: 6.

7. *SSSP Newsletter*. "Elizabeth Briant Lee Wins Award." Vol. 20 (Summer 1989): 6.

8. Arthur J. Vidich and Stanford M. Lyman. *American Sociology: Worldly Rejections of Religion and Their Directions* (New Haven: Yale University Press 1985): xi.

9. Ibid.: 3.

10. Darian Connecticut *Review*. "Dr. Lee is Honored by Sumner Club." (April 11, 1940).

11. Alfred McClung Lee. *Sociology for Whom?* (Syracuse, NY: Syracuse University Press, 1986): 7.

12. Ibid.: 7–8.

13. Alfred McClung Lee. "A Response to Dusky Lee Smith and Larry T. Reynolds, 'The Sociologist as Critical Apologist: William Graham Sumner as an Anti-Imperialist.' " *Humanity and Society* 11 (1988): 205.

14. Alfred McClung Lee. "Introduction." *Earth Hunger and Other Essays* (New Brunswick, N.J.: Transaction Books, 1980): xxiii.

15. Ibid.: xvii.

16. Dorothy Ross. *The Origins of American Social Science* (Cambridge: Cambridge University Press, 1991): 88.

17. Vidich and Lyman op. cit.: 36.

18. Ibid.: 41.

19. Ibid.: 47.

20. Ross op. cit.: 91.

21. Ibid.: 92.

22. Lee 1988 op. cit.

23. William Graham Sumner. *Folkways: A Study of the Sociological Importance of Usages, Manners, Customs, Mores, and Morals* (Boston: Ginn and Company, 1940): 169.

24. Vidich and Lyman. op. cit.

25. Ross op. cit.: 126.

26. Ibid.

27. Vidich and Lyman op. cit.

28. Ibid.

29. Ross op. cit.

30. Ibid.

31. Robert C. Bannister. *Sociology and Scientism: The American Quest for Objectivity, 1880–1940* (Chapel Hill: University of North Carolina Press, 1987).

32. Ibid.

33. Ross op. cit.

34. Edward Shils. "Tradition, Ecology, and Institution in the History of Sociology." *Daedalus* 99 (Fall 1970): 760–825.

35. Don Martindale. *The Nature and Types of Sociological Theory* (Cambridge: Houghton Mifflin, 1960).

36. Lewis A. Coser. *Masters of Sociological Thought: Ideas in Historical and Social Context* (New York: Harcourt Brace Jovanovich, Inc., 1971).

37. Ibid.: 369.

38. Robert Ezra Park. *Race and Culture* (Glencoe, IL: The Free Press, 1950): 159.

39. Shils op. cit.

40. Bannister op. cit.: 223.

41. Vidich and Lyman op. cit.: 229

42. Herbert Blumer. "Science without Concepts." *American Journal of Sociology* 36 (January 1931): 515–33; Bannister: 176.

43. Blumer: 525.

44. Kenneth Baugh, Jr. *The Methodology of Herbert Blumer* (Cambridge: Cambridge University Press 1990): 2.

45. Bannister op. cit.: 194.

46. Vidich and Lyman op. cit.: 157.

47. Ibid.: 159.

48. Ibid.: 286.

49. Mary O. Furner. *Advocacy and Objectivity: A Crisis in the Professionalization of American Social Science, 1865–1905* (Lexington: University of Kentucky Press, 1975): 150.

50. Ibid.

51. Ibid.

52. Ibid.: 162.

53. Mark S. Gaylord and John F. Galliher. *The Criminology of Edwin Sutherland* (New Brunswick, NJ: Transaction Books, 1988).

54. Bannister op. cit.: 113; *Jessie Bernard: The Making of a Feminist* (New Brunswick, NJ: Rutgers University Press, 1991): 198.

55. Ibid.

56. Ibid.

57. Gaylord and Galliher op. cit.

58. Bannister 1987 op. cit.

59. Edwin H. Sutherland. *The Professional Thief* (Chicago: University of Chicago Press, 1937).

60. John F. Galliher and Cheryl Tyree. "Edwin Sutherland's Research on the Origins of Sexual Psychopath Laws: An Early Case

Study of the Medicalization of Deviance." *Social Problems* 33 (December 1985): 100–113.

61. Galliher and Gaylord op. cit.: 66.

62. Ibid.

63. John H. Laub and Robert J. Sampson. "The Sutherland-Glueck Debate: On the Sociology of Criminological Knowledge." *American Journal of Sociology* 96 (May 1991): 1423.

64. Edwin H. Sutherland. "The Sexual Psychopath Laws." *Journal of Criminal Law and Criminology* 40 (January-February 1950): 554.

65. Galliher and Tyree op. cit.: 109.

66. Paul W. Tappan. "Who is the Criminal?" *American Sociological Review* 12 (February 1947): 96–102.

67. Edwin H. Sutherland. "'Is White Collar Crime,' Crime?" *American Sociological Review* 10 (April 1945): 132–39.

68. Gilbert Geis and Colin Goff, eds. "Introduction." *White Collar Crime: The Uncut Version*. Edwin H. Sutherland (New Haven: Yale University Press, 1983): xv.

69. Alfred McClung Lee. *Sociology for Whom?* 2nd ed. (Syracuse, NY: Syracuse University Press. 1986): 212.

70. Sutherland 1937 op. cit.

71. Sutherland 1950 op. cit.: 545.

72. Bannister 1987 op. cit.

73. Ibid.

74. Ibid.: 6.

75. Ibid.: 230.

76. Ibid.: 112.

77. Ibid.: 201.

78. Ibid.: 189.

79. John F. Galliher and Robert A. Hagan. "L.L. Bernard and the Original *American Sociologist*." *The American Sociologist* 20 (Summer 1989): 136.

80. Talcott Parsons. "*The American Sociologist*: Editorial Statement." *The American Sociologist* 1 (November 1965): 2–3.

81. Elizabeth Briant Lee and Alfred McClung Lee. "The Society for the Study of Social Problems: Parental Recollections and Hopes." *Social Problems* 24 (October 1976): 6.

82. Bannister 1987 op. cit.: 112.

83. Bannister 1987 op. cit.

84. Ibid.: 140.

85. Vidich and Lyman op. cit.: 174.

86. Shils op. cit.

87. Barry Skura. "Constraints on the Reform Movement: Rela-

tionships between SSSP and ASA, 1951–1970." *Social Problems* 24 (October 1976): 17.

88. Howard Becker. "Marihuana Use and Social Control." *Social Problems* 3 (July 1955): 35–44.

89. Harold Finestone. "Cats, Kicks, and Color." *Social Problems* 5 (July 1957): 4–5

90. Shils op. cit.

91. Robert S. Lynd. *Knowledge for What?* (Princeton, NJ: Princeton University Press, 1939).

92. Ibid.: 1.

93. Ibid.: 184.

94. Ibid.: 228.

95. Ibid.: 220.

96. Ibid. 227.

97. Ibid., 241.

98. Lee. 1986 op. cit.

99. Alfred McClung Lee. *Sociology for People* (Syracuse, NY: Syracuse University Press, 1988).

100. Joseph A. Scimecca. *The Sociological Theory of C. Wright Mills* (Port Washington, N.Y.: Kennikat Press, 1977).

101. C. Wright Mills. "The Professional Ideology of Social Pathologists." *American Journal of Sociology* 49 (September 1943): 165–80.

102. Scimecca op. cit.

103. Ibid.

104. Ibid.: 13.

105. Irving Louis Horowitz. *C. Wright Mills: An American Utopian* (New York: The Free Press, 1983).

106. C. Wright Mills. *The Sociological Imagination* (New York: Oxford University Press, 1959).

107. C. Wright Mills. *Listen Yankee! The Revolution in Cuba* (New York: McGraw-Hill, 1960).

108. C. Wright Mills. *The Causes of World War III* (New York: Simon and Schuster, 1958).

109. Horowitz op. cit.

110. Alvin W. Gouldner. "Anti-Minotaur: The Myth of a Value-free Sociology," *Social Problems* 9 (Winter 1962): 212.

111. ———. *The Coming Crisis of Western Sociology* (New York: Basic Books, 1970): 335.

112. ———. "On the Quality of Discourse Among Some Sociologists." *American Journal of Sociology* 79 (1973): 152–57.

113. *Transaction*. "Alvin Ward Gouldner July 29, 1920–December 15, 1980." Vol. 18 (March/April 1981): 82.

114. Alvin W. Gouldner. "Theoretical Requirements of the Applied Social Sciences," *American Sociological Review* 22 (1957): 92–102.

115. Richard Wightman Fox. "Epitaph for Middletown: Robert S. Lynd and the Analysis of Consumer Culture." *The Culture of Consumption: Critical Essays in American History, 1880–1980.* Richard Wightman Fox and T. J. Jackson Lears, eds. (New York: Pantheon Books 1983): 101–41.

116. American Sociological Association. "Advice to Future Sociologists by the 20 Living Former Presidents of the American Sociological Society." First Played at the 1953 Annual Meeting, Berkeley, California.

117. Ibid.

118. Ibid.

119. Ibid.

120. Vidich and Lyman op. cit.: 288.

121. American Sociological Association.

122. Ibid.

123. Robert W. Friedrichs. *A Sociology of Sociology* (New York: The Free Press 1970): 77.

124. Robert Bannister. "Principle, Politics, Profession: American Sociologists and Fascism, 1930–1950." *Sociology Responds to Fascism.* Stephen P. Turner and Dirk Kasler, eds. (London: Routledge, Kegan & Paul, 1992).

125. Ibid: 196.

126. Ibid.: 190.

127. Ibid.: 197.

128. William Buxton and Stephen Turner. "From Edification to Expertise: Sociology as a 'Profession.' " *Sociology and Its Publics: The Forms and Fates of Disciplinary Organization.* Terence C. Halliday and Morris Janowitz, eds. (Chicago: University of Chicago Press, 1992): 378–407.

129. Uta Gerhardt. *Talcott Parsons on National Socialism* (New York: Aldine De Gruyter, 1993): 22.

130. Ibid.

131. Ibid.: 15.

132. Ibid.: 101.

133. William Buxton. *Talcott Parsons and the Capitalist Nation-State: Political Sociology as a Strategic Vocation* (Toronto: University of Toronto Press, 1985).

134. Gerhardt op cit.: 107.

135. Bannister 1992 op. cit.: 202.

136. Talcott Parsons. "The Sociology of Modern Anti-Semit-

ism." *Jews in a Gentile World.* Isacque Graeber and Steuart Henderson Britt, eds. (New York: The Macmillan Company, 1942): 115–16.

137. Jon Weiner. "Talcott Parsons' Role: Bringing Nazi Sympathizers to the U.S." *The Nation* (March 6, 1989): 1, 306, 308, 309.

138. Ibid.: 308, 309.

139. Sigmund Diamond. *Compromised Campus: The Collaboration of Universities with the Intelligence Community, 1945–1955.* (New York: Oxford University Press, 1992): 89–90.

140. Ibid.: 93.

141. Ibid.: 95.

142. Jens Kaalhauge Nielsen. "The Political Orientation of Talcott Parsons: The Second World War and its Aftermath." *Talcott Parsons: Theorist of Modernity.* Roland Robertson and Bryan S. Turner, eds. (London: Sage Publications, 1991): 224.

143. Gerhardt op. cit.: 39.

144. Bannister 1991 op. cit.: 129.

145. Ibid.

146. Ibid.: 110.

147. George A. Lundberg. "Sociologists and the Peace." *American Sociological Review* 9 (February 1944): 3.

148. Bannister 1992. op. cit.: 192.

149. Ibid.

150. Martin Oppenheimer, Martin J. Murray, and Rhonda F. Levine, eds. "Introduction: The Movement and the Academy." *Radical Sociologists and the Movement: Experiences, Lessons, and Legacies* (Philadelphia: Temple University Press, 1991): 12.

151. Edward Shils. "Totalitarians and Antinomians." *Political Passages: Journeys of Change Through Two Decades, 1968–1988.* John H. Bunzel, ed. (New York: The Free Press, 1988): 19.

152. Dick Flacks. "The Sociology Liberation Movement: Some Legacies and Lessons." *Radical Sociologists and the Movement: Experiences, Lessons, and Legacies.* Martin Oppenheimer, Martin Murray, and Rhonda Levine, eds. (Philadelphia: Temple University Press, 1991): 20.

153. Ibid.: 18–19.

154. Martin Nicolaus. "Remarks at ASA Convention," *The American Sociologist* 4 (May 1969): 155.

155. Friedrichs op. cit.: 118.

156. Peter L. Berger. *The Precarious Vision: A Sociologist Looks at Social Fictions and Christian Faith* (New York: Doubleday and Company, Inc., 1961).

157. Jack Greenberg and Jack Himmelstein. "Varieties of Attack on the Death Penalty." *Crime and Delinquency* 15 (January 1969):

112–20; Hugo Adam Bedau. *The Death Penalty in America* (New York: Doubleday and Company, Inc., 1964); Thorsten Sellin, ed. *Capital Punishment* (New York: Harper and Row, 1967).

158. Jack P. Gibbs. "Crime, Punishment and Deterrence." *Southwestern Social Science Quarterly* 48 (March 1968): 515–30.

159. Charles R. Tittle. *Sanctions and Social Deviance: The Question of Deterrence* (New York: Praeger Publishers, 1980).

160. Isaac Ehrlich. "The Deterrent Effect of Capital Punishment: A Question of Life and Death." *American Economic Review* 65 (1975): 414.

161. Isaac Ehrlich. "On Positive Methodology, Ethics, and Politics in Deterrence Research." *British Journal of Criminology* 22 (1982): 137.

162. David P. Phillips. "The Deterrent Effect of Capital Punishment: New Evidence on an Old Controversy." *American Journal of Sociology* 86 (July 1980): 139.

163. David P. Phillips. Letter to John F. Galliher (October 23, 1980).

164. Donald R. Cressey. "The Scientist and the Writer," *Contemporary Sociology* 9 (May 1980): 345–46.

165. Elizabeth Briant Lee and Alfred McClung Lee. "Struggles Toward Equality and Justice," Presentation at the annual meetings of the Society for the Study of Social Problems (1991).

166. Ted R. Vaughan. "The Crisis in Contemporary American Sociology: A Critique of the Discipline's Dominant Paradigm." *A Critique of Contemporary American Sociology.* Ted R. Vaughan, Gideon Sjoberg, and Larry T. Reynolds, eds. (Dix Hills, N.Y.: General Hall, Inc., 1993): 15.

167. Martin Bulmer. "The Growth of Applied Sociology after 1945: The Prewar Establishment of the Postwar Infrastructure." *Sociology and Its Publics: The Forms and Fates of Disciplinary Organization.* Terence C. Halliday and Morris Janowitz, eds. (Chicago: University of Chicago Press, 1992): 317–45.

168. Gouldner 1970: 139.

169. Ibid.

170. Ibid.: 50.

171. Vaughan op. cit.

172. Mills 1959 op cit.

173. Vaughan op. cit.

Chapter 2

The Significance of Two Careers and Lives Together

BOTH TOGETHER IN EVERYTHING: A REVISIONIST HISTORY

For both Betty and Al the commitment to family has been just as profound as their commitment to humanity. Al and Betty collected many volumes of scrapbooks devoted to the development of their family and their careers, mixed together, showing equal commitment to both. A psychologist who attended both high school and college with Al recalls that the Lees' commitment to each other, to their children, to their extended family, and to people in general may be the key to understanding their careers: "I suggest that this concept of commitment may provide the theme which may guide the exposition of their careers. . . . Such demonstration of commitment is an all-too-rare personal attribute in the 20th century, wherein personal selfish insecurity is almost totally taken for granted."[1] We will see in the chapters which follow that some others have characterized this commitment as a weakness rather than a strength.

The Lees' professional careers are best captured, according to Betty Lee, by the Italian phrase, *tutti e due insieme*, or both together in everything. This phrase should serve as a methodological note on a revisionist history of two lives in one career. If revisionist history has as a primary mission the discovery and analysis of institutionalized oppression left unexamined in more traditional historical accounts, this is precisely what is attempted here. Over the years Al often suggested that Betty be a coauthor of his books and articles, but she typically declined. Betty was involved in countless discussions with Al in helping to formulate ideas, and in reading all drafts of manuscripts. Betty observed in an interview that: "Al did most of the initial writing and I do the editing—I'm an excellent proofreader." Her reading and criticism, of course, was that of a colleague and not merely as a copyeditor. Al's profound gratitude to Betty was reflected in 1966, when he dedicated a book (as he often did): "To my closest associate, collaborator, and fellow sociologist, my wife, the spirit of my Pierian spring."[2]

It has been observed that a "pattern of uneven attribution of credit was common for many academic couples in these times, a gendered practice where women's contributions were much less visible than their husbands'."[3] A colleague and friend agreed that "Al would have been the first to say Betty has not had her share of the acclaim. By today's long-overdue standards Betty certainly has not been done right by."[4] A prime example of her tireless work behind the scenes is that in 1978 Betty typed the entire AHS program on Al's manual typewriter.[5] One of Al's female colleagues from Brooklyn College noted: "Even though Al and Betty are sensitive to issues of equality, they are still people of their times, when female intellectuals were not treated fairly. Other sociological couples of their age cohort show the same patterns. Everett and Helen Hughes as well as John and Matilda Riley are other examples. In all these cases the women wrote a lot that never got their name on it."[6]

Thus this biography is not merely a revisionist history of these careers, but a revisionist history with a feminist slant to give Betty her fair share of credit, which she has been denied, and in fact which she has denied herself, due to the legacy of institutionalized and internalized sexism. Such a feminist-revisionist history is one with which both Betty and Al would have no quarrel. To produce this revisionist history in the text which follows we will refer to all of the Lee books, articles, and other papers as joint productions, which in fact they were, even in those cases where Al's name alone appears. The appendix and notes will show the exact citation as published.

EARLY LIFE BEFORE MARRIAGE AND AS NEWLYWEDS IN GRADUATE SCHOOL

Al was born August 23, 1906, and Betty, September 9, 1908.[7] They first met on a so-called "blind" date at the home of friends in Oakmont, Pennsylvania, in 1926. They then wandered around in the quiet of a local cemetery. A year later, after Betty had finished her sophomore year of college and Al had graduated, they were married. Both Betty's and Al's parents were deeply committed to higher education, although it was not an easy task for them because both families struggled financially. After Al's father graduated from the state normal school at Indiana, Pennsylvania, he decided to become an attorney, as had two of his uncles and his older brother. While attending the University of Pittsburgh law school he supported himself by working as a newspaper reporter.

Both Betty's and Al's fathers were opposed to militarism and were active Christians. Betty was reared a Baptist. As a child and young man Al sang in the choir at the St. Thomas Episcopal Church in Oakmont, Pennsylvania. Al recalled that one attraction for the younger members of the choir was that they were given a small weekly allowance for singing. His life was made all the richer by the love he found at home. For example, Al remembered "wonderful experiences with the horse my father bought for my brother and me, a mustang named Bess."

Al's father was a Pittsburgh attorney who was known in the area for his defense of African Americans, immigrants, and other powerless people. Al recalled that on one occasion his father learned that the local Ku Klux Klan planned a raid on a local black church during the Sunday evening services. His father asked the minister if he could be the featured guest speaker that evening. When the KKK arrived his father confronted them in the center isle of the church and pulled off the leader's mask, thus identifying him. Perhaps as a result of this surprise they left without a word. Later, however, reflecting the KKK's special brand of cowardice, a cross was burned in the front yard of the family's home. Al recalled his father's influence: "Since my father was an attorney who served the poor and since several of his sisters were local volunteer social workers, I early gained from them a sense of there being real people in groups other than our own. Those others were different from us, but they included people of integrity and dignity. The mixture of pupils in our nonsegregated public school helped me to look across intergroup gaps more accurately."[8] Elsewhere Al has written: "My father, the late educator, journalist, and attorney for whom I am named, took me as a child and youth behind the scenes of society and gave me intimate glimpses of human beings struggling with their problems in groups quite different from our own."[9] Al noted that "I did not know until later what father's idealism in this and other respects cost him in 'respectable' clients." Fueled by the democratic spirit of his family, as a boy Al organized his own scout troop, number three, as an alternative to the one he had initially joined. His troop was intentionally nonmilitaristic and had no salutes or any marching. The excellence of the group is reflected in the fact that 28 of the 32 boys in the troop achieved the Eagle rank. Al's father was the scout master. Al knew a good deal of the history of his family and noted that "the bulk of my forebears were starved or driven out of Ireland and Wales during one or another period of famine or repression in the seventeenth and eighteenth

centuries." He traced his ancestry back to an Irish sailor John Mc-
Clung and his wife Sarah, a couple whose last name he proudly
carried.

Betty's father was a part of middle management in a steel plant,
but in the depression of the 1930s was replaced by a relative of the
owner. He then spent his last years as a farmer and an "agitator for
socialism." While Betty's family was one of modest means, unlike
many families of the time they insisted that all of their children,
including their daughter, go to college. Betty had two brothers; one
became a physician and the other a dentist. Betty recalled that she
came from a middle-class family, which her mother felt qualified
them to be a part of the "genteel poor." "My mother was proud of
her family background and we always had white linen tablecloths and
napkins for the evening meal." Like Al, Betty indicated that she has
been interested in Ireland for a long time. She traced her interest to
that fact that her mother's maiden name was Riley. Betty recalled:
"My mother didn't want any connection with this. She always
claimed that the family had actually immigrated to Ireland from
Germany several centuries prior to coming to the United States. The
200 or so years she felt didn't make them Irish. But as a young girl I
imagined that I would like Ireland because I enjoyed Irish fairy tales.
And I once told my mother that if I could not be an American I would
like to be Irish. She was not at all pleased to hear it."

Betty's interest in things Irish would surface years later in research
on Northern Ireland. Betty's mother had other prejudices as well:
"My mother was from Virginia and had a very different attitude
toward people than mine. For example, my mother went to my grade
school and objected vociferously because I had to walk into the
classroom with a black child, Eva. We went in two abreast according
to height and Eva was the shortest and happened to be black and I
was the next shortest."

Betty and Al ascribed great importance to the influence of their
childhood homes. Betty was an outstanding high-school student and
graduated as the salutatorian of her senior class. Early on Betty
demonstrated a keen awareness of art, and in her June 1925 graduation
address to her classmates, she urged them to make homes for themselves filled with art, a practice she followed herself. Betty had tied
with a male for the highest grades in her senior class, but then the
school authorities determined that the tie could be broken since the
boy had taken one more course than had Betty. "My mother was
furious for she thought the selection was rigged. The problem was
that only the valedictorian got an automatic scholarship to college.
But mother was working for a woman who had direct family connec-

tions to a foundation and this woman saw to it that my tuition to Pitt was covered." Betty was awarded the Sarah Sloan Scholarship in 1925 to attend the University of Pittsburgh, where she majored in English literature. "By the end of my sophomore year in college Al and I had decided to get married even though none of our parents liked it at all. I was 19 and Al was 21. Al's mother didn't care for college women." Even so, she and Al were married in the Episcopal Cathedral in Pittsburgh.

> After I was married I was very different from everyone else in college. Even the girls in the Kappa Kappa Gamma house [Betty's sorority] were standoffish. They didn't understand the idea of a female going to school because you liked learning and wanted a profession—they seemed to feel that simply being married was enough. None of them was friendly with me. Their elitism disturbed me greatly. Some older members objected to pledging one woman on the basis that she chewed gum, another because she wore pearl earrings to school—which was considered to be in poor taste, but we got them in anyhow. Looking back on the situation is amusing because these same elitist girls refused to recognize the fact that one member of the sorority was probably working her way through college as a prostitute, even while she was living in the house. She often had more than one engagement with different men on the same evening and often received very lavish gifts from them.

As an undergraduate Al majored in mathematics and English composition. Even though Al served in the ROTC as an undergraduate at Pitt, he was a conscientious objector during WWII, as were both of Al and Betty's sons during the Korean and Vietnam wars. Curiously, Al's only sibling, a brother George, earned a Ph.D. degree in engineering and eventually retired with the rank of a three star general at the Pentagon, as Chief scientist of the U.S. Ordnance Corps. Earlier George had taught at the U.S. Naval Academy. Given the great gulf in the political views of Al and his brother it was predictable that they were never really close. Betty recalled: "Whenever George was in New York City he would arrange to have lunch with Al. And over the years during their conversations George would often ask Al if he was a Communist. Just for fun Al never gave him a straight answer and so when they got together again George would ask the same question. Part of the reason for George's concern was that he may have been worried about radical relatives creating problems with his government security clearance."

In 1945 Al and Betty left the Episcopal church over the issue of racism in the church, after Al's having been a vestry member in a Detroit congregation. Al recalled that "the clergy did not like a talk I gave at a church meeting on racism in the church. We gradually left and put our kids in a Unitarian Sunday school." After that time the Lees remained active Unitarians and also participated in Friends' Meetings. Al served as president of the American Unitarian Fellowship for Social Justice.

Beginning Graduate School at the University of Pittsburgh

In 1930 Betty received her B.A. degree and in 1931 the M.A. degree at Pittsburgh. Betty recalled:

> Dr. Florence Teagarden in the psychology department was one of the few women on the faculty then. I took various courses from her and I also worked for her in a hospital with the mentally ill. She had me following up on patients six months after they were released. She really got me conscious about wanting to go to graduate school. She told me about a good course that was going to be offered in the upcoming semester that I should take which would prepare me for graduate school. She said: "You are going to graduate school aren't you?"

At the University of Pittsburgh Betty worked as a graduate assistant for George Lundberg and for F. F. Stephan, a statistician later at Princeton. At the University of Pittsburgh Manuel C. Elmer had asked if Betty could receive a fellowship awarded by the sociology honorary society, Alpha Kappa Delta. However, she was ruled to be ineligible because she was married; it was reasoned that as a married woman with a husband to provide for her, she didn't need it. The response to her request for a fellowship was that "any married woman who takes graduate work must have incentive enough and does not need further encouragement."[10] Her M.A. thesis, titled "Personnel Aspects of Social Work in Pittsburgh," focused on the patterns of employment of social workers in the city in an effort to assess the needs and gaps in the availability of such services. As the title indicates, this was a survey and description of social workers and their agencies in the city. At the time of her research the profession of social work was almost wholly composed of females and this undoubtedly was responsible for Betty's interest in this topic. The survey information Betty collected for her MA thesis was used to establish the need for a school of social work at the University of Pittsburgh.[11] Her interest in women's issues continued and later was reflected in her choice of a dissertation topic.

Al's M.A. thesis at Pitt, "Trends in Commercial Entertainment in Pittsburgh as Reflected in the Advertising in Pittsburgh Newspapers (1790–1860)," was completed and the degree awarded in 1931, the same year as was Betty's. Al's thesis research demonstrated a nearly steady increase between 1790–1860 in newspaper space devoted to total paid advertising, as well as in entertainment advertising. He observed a quite different pattern in liquor advertising, which peaked around 1820 and then tapered off. Al noted that the objective of the thesis was not primarily to develop a historical record, but rather the testing of the "validity of certain statistical data as quantitative indications of social trends . . . [and] the determination of relationships existing between the social trends studied statistically and other influencing social factors in the community. This investigation was, in other words, an experiment in sociologic method rather than an effort to exercise some historic technique."[12] At this early stage in his career Al seemed well on his way to becoming a contented mainstream social scientist.

While Betty was an M.A. candidate at Pittsburgh, and while waiting for a class to begin, she overheard two students talking about graduate fellowships at Yale for students who had a parent who was a member of the Allegheny County Bar Association. Al checked it out. His father was a member of the bar association, and Al found that his great uncle was a member of the committee that awarded such fellowships. Al applied for the fellowship and not surprisingly it was awarded to him. Thus both Betty and Al were able to use personal and family connections to help finance their higher education at a time when few without independent means could realistically aspire to university training.

MAN AND WOMAN AT YALE

With the funds from Al's scholarship Betty and Al were off to Yale. To help make ends meet while at Yale Al also worked as a reporter (as had his father before him). Al worked for the New Haven *Journal-Courier* and also handled public relations for a political campaign. His opportunity to work in the political campaign developed when Al took a course in the government department from Milton Conover. Professor Conover learned that Al had worked as a journalist and asked for his assistance in his campaign for the United States Senate. He ran as an Independent Republican in hopes of taking enough votes away from the regular Republican candidate, Hiram Bingham, to insure his defeat. Conover's plan worked. With Al's help Bingham was defeated.

Betty found the going somewhat difficult at Yale because she was one of the first women to enroll there in the sociology graduate program. In those days sociology and anthropology were combined and one of the senior anthropologists took great pleasure in mocking and belittling her. For example, the foreign language requirements were handled in each department by designated professors. This anthropology professor handled the German tutorials for all graduate students in the combined department. He met from time to time with a small group of students to provide instruction in German and to test their mastery of the language. Betty recalled: "I had trouble with German and as he tried to teach us he made fun of me repeatedly. He was a mocking kind of person. When I first took the exam from him he said I would have to take it again, which I did. But after the retake I went to the graduate school to check on my performance only to learn that he had actually passed me on the first exam and had me take the second for no reason." Betty felt this gender-related bias manifested itself in other ways:

> The department required Al to take a difficult and advanced course on theoretical sociology, but not me. They didn't even want me to be prepared. Professor Keller, on the other hand, was always fair with me, but even he had advised me to drop out of school, stay home, and have a baby. I did drop out of school temporarily to have the baby and to type Al's dissertation since we had no funds for a typist. I eventually finished my dissertation after we left Yale. Just prior to our leaving, the anthropologist who had always mocked me came by our house to invite Al to contribute a paper for a festschrift for Keller. He then looked at me, smiled, and said that I couldn't contribute because I hadn't finished my dissertation.

After all the intervening years, and long after the death of this well-known anthropologist, Betty still felt that good manners precluded mentioning his name.

DISSERTATIONS

Betty Lee completed her dissertation in 1937, the second woman to complete graduate training in sociology at Yale. The dissertation, titled "Eminent Women: A Cultural Study,"[13] is squarely placed in a feminist tradition. Since it has never been published, it deserves special attention. Betty Lee used the 1928 through 1936 editions of the *Dictionary of American Biography* to compile a list of the 628 women, born between 1750 and 1894, who had achieved at a level to be included in this publication. Her dissertation included all of those women who had achieved eminence in the areas of writing, art, education, religion, philanthropy, business, and other learned professions, including medicine and law. She looked into the family backgrounds of these women, as well as their religious affiliations, education, marital status, and economic situation.

Betty Lee's review of existing literature on eminence cited a 1906 study of royalty that came to the absurd conclusion that the nobility's distinction was due to their "high level of mental activity" (1–16). Her literature review also demonstrated that most of the previous literature dealt solely with the eminence of men. This shortcoming characterized the work of such notables as William Graham Sumner and Charles H. Cooley. However, Betty noted that, to his credit, Cooley recognized that an advantaged social environment is responsible for achievement rather than race: "Social conditions can cause genius to remain hidden" (1–12). Unfortunately Cooley said nothing about gender. Betty Lee displayed a dry sense of humor usually missing in dissertations, for in her review of the literature on eminence she included the study of a German scholar who noted that the reason for there being few eminent women was that they are usually better suited to biological reproduction than to aiding the progress of culture. While Betty indicated there were a few studies of eminent women, there were no attempts to relate eminence of females to social structure. Betty asked (1–33): "Have there been women of genius in America comparable to those in our more lengthy lists of unusual men?" And: "the investigator hoped to find out whether or not any common influences in life conditions would appear to have stimulated extraordinary achievement." (1–34).

Physicians, college presidents, professors, clergy, and lawyers made up two percent of the total population, but nearly 22 percent of these women's fathers. Of the 628 women, 155, or almost 25 percent, had relatives who were also in the Dictionary—9.1 percent of their fathers and 19.6 percent of their husbands. More eminent women were born in New England than in any other region of the country and as adults lived in the Middle Atlantic region more often than any other area. These geographical patterns undoubtedly tell us a lot about regional cultural differences in the emancipation of women during these early years of American history.

The 429 married women on the list had an average of 1.9 children, far fewer than the national average during these periods, when large families were the norm. Lee noted that their comparatively small families undoubtedly contributed to these females' freedom to achieve excellence. Education for females was not stressed during these periods in American history and thus the eminence of these women is especially noteworthy. Of course, sufficient money was needed to finance a formal education, but not so much as to discourage educational attainment. Women born to wealthy families "felt no need and small urge to follow a lucrative profession, but the folkways called for her to be a fashionable lady." (4–25). Moreover, Protestants outnumbered Roman Catholics. There were only 32 of the latter. Liberal religious training found among groups such as the Quakers and Unitarians encouraged achievement, while Protestant religious sects viewed women as belonging only in the home. Betty undoubtedly was especially sensitive to issues such as child rearing obligations since, as indicated above, she had temporarily dropped out of graduate school to type her husband's dissertation and also to have her first baby in 1934.

The largest single group of these women was writers (n = 232), including poets, novelists, and journalists. The period of greatest achievement was between 1830 and the Civil War. For example, Harriet Beecher Stowe (1811–1896) wrote *Uncle Tom's Cabin* (1851–52), which attacked slavery and became a nationwide sensation. Another similar attack was Lydia M. F. Child's (1802–1880) *An Appeal in Favor of the Class of Americans Called Africans* (1833). Also found in this period was the famous suffragist and reformer, Susan B. Anthony (1820–1906). Others include Dorothea Dix (1802–1887), who established hospitals and asylums to replace prisons for the insane. Clara Barton (1821–1912) established the Red Cross and Eliza D. Steward (1816–1908) founded the Woman's Christian Temperance Union. Lee does not glorify these women, for she noted that Mary Baker Eddy (1821–1910), who founded Christian Science, has been presumed by her biographers to have been suffering from several types of mental disease. This dissertation is a prime example of early feminist research that preceded by nearly half a century the resurgence of the women's movement in the United States. It not only predated the contemporary woman's movement by several decades, but also was far ahead of the interests of most sociologists.

Yet Betty's work was not always appreciated. At Yale one visiting sociologist, when told of her interest in women, snorted, "That's not a field!"[14] Nearly 60 years later, the oral defense of the dissertation has left unpleasant memories: "Two members of my committee, including the mocking anthropologist, didn't like the idea of a dissertation on American women and made fun of me during the oral defense. But Professor Keller became angry with them and shouted at them in defending me." This history of eminent women demonstrates the point that the writing by women "is likely to be devalued and discounted, particularly if it is about women"[15] for it traditionally has been assumed by male scholars that women studying women will bring biases and distortions to the task. At the time Betty wrote her dissertation, even some female historians did not challenge the basic assumptions of the field.[16]

Betty recalls that even her family didn't always understand her: "My older brother's wife was jealous of my being a graduate student at Yale. Once when Al and I were back in Pennsylvania visiting family she sniffed, 'It isn't enough for Betty to be a wife and mother.' " And even Betty's supporters on the faculty did not offer much professional encouragement: "While I was finishing up my studies at Yale the only position that Keller could find for me was as a dean of women, volleyball coach, and sociology instructor at a small college in Pennsylvania."

Unlike Betty's dissertation, Al's dissertation, *The Daily Newspaper in America*, was published as a book in 1937 and was still in print in 1991.[17] The scope and table of contents shows an encyclopedic coverage in its 797 pages. The book has chapters on the history of the daily newspaper, various types of dailies ranging from large-city dailies to foreign language dailies, material needs including printing equipment and ink, labor costs and unions, ownership and management, newspaper chains, circulation, Sunday papers, wire services, propaganda in the press, and advertising and editorial policy. Al felt this book had a critical edge in examining the relationship between editorial policy and advertising. He noted in the book, "On the whole, principles agreeable to advertising interests or to certain advertisers dominate editorial policy largely because publishers and their editorial employees accept the dominant mores of their communities and of the class to which they and the advertisers belong."[18] The book observed that, while testifying before a U.S. House subcommittee in 1935, the manager of a chain of stores admitted that such chains control the ways relevant news stories are framed and the content of relevant editorial policy. Yet compared to later writings, in this first book Al Lee seemed tentative and almost timid. He wrote regarding advertising and the elite control of the press: "Here, as elsewhere in society, the lines are not so clearly drawn that an airtight case may be constructed to defend any precise answer."[19]

At this early stage in their careers the deep vein of egalitarianism that would come to characterize them was more apparent in Betty's dissertation than in Al's. Yet Al's dissertation has been very important, in that its analysis of the significance of wire services, "helped in the Supreme Court decision to break up the Associated Press news monopoly."[20] Reviews of the book were seen across the country, for ironically the AP reviewed it in the most favorable terms in copy sent to over 1,000 newspapers. The AP review concluded: "Let nobody think he is a long-haired radical, an agitator or any of those things.

He is merely a first rate historian with a sense of humor and a passion for documentation."

BETTY LEE'S ACADEMIC APPOINTMENTS

Receiving her Ph.D. during the late 1930s, Betty's timing could not have been worse. Earlier and later generations of women found less in the way of employment discrimination than did those attempting to enter the job market from approximately 1945 to the 1960s.[21] Women were then widely expected to take as their highest priority the support and furtherance of their husband's career rather than being concerned with their own independent advancement.[22] Recalling that all of her professional appointments were part time or temporary, Betty commented at length about antifeminism masquerading as rules against nepotism.[23] During the full length of her career this was surely a serious obstacle to her pursuit of full-time employment. But unlike some, Betty asks women to act at a higher standard than do men and not be content merely to replace an "old boy" with an "old girl" network.[24] Although claiming no bitterness about her treatment, the widespread fears of nepotism clearly did limit her career opportunities:

> Al came to Brooklyn College in 1949 as a full professor. The department asked if I would teach a couple of courses in the evening school. I taught criminology and the family. At the end of our first year there the faculty asked Al to become the department chair and it was evident that they had really had this in mind all along. Because of people's fears that Al would not be fair in evaluating me I felt I could not continue teaching, even part-time at night.
>
> It was clear at the time that other departments always preferred to hire a man with a wife and children and thus women were not hired—especially a woman who was married to a man with a job. So throughout my life I have mostly taught just a course or two at a time, often fringe courses for very small compensation, typically at an hourly rate. For example, at Wayne State I taught a special sociology course emphasizing cross cultural literature to nursing students who were headed for war in the Pacific. Wherever I taught I was never invited to faculty meetings. Especially at the small colleges where I taught it was probably threatening to men on the faculty to be faced with a woman who had a Ph.D. when they didn't have one. The first and only time I felt I had a real academic job with a decent salary was at the Connecticut College for Women where I replaced the department chair for one year.

Caroline Rose, the wife of Arnold Rose of the University of Minnesota, had experiences similar to Betty's. Caroline worked at the margins of the profession, teaching in night school, never really having the opportunity to get a research career initiated and in general giving more support to her husband's career than he gave to hers. Both Arnold and Caroline Rose "had an outstanding share in the writing of *An American Dilemma*"[25] with Gunnar Myrdal. Arnold's name appeared with Myrdal's on the front page, but Caroline only received acknowledgement in the Preface. It has been observed that the practice of "uneven attribution of credit" for research and writing clearly applied to Caroline and Arnold Rose.[26] While Arnold was made an associate professor at the University of Minnesota in 1949, it was only after Arnold's death in 1968, nearly two decades later, that Caroline was offered an appointment in the department at that rank. She was offered an appointment at this junior rank "despite her record of scholarly productivity,"[27] which included several books and journal articles. Among the junior faculty it was widely believed that Caroline was a better writer than Arnold and that she had actually written many of Arnold's publications.[28]

Eleanor Glueck, of the famous husband and wife delinquency research team at Harvard, while having an earned doctorate, was a research assistant from 1930–1953, and was finally "promoted" to research associate, which was her rank until 1964.[29] By comparison her husband became a full professor in 1931. "In short, Eleanor Glueck's entire career at Harvard University consisted of a social position akin to what many Ph.D. candidates face today *before* graduation. As such, she was an outcast from mainstream academia at Harvard."[30] Some of the same problems were also encountered by Helen Hughes, wife of Everett Hughes, who received her Ph.D. from Chicago. After receiving the degree, in 1944 she became an editorial assistant for the *American Journal of Sociology* for only token remuneration, a position she held for 17 years.[31] In this position she was allowed to edit articles and select reviewers for both articles and books, but in these 17 years she never received a promotion.

A sense of bitterness is especially evident in reflections by Alice Rossi regarding her treatment in the early 1960s:

> It was not, however, passing the then dreaded fortieth birthday that made 1962 significant; rather it was a jolting experience of sex discrimination that was the precipitant: I was fired by the principal investigator of a kinship study I had designed, supervised the fieldwork for, and was happily analyzing at the time my draft of a proposal for continued support by the National Science Foundation. I was "let go" within days of receiving word of the grant's approval, when the principal investigator decided the study was a good thing he wished to keep to himself. In those years, there was no legal

recourse. . . . [T]he social science dean simply told me . . . I, as a
mere research associate, was "expendable." This was, of course,
structural discrimination against women, for most young men in
academe were assistant professors; it was predominantly women
who were the "expendable" research associates.[32]

Like Helen Hughes and Alice Rossi, Betty feels betrayed by this
systematic discrimination. A much younger female sociologist who
first met Betty in the mid-1970s recalled: "I wasn't sure how I felt
about Betty in the beginning, because I could feel how deeply angry
she was, and I wasn't comfortable with it. As my consciousness
grew, I grew more familiar and more accepting with my own—and
Betty's—anger and sense of loss. I now consider her a very important
role model; I like the fact that she took herself seriously as an
artist and mother and wife and human being, and not just as a
sociologist."[33]

Some sense of the complexity of the issue of gender discrimination, is seen in the views of still other sociologists. Jessie Bernard,
another of Betty's contemporaries in the profession, took motherhood very seriously,[34] as did Betty. If Jessie Bernard and Betty
agreed on the significance of motherhood, they disagreed on sex
discrimination in the academy. Jessie Bernard saw doors opened to
her because she was a woman; positions, salaries, and promotions.
She claimed that, rather than due to discrimination, women were
grossly underrepresented in academia due to their preference for
motherhood. According to Jessie Bernard, women were not victims
of forces beyond their control. Rather, they wanted things the way
they were. Thus, Bernard "in sum, effectively blamed the victims for
market forces beyond their control."[35] Bernard claimed that it was
not the case of " 'women seeking positions and being denied', but
rather their 'finding alternative investments of time and emotion more
rewarding.' "[36] Margaret Peil, a University of Chicago Ph.D. from
1963, agreed that she encountered no discrimination as a student even
though there were no women on the Chicago faculty.[37]

Ruth Useem, who has been a long-time friend of Betty's and
who is a part of her age cohort recalled: "After receiving my Ph.D.
traditional nepotism rules made it impossible for faculty wives to get
a faculty position. Concerns ran the gamut from the worry that the
husband and wife would vote as a block on all issues to the concern
about what would happen to relations in the department if the
marriage fell apart. And moreover in joint publications the male often
would dedicate a book to his wife without even naming her when she
was in fact a co-author."[38]

But her husband John Useem observed that as far as academic husbands were concerned, "even early on there was no universal pattern about how professional women ought to be treated."[39] Thus, according to Ruth Useem, the academic and family relationships provided a complex situation for these professional women: "My husband John Useem and Al Lee were two men who gave their wives enough backing to accomplish things we were able to do."[40] And John Useem added: "Al made it possible for Betty to have some recognition in a male dominated world."[41] For example, Ruth Useem noted: "In *The Fine Art of Propaganda* Al included Betty as a co-author which was almost unheard of at the time and this was true even if the woman did most of the writing and research."[42] With this help early on doors were opened to these women that might otherwise have remained closed. With a little help from their spouses Betty was elected Vice President of the SSSP and Ruth served on the ASA Council. Deutscher agreed: "Al began to make amends to Elizabeth as they established themselves in a new dual career."[43]

To add to the complexity, Matilda White Riley, also married to a sociologist, recalled only one major instance of sex discrimination in her professional life. Similar to Betty's experience, she was rejected for a graduate teaching fellowship simply because she was a woman: "I was told that I was the best qualified candidate but, 'You will get married, have children, and that will be the end of it.' I was hurt; but the following year I was fortunate enough to become the first Research Assistant in the just established department at Harvard where my husband was one of the first graduate students. My small stipend supported us both! . . . I went on to establish myself in market research and subsequently became head of the largest firm in the world at that time."[44]

She recalled that several joint projects with her husband, John, were published in the first volume of the ASR and that over the years they have frequently collaborated.[45] Her husband was at Rutgers, where she was eventually offered a faculty position and "[s]ince I was able to bring in research funds, what there was of a nepotism rule at Rutgers quickly disappeared."[46] She concluded: "My career has been energized both by my gender and by my marriage."[47] By any measure her career has been immensely successful. She became the first Executive Officer of the ASA and later was elected ASA President.

Alva Myrdal (1902–1986), the wife of Gunnar Myrdal, was an equally successful woman of this same generation. Both Alva and Gunnar were brilliant, well-educated Nobel laureates, widely remembered as advocates of human rights. But Alva Myrdal found that even a marriage to such a good and sensitive man as Gunnar created difficult problems. "Unlike the great majority of men at the time, he had every intention of encouraging her career. But he did not expect this to entail any sacrifices on his part. He took for granted her subservience and with it men's dominance in general."[48] Until Alva was forty-seven years old she never had an opportunity for a career of her own, tied as she was to Gunnar's career requirements. Gunnar and his work had to come first, even she agreed. "Whenever they traveled, she assisted him with languages and library work; when they returned home, he needed her help in sorting out all the material he had brought back. She spent the year of 1926 typing and going over his doctoral dissertation so that it could be ready the following spring. She knew how much he needed her help in order to maintain his momentum."[49] As a wife and mother she sometimes felt torn while caring for their children and at the same time attempting to satisfy her husband's demands on her time, not to mention the tug of her own scholarly pursuits. Betty's experiences were remarkably similar.

AL LEE'S EARLY CAREER MOVES: UNIVERSITY OF KANSAS AND THE RETURN TO YALE

The University of Kansas, 1934–1937

From the beginning the Lees hated the weather in Lawrence, it was far too hot and humid in the summer for their eastern tastes. Betty recalls that shortly after arriving at KU with her husband and new baby she was invited to a meeting of faculty wives:

> One of the wives asked me about the progress on my dissertation whereupon the wife of the head of the English department glared at me saying "And I thought you were such a nice person." Yet I think I defied their stereotypes and showed them that you can be a Ph.D. and don't have to have runners in your stockings and a slip that hangs. But others continued to talk behind my back that I couldn't write a dissertation and give proper attention to my child. But I wrote at home between his naps and had a little part-time help with housework and so clearly the baby didn't suffer.

One of Betty's contemporaries recalled with regret: "Women in my generation who were professionals liked to sew and cook and to be mothers. Yet we got no support from the wives of male academics because they never invited us to their parties and informal get-to-gethers. And in this way we felt isolated from other women."[50] Clearly this isolation is what the wife of the Kansas English department head had intended.

> One of Al's former journalism students at KU recalled those days fondly:

Dr. Alfred McClung Lee was a Ph.D. fresh out of Yale and his very presence seemed to change the aura of a department that until fall '34 was looked upon as a well-respected trade school. Its graduates knew their craft well, mechanically. No one seemed to be concerned whether they could think. . . . Lee's journalism students began to take sides in print, in campus politics, and on local, state and national issues. . . . Soon it appeared more moderate segments of the citizenry were being swept into the emotional crusade to get rid of the KU "Socialist."[51]

Even early in the careers of Betty and Al their pacifism was apparent and, to add to the pique of some University of Kansas administrators and state politicians, Betty and Al gave critical encouragement to a nascent campus antiwar student group named the Veterans of Future Wars (VOFW), which took its name as a parody of the Veterans of Foreign Wars (VFW). The local Kansas chapter was called Deathwatch Post No. 1. As early as 1935, these students saw that war was coming, so they started an exhaustive search to locate the future unknown soldier and to locate a campus site to erect a monument to future soldiers. The group requested that the university establish a school for the purpose of training writers to produce atrocity stories to insure the nation's entrance in the future war. The group even petitioned Washington for a $1,000 bonus for the war in which they would fight. The goal was to use satire and burlesque in a "sincere and conscientious attempt to forward peace."[52] Yet in spite of the irritation he caused, it was not necessary to fire Al Lee, for the combination of the Kansas weather plus the lure of a research appointment at his alma mater, Yale, was too much for him to pass up. At this point, however, Al nearly went to the *Chicago Sun* as an editorial writer. It would have paid $2,000 more than Yale, and, as it turned out, he probably would have been happier.

ADVENTURES IN GHOSTWRITING FOR YALE AND
FOR MARSHALL FIELD

Al and Betty returned to Yale for the 1937–1938 school year, with their young son in tow. Al was disappointed to learn that the Yale anthropologist Peter Murdock had arranged that during his year back at Yale he would be responsible for writing a book for another scholar. A grant had been awarded to a Yale researcher for a project, but it shortly became clear that this person was incapable of completing the task. Thus Al became the ghost writer for *South Italian Folkways in Europe and America: A Handbook for Social Workers, Visiting Nurses, School Teachers and Physicians*.[53] Al received neither recognition nor acknowledgement in the book from Phyllis Williams, listed as the book's author. The book was sponsored by the Yale Institute of Human Relations, where Phyllis Williams was a research assistant. It was the second in a series dealing with the population of New Haven, and in this case the problems South Italians were having in adjusting to life in America. "It is published not as a scientific report but rather as a manual for social workers, lawyers, physicians, and other professional groups" according to the Foreword written by Mark A. May, the Institute Director. The chapters covered topics as diverse as: problems in employment, housing, diet, clothing, marriage, recreation, religion, and health. After this humiliating exploitation, Al was more than ready to leave Yale after one year, during which time another son was born. He was ready to leave even though jobs were very hard to locate during these depression years and even though it was made clear to him that he could have "stayed at Yale and written a shelf full of books for others."

At the end of the year of ghostwriting almost anything seemed better, and Al, Betty, and the two boys were off to New York University, where Al remained from 1938 to 1942. During the first year Al taught only one course at NYU, in the department of marketing, and also worked with Raymond Rich Associates, which was a public relations firm that did work for not-for-profit organizations. During this period Al also served with the Institute for Propaganda Analysis in New York City, eventually becoming its director. In 1939 Al began to teach full time at NYU. But by 1942 he would be ready to leave NYU when offered a position as professor and chair at Wayne State University in Detroit. It was during these years at Wayne State that Al engaged in yet another ghost-writing project. Perhaps two growing children to support made another ghost-writing task attractive to Al. In return for a handsome $20,000 commission, Al wrote *Freedom is More than a Word* for Marshall Field.[54] It is essentially an inspirational book based on Field's personal philosophy.

The book describes how Field bought the progressive New York City newspaper, *PM*, and founded the *Chicago Sun*. Several illustrations show how over the years the Chicago *Tribune* had supported fascism and thus how the *Sun* was sorely needed. Field condemns corporate monopolies, expresses support for minorities, condemns racial discrimination, and criticizes "ritualistic" and "mechanical" education.[55] "The tendency for education to be used to produce 'docile instruments' is perhaps one of the most fundamental challenges to democracy."[56] According to Field, true freedom requires that all people have the opportunity to "develop their full capabilities and potentialities" and thus is inconsistent with poverty and racial segregation.[57] Consistent with this position Field bemoans the fact that "often in the past we have seen a plethora of goods and food in one part of the world and starvation in another part."[58] He argued that this inequality must be eliminated if war is ever to be abolished.

Field acknowledged that "I am most grateful to many friends who have read this book manuscript and have helped me with it, particularly to Alfred M. Lee, whose knowledge of the history of the newspaper business and whose research have been invaluable."[59] This is certainly much more than Williams ever acknowledged. The majority of the book could have been written about Betty and Al Lee's beliefs, but there are exceptions, such as the following: "But to wage war successfully, men must completely subordinate themselves, their abilities, and the expression of their opinions to the common objective."[60] Unlike the Lees, who were by this point in their lives committed pacifists, Field was a veteran of WWI, having fought in the land war in Europe, and at the book's printing Field's son was in the Navy. Al Lee's hand and values are obvious throughout the book, except in this one instance.

Field also criticized the fact that there are fewer and fewer daily newspapers. Because the *Sun* could not buy services from the Associated Press (AP) due to objections of the competing Chicago *Tribune*, Marshall Field filed a complaint with the Department of Justice against monopolistic practices. Indeed, Al's list of publications shows that he and Betty filed a brief in 1943 in support of this complaint. The Lees presented evidence to the Federal Trade Commission on the monopoly of the AP during the 1940s, a clear example of applied or clinical sociology,[61] which is a sociology with a direct bearing and use in human affairs. As we will see in the following chapter, clinical sociology became the major focus of the Lees' careers.

NOTES

1. Frederick Elwood. Letter to John F. Galliher (April 13, 1990).

2. Alfred McClung Lee. *Multivalent Man* (New York: George Braziller, 1966): vi.

3. Carla B. Howery. "Caroline Baer Rose (1913–1975)." *Women in Sociology: A Bio-Bibliographical Sourcebook.* Mary Jo Deegan, ed. (New York: Greenwood Press, 1991): 338.

4. S. M. Miller. "Portrait of Our New President." *ASA Footnotes* 3 (August 1975): 6.

5. Alfred McClung Lee. Letter to Leo Chall (October 12, 1978).

6. Setsuko Nishi. Interview (February 13, 1991).

7. For additional details of the early life of Elizabeth Briant Lee, see Jan Marie Fritz. "Elizabeth Briant Lee (1908-   )" *Women in Sociology: A Bio-Bibliographical Sourcebook*. Mary Jo Deegan, ed. (New York: Greenwood Press, 1991): 249–55.

8. Alfred McClung Lee. *Sociology for Whom?* 2nd ed. (Syracuse, NY: Syracuse University Press, 1986): 220.

9. Lee 1966 op. cit.: v.

10. Elizabeth Briant Lee. "A History of Women's Participation in the Eastern Sociological Society." *SWS Network* 10 (July 1980): 5.

11. Elizabeth Briant Lee and Alfred McClung Lee. "Two Clinicians Tandem in Social Action." *Clinical Sociology Newsletter* (Fall 1981): 3–4.

12. Alfred McClung Lee. "Trends in Commercial Entertainment in Pittsburgh as Reflected in the Advertising in Pittsburgh Newspapers (1790–1860)." M.A. Thesis in Sociology, University of Pittsburgh (1931): 156.

13. Elizabeth Briant Lee. "Eminent Women: A Cultural Study." Ph.D. Dissertation in Sociology, Yale University (1937).

14. Lee 1980 op. cit.: 5.

15. Julia A. Sherman and Evelyn Torton Beck, eds. "Introduction." *The Prism of Sex: Essays in the Sociology of Knowledge* (Madison: University of Wisconsin Press, 1979): 4.

16. Nancy Schrom Dye. "Clio's American Daughters: Male History, Female Reality." *The Prism of Sex: Essays in the Sociology of Knowledge* (Madison: University of Wisconsin Press, 1979): 18.

17. Alfred McClung Lee. *The Daily Newspaper in America: The Evolution of a Social Instrument* (New York: The Macmillan Company, 1937).

18. Ibid.: 370–71.

19. Ibid.: 370.

20. John F. Glass. "Portrait of a President." *AHP Newsletter* (December 1975): 1.

21. Leila J. Rupp and Verta Taylor. *Survival in the Doldrums: The American Women's Rights Movement, 1945 to the 1960s* (New York: Oxford University Press, 1987).

22. Janet Finch. *Married to the Job: Wives' Incorporation into Men's Work* (London: George Allen & Unwin, 1983).

23. Lee 1980 op. cit.

24. Ibid.: 6.

25. Helen MacGill Hughes. "Women in Academic Sociology, 1925–75." *Sociological Focus* 8 (August 1975): 216.

26. Howery op. cit.

27. Ibid.: 215.

28. John P. Clark. Interview. January 30, 1993.

29. John H. Laub and Robert J. Sampson. "The Sutherland-Glueck Debate: On the Sociology of Criminological Knowledge." *American Journal of Sociology* 96 (May 1991): 1402–40.

30. Ibid.: 1406.

31. Helen MacGill Hughes. "Maid of All Work or Departmental Sister-in-Law?" *American Journal of Sociology* 78 (January 1978): 767–72.

32. Alice C. Rossi. "Growing Up and Older in Sociology, 1940–1990." *Sociological Lives*. Matilda White Riley, ed. (Beverly Hills: Sage Publications, 1988): 45–46.

33. Victoria Rader. Letter to John F. Galliher. n.d.

34. Robert C. Bannister. *Jessie Bernard: The Making of a Feminist* (New Brunswick, NJ: Rutgers University Press, 1991).

35. Ibid.: 150.

36. Ibid.: 156.

37. Mary Jo Deegan. "The Second Sex and the Chicago School: Women's Accounts, Knowledge and Work, 1949–1960." Presented at the Second Chicago School Symposium (Atlanta, March 1991).

38. Ruth Hill Useem. Interview. January 29, 1993.

39. John Useem. Interview (January 29, 1993).

40. Ruth Hill Useem op. cit.

41. John Useem op. cit.

42. Ruth Hill Useem op. cit.

43. Irwin Deutscher. "Revisiting History: Hughes and Lee," *ASA Footnotes* 21 (January 1993): 7.

44. Matilda White Riley. Letter to John F. Galliher. March 14, 1993.

45. Ibid.

46. Ibid.

47. Ibid.

48. Sissela Bok. *Alva Myrdal: A Daughter's Memoir* (New York: Addison-Wesley Publishing Company, Inc., 1991): 72.

49. Ibid.: 75.

50. Ruth Hill Useem op. cit.

51. Fred Harris. "Controversial Journalism Prof Alive and Well in Retirement." *Chanute Tribune* (January 13, 1976).

52. Dean Moorehead. "Future Vets Demand Bonus." *Jayhawker* (1935–36): 341.

53. Phyllis H. Williams. *South Italian Folkways in Europe and*

America: A Handbook for Social Workers, Visiting Nurses, School Teachers and Physicians (New Haven: Yale University Press, 1938).

54. Marshall Field. *Freedom is More Than a Word* (Chicago: University of Chicago Press, 1945).

55. Ibid.: 53.

56. Ibid.: 50.

57. Ibid.: 28.

58. Ibid.: 171.

59. Ibid.: xv.

60. Ibid.: 165.

61. Alfred McClung Lee. *Toward Humanist Sociology* (Englewood Cliffs, N.J.: Prentice-Hall, Inc., 1973): 189.

Chapter 3

The Birth of Clinical Sociology: Clinical Sociology in Society

The specific type of clinical sociology relevant to human affairs and public policy that interested the Lees centered around race and religion; in the various activities of the Lees the themes of *racism* and *religious bigotry* provided the fuel for research that spanned five decades. The Wayne State University *Collegian* noted that Al Lee had been elected vice-president and chair of the department of social service of the Detroit Council of Churches.[1] Over the years Betty and Al would be continually involved in myriad community activities, publishing many articles in nonsociological magazines and journals. Taking sociology into the community required this involvement. An early member of the Society for the Psychological Study of Social Issues (SPSSI) illustrates Al's activity:

> An early example of Al Lee in action comes to mind. Sometime in the early fifties, Al got after a philosopher and me, a social psychologist, to join him in speaking to a large group in a well-to-do suburban community outside New York. I don't recall the exact topic but it had to do with academic freedom, civil liberties, and social science teaching in the schools. I recall that Al was particularly good at challenging supporters of the *status quo* and evoking discussion from them. His mastery of facts—social, educational, political, economic—was impressive and gave real support to the small contingent of progressives in the community.[2]

DEFINITION OF CLINICAL SOCIOLOGY

In Henry Pratt Fairchild's *Dictionary of Sociology* the Lees contributed the definition of the term of Clinical Sociology.[3] Louis Wirth, Al noted, has also been credited with introducing the term into sociological discourse, although Wirth's use of the term was more psychological. The Lees provided this definition of clinical sociology:

That division of practical or applied sociology that reports and synthesizes the experiences of (a) social psychiatrists with functional problems of individual adaptation and (b) societal technicians with functional problems of institutional adjustment. Chiefly in the first group, at least in emphasis, is the experience of social workers, personnel managers, psychiatrists, career guidance experts, etc., and chiefly in the second group is that of public relations counselors, professional politicians, sentiment and opinion analysis propagandists, advertisers, etc. Clinical sociology thus stresses the development of effective manipulative and therapeutive techniques and of accurate functional information concerning society and social relationships.[4]

A decade later the Lees added that " 'patients' are social aggregates rather than individuals, but their exchanges of observations, techniques, and insights have points in common with . . . psychiatrists."[5] Even later the Lees added that "the clinical approach to social interrelations must take the clinical sociologist into the field, into participant observation, into opportunities to observe how individuals and organizations actually behave in a range of different conditions."[6] And: "Clinical sociology is the kind of applied sociology or sociological practice which involves intimate, sharply realistic investigations linked with efforts to diagnose problems and to suggest strategies for coping with those problems."[7] Clinical sociology can be used on the "microlevel" with individuals or the "macrolevel" in dealing with organizations.[8]

The Lees contrasted their view of typical social science with clinical sociology. The former 1) conducts studies without consideration of the broader social context; 2) has a general acceptance of the *status quo*; 3) uses sample survey data as opposed to participant observation; and 4) alleges it is value free.[9] Clinical sociologists, on the other hand, are concerned as therapists with serving their " 'clients' or 'audiences' problems."[10] For example, one can use confrontation in a laboratory setting to increase communication and understanding between ghetto residents and the police. Yet the Lees recognized that some are critical of such techniques and see them merely as a means of co-opting the oppressed, leaving institutionalized inequality intact when in fact only violent revolution can modify this oppression.

Beginning Propaganda Analysis

The Fine Art of Propaganda was published originally in 1939 and, like Al's dissertation, was still in print during the 1990s. This book was based on an analysis of Father Charles Coughlin's speeches, which were filled with anti-Semitic utterances. In retrospect it seems unlikely that two very junior sociologists, with so few sociological role models to follow, would have attacked a figure who at the time had great prominence through his nationally syndicated radio program. According to the Lees' analysis, propagandists' "tricks of the trade"[11] include name calling, prestige association, testimonial by a respected or hated person, selective use of facts, and the so-called "bandwagon" argument that everybody agrees with a given position. In arguing for the teaching of religion in all schools, Coughlin reasoned as follows, using "glittering generalities" or associating something with a "virtue" word: "Once more, nations will either reassert their belief in the supernatural Messiah and the supernatural order of life which He instituted, or they will complete their rejection of Him, logically proceeding to exterminate Him in the personal life of the individual."[12]

In attacking Jews, Coughlin went on to say: "I am not so illogical as to charge that the Jews alone have been responsible for banishing religion from our educational institutions."[13] Yet he engaged in what the Lees referred to as card stacking, which involves the selective use of illustrations and facts to support a position. While Coughlin admitted that Jews alone were not to blame, he nonetheless gave no further illustrations of other guilty parties, thereby leaving the impression that this one group alone really stood accused. Coughlin also argued that in 1919 innocent German hostages had been murdered by communists who were "Jewish Soviet commissars,"[14] and that "the intellectual leaders . . . of Marxist atheism in Germany were Jews."[15] With the hindsight that came after the Holocaust, the enormous evil in Coughlin's utterances is easy to see. Betty and Al saw it clearly even prior to the war. Betty recalled: "We felt that it was a shame for this clergyman to take all the money he did from his parishioners and others by misleading them."

The audience for this book by the Lees was primarily the general public. The Lees felt it necessary to challenge Coughlin among the general public, for this is where he had attracted considerable support. The enduring quality of this book, which explains why it was still in print in the late 20th century, is that it is as relevant as it was during the 1930s. For example, television evangelist Jimmy Swaggart argued during the 1980s that Jews themselves were to blame for the Holocaust, saying that whenever a person "does not accept Jesus Christ, he takes himself away from God's protection . . . [and] places himself under Satan's domain."[16]

Betty was a co-author of *The Fine Art of Propaganda* and explains her major and visible role in this way:

Al had a full-time job with a public relations firm and was also teaching two courses at NYU on the side, as well as working for the Institute for Propaganda Analysis. The Institute had decided it wanted to get out a book on propaganda. But Al was too busy to do it alone. So I helped out. My oldest son was four at the time. Sometimes he would ask me to do something with him and I would say that I had to work. He would then say "No more bookie, mom!" I also clearly recall that the secretary who worked with us on this book was very worried about our welfare because we criticized Coughlin. She even suggested that we get out of town.

As usual, the Lees remained undaunted.

An early review in the *Journalism Quarterly* in 1939 noted that this book was intended for the layman.[17] It was widely reviewed in the print media, including the *Saturday Review*,[18] *The New Republic*,[19] and many newspapers. A review in *The Communist* was extremely critical: "First of all, it does not understand the class nature of fascism. . . . As a result of this treatment of Coughlinism as unrelated to finance capital, the unguarded reader of the book would be totally unable to penetrate the present 'peace' demagogy of Coughlin."[20] Those presumably further to the political right also were not pleased by what they saw as a disservice to a Christian leader. In the *American Sociological Review* Kimball Young argued that the work

> turns out to be not an objective account but a case of special pleading and propaganda itself. The book, in short, is a good illustration of "the fine art of propaganda" where by dressing up a discussion in the acceptable language of science, it is possible to launch out on a line of promotion against a movement which is evidently considered by the sponsors as evil. . . . It seems to the reviewer that two effects may flow from such a work. First, to the observing reader it is not an effective treatment but a tract, hence it enhances the popular disregard for so-called social science. Second, for the less wary it serves as propaganda of an effective sort since its appearance of impartiality provides an efficient vehicle for what amounts to counter-propaganda against a contemporary leader.[21]

But more recently, in *The Quill*, a journalism professor writes, "If ever a book on the subject of propaganda ever deserved to be called a classic, this book did."[22]

In 1941, Al was elected executive director of the Institute for Propaganda Analysis which had published the book. That same year two university professors who were members of the board of directors of the institute resigned, "because they believed the institute was too critical of the defense policies of the Roosevelt Administration." One of these professors was quoted: " 'I am all out for intervention,' he declared. 'They did not seem to be.' "[23] Because the former director of the institute had openly called for tolerance of communist candidates for U.S. political office and for American support for the antifascist forces in Spain, in the minds of some, doubt was cast on the patriotism of all those associated with the institute. A congressional investigation was threatened in the U.S. House Committee on Un-American Activities, which was headed by Representative Martin Dies of Texas. According to the *New York Times* report, Al was undaunted:

> Dr. Lee referred to the Dies committee as "a disgrace to the United States" and said that he was speaking "as a conservative." "I'm no radical," he continued. "I teach advertising at the School of Commerce at N. Y. U. . . . . I should think that if Mr. Dies is going to raise a hullabaloo about pinkish cast he should present definite evidence." Dr. Lee went on. "I don't like this innuendo. If he knows of any evils, they should be placed before our board."[24]

Aside from publishing Betty and Al's book on propaganda, the institute had other activities: "One million children in 3,000 public and private high schools of this country are being taught to develop critical, questioning attitudes of what they read in the newspapers, hear on the radio or see in the motion pictures through monthly bulletins, teaching guides and other materials prepared for classroom use by the Institute for Propaganda Analysis."[25]

In spite of all this activity, or perhaps because of it, the organization was in serious trouble. In 1941, as the war in Europe loomed larger, the trustees of the estate that had been the major source of funds for the institute became increasingly reluctant to continue their support. Moreover, many of the institute's board members were moving into war-related government positions and thus found it necessary to resign from the board.[26] The *New York Times* reported: "After more than a year of trying to dodge full-dress discussions of the war, the Institute for Propaganda Analysis last month gave it up as a bad job and decided to go into hibernation until the shooting has ended. . . . [I]t has closed its Manhattan offices and suspended publication of its bulletin."[27]

Al later recalled: "[G]ood friends and former supporters became convinced that since we could not be partisan, their own effort to aid democracy in the crisis should be made elsewhere; that long-time programs like the institute's could 'wait.' "[28]

The last bulletin of the institute was published in January 1942, after four years of institute operation. The institute's secretary was quoted by the Lees as follows: "The institute did not have enough funds to continue work. . . . I am reasonably sure we could have obtained money from interventionist sources but we would have had to weight our analyses accordingly; it is possible, too, we could have gotten money from isolationist sources, but again our analyses would have had to be weighted. We could not solicit or accept such money and still retain our integrity."[29]

It should be noted that to be non-aligned in an international conflict is not the same as being value-neutral. The Lees were passionately opposed to the violence committed by both sides during the war.

A long-term friend and supporter remembered: "Al was quite gloomy a great deal of the time. I recall his quoting a critic to the effect that the institute had only one idea at the beginning and was now played out. Al, as I recollect, was inclined to agree. . . . Al I now perceive as a mixture of the cynical realist newspaperman (actually public relations specialist), who sees how politics really work, and the liberal democratic idealist."[30]

If Al was gloomy, it was because he saw the tremendous need for such an organization to overcome the widespread warmongering propaganda in the mass media, which was supplied by some of the most influential academicians. The Lees noted that "[d]uring World War I, American newspapers and magazines widely reviewed, digested and reprinted atrocity books, including those of the British historian Arnold Toynbee. . . . Toynbee then served the purposes of the Allies by grinding out books with titles such as *The German Terror in Belgium*, *The German Terror in France*, and *The Murderous Tyranny of the Turks*."[31]

There is abundant evidence from the latter part of the 20th century that American politicians still have reason to believe that cynical manipulation of the public through the mass media is not only possible, but essential for political success.

THE LEES' ARTICLES ON THEORY AND METHOD

In addition to their journalistic accounts of propaganda, the Lees attempted to add to the existing literature on sociological theory and methods. A 1947 *American Sociological Review* (*ASR*) article reviewed the details to be considered in conducting surveys, including: selection of issues, development of interview schedules, selection and training of interviewers, sampling, problems of various interview situations, analysis of results, possible social consequences of polling itself, and how the financial interests commissioning opinion surveys can distort the results.[32] The article concluded that, given the costs of surveys and the necessity of securing grant support, serious doubt is cast on the entire enterprise.

As early as 1945, again in the *ASR*, the Lees discussed the notion of value conflicts at the individual, group, and societal levels.[33] This is a theme they would draw on throughout their careers. Later, they observed, "Even relatively isolated groups contain persons who have internalized cultural and subcultural contradictions and who pass them on to their children."[34] The Lees' conception of cultural contradictions stands in stark contrast to the view of human behavior in Talcott Parsons' *The Social System,* which characterized human interaction as totally integrated into an overall master plan.[35]

A 1945 *American Journal of Sociology (AJS)* article by the Lees asserts that, given the presence of these struggles and contradictions, "propaganda grows out of and plays a part in social tensions and struggles, and its effectiveness is controlled in this societal sense by the trend of popular sentiments and by the limits to societal change set by environmental conditions."[36] One example they provide is the conflict typically found between management and workers. At the social-psychological level, "[w]ithin societal limitations, propaganda's effectiveness depends upon either luck or the propagandist's 'intuitive' or conscious knowledge of how his audiences will react to mass-communication stimuli."[37] They noted that "the attempt is made to ascertain the kind and character of the publicity mediums being used and especially to learn the actual degree of currency being achieved by the propaganda."[38] With a psychological approach, "[s]ocial struggles and their resulting propagandas attract personalities of types that find needed self-expression in their appeals, promises, and activities."[39] Knowing all this, one should remember that "[p]ropagandists use certain 'tricks of the trade,' or 'propaganda techniques,' " including name-calling.[40]

APPLYING PROPAGANDA ANALYSIS TO SOCIAL ISSUES: RELIGION AND RACISM IN SOCIETY

In *The Fine Art of Propaganda,* as well as in those books to come later, such as *Dry Propaganda*[41] and *Race Riot,*[42] we find prime examples of what the Lees referred to as clinical sociology. These books were written in a timely fashion in response to some critical social problem and attempted to use sociology to help solve the problems associated with a particular crisis. *Dry Propaganda: An Analysis of the New Prohibition Drive* was accepted for publication by the Dryden Press and was scheduled for release in 1943. However, these were the war years and publishers were experiencing severe financial distress. Dryden could afford to produce the manuscript only in mimeograph copy. A small portion of the book-length manuscript was published in the *ASR* in 1944,[43] but the bulk of it never has been published. Thus, more attention will be paid to this research than might otherwise be the case.

Dry Propaganda drew heavily on the ideas developed in *The Fine Art of Propaganda*. The dominance of rural and protestant America was threatened by the combined forces of urbanization, industrialization, and immigration. The nonpuritanical cities were growing rapidly and gaining considerable social, economic, and political power. In this context the targets of prohibition included Roman Catholics and African Americans. "Rum, Romanism, and Rebellion" was the refrain (5–4). The Lees reported that in the South "the presence of the Negro made Prohibition attractive as a way of keeping him 'in his place' " (12–3). Moreover, the identification of beer with German immigrants served to discredit it during WWI. H. L. Mencken was quoted as having said of prohibitionists that they have a "haunting fear that someone, somehow, somewhere is having a good time" (14–2). The "Committee of Fifty," a group of leading scientists, educators, and religious leaders, reported the results of a ten-year study of the effects of prohibition. The committee concluded that "the traffic in alcohol beverages has been sometimes repressed or harassed, but never exterminated or rendered unprofitable. . . . [Prohibition has reduced] public respect for courts [and caused] perjuries" (10–3).

The head of the Woman's Christian Temperance Union is quoted: "Prohibition is religiously, morally, industrially, economically and socially right. Therefore it must prevail" (1–4). Prohibitionists engaged in name calling, associating alcohol with words such as drunkard, bar fly, and alcoholic, and prohibition with Christianity, civilization, love, patriotism, science, medicine, and health. The WCTU was one of the primary proponents of prohibition and "bristles with testimonials from physicians, ministers, [and] educators" (17–2). Yet the prohibitionists also sought to identify their cause with "plain folks" such as "farmers, mothers, housewives" (18–2).

After the legislative victory by prohibitionists in 1919, they immediately turned their attention to neighboring countries, for they recognized that American prohibition would be more difficult to enforce with legal alcohol available in neighboring nations. As one prohibitionist said: "When we had county option we could do but little with wet counties around us" (5–3). [Now] "Mexico must be cared for. South America must be cared for. The nations of the earth must be helped." At the 1919 Victory Convention of the Anti-Saloon League of America the organization took the following position:

"Consequently, in the same way that municipal and township prohibition were not capable of complete enforcement without county prohibition, and county prohibition was not capable of complete enforcement without state prohibition, and state prohibition was not capable of enforcement without national prohibition, so today national prohibition is incapable of complete enforcement without world prohibition." With this in view, they launched a program with a budget of $15 million to prohibitionize the globe (14–3).

Later, after the repeal of national prohibition, another supporter of prohibition blamed the fall of France into Nazi hands during WWII on alcohol: "[W]idespread alcoholism in France, especially in the army, was not an unimportant factor in the collapse of that country in June, 1940" (2–5). The fall of Rome, the beginning of WWI, and even Pearl Harbor were blamed on alcohol and drunkenness. Shortly after Pearl Harbor, prohibitionists sought to "disseminate the theory that Japanese saloon keepers [in Hawaii] were to blame, that liquor kept 'our boys' from 'being ready' " (19–2). A Texas minister spoke at a Free Methodist Church in St. Louis, Missouri, and condemned alcohol and brewers. "Strong drink causes more teen-age, unwed girls to hug illegitimate children to their breasts than anything else in this world, and the brewers know it, the beer advertisers know it, and the beer sellers know it. . . . The brewers are the most unpatriotic bunch there ever was. I hope they have representatives here tonight. I want to tack their hides to the barn door" (2–6). He specifically named two large St. Louis brewers, Anheuser-Busch and Griesedieck Brothers. Prohibitionists had the supreme bad judgment to attack business leaders and government and military leaders, and such attacks were particularly ill-timed, with the nation at war.

The prohibitionists tried to use WWII just as they had used WWI. The president of Colgate University, speaking before a Northern Baptist Convention in Cleveland in May of 1942, criticized the military policy of the U.S. government and said "the fundamental strategy seems to be to drink our way to victory" (5–5). Four months prior to this speech, President Roosevelt's investigating committee had concluded that there was no basis in fact for such divisive propaganda (6–5). The *St. Louis-Post Dispatch* commented on this disparity in the Colgate president's speech: "Does he not realize that by doing so he is disputing the word of an official commission and, worse than that, he is smearing the men and officers of the nation's fighting services (6–5)?"

The members of Alcoholics Anonymous were generally very resentful of prohibitionists because of their apparent lack of either sympathy or understanding of alcoholism, blaming it as they did on individual moral failure (10–5). Most leaders of the business community had learned their lesson from the earlier experience with prohibition and now knew that a new prohibition law would not necessarily make their workers more productive. Much of the understanding of prohibition movements that appeared in *Dry Propaganda* would appear decades later in the works of Gusfield,[44] Timberlake,[45] and Rumbarger.[46]

Undaunted by their failure to publish *Dry Propaganda*, the next year the Lees completed another book-length manuscript on the issue of prohibition based on much of the same material, titled *Techniques of Agitation: Drys and Wets on the March*. Like *Dry Propaganda*, it was never published. In this manuscript they noted that prohibitionists had argued that cigarettes were a stepping stone to alcohol and that as stepping stones to hard liquor, beer and wine were worse than whiskey itself. Moreover, during the drive toward the 18th amendment, business interests looked upon drinking as harmful to their employees and thus as harmful to profits. Forty-five years later, Rumbarger discovered evidence similar to the Lees'.[47] Prohibition was an attempt by farmers and villagers to maintain the influence of their ideals over the nation even while rapidly losing population to the cities. Later Gusfield found similar evidence.[48] The Lees also anticipated the work of David Musto[49] when they found that during both WWI and WWII prohibitionists argued that abstinence was required as a wartime sacrifice because drinking weakens the collective will to fight.

Race Riot by the Lees and Norman Daymond Humphrey is an analysis and a detailed chronology of events leading to and including the Detroit race riots of June 1943, hurried into print that same year.[50] Living in Detroit at the time, the Lees and Humphrey were ideally suited to tell this story. According to the book, these riots were at least partially a consequence of the massive immigration of southern blacks and southern whites (with the southern white traditions of racism) into the city of Detroit during the years immediately prior to the riot. But the book also noted how fascism and American demagogues such as Father Charles Coughlin, Huey Long, and the Rev. Gerald L.K. Smith contributed to the problem, and how those demagogues in turn were autocrats similar to Hitler and Mussolini. The authors also noted that such riots soil the international reputation of American democracy and, most significantly represent, a real danger to democracy itself.

The authors did not shun publicity for this book. In fact, publicity is needed for clinical sociology to have the maximum impact upon the community. The reviews of the book were numerous and very positive. The *Christian Science Monitor* review, for example, gave special praise to the book for emphasizing that demagogic groups and police misconduct increase the likelihood of riots, as do overcrowded housing and unequal employment opportunities.[51] The *Chicago Tribune* review concluded: "The book proves conclusively that Axis agents did not touch off the spark; it lays the blame for the delay in calling in federal troops squarely on city officials."[52] A *Social Forces* review noted also that the book demonstrated conclusively that in integrated neighborhoods the neighbors did not riot.[53] The book even got the attention of the noted columnist Walter Winchell, who was quoted in one of the book's advertisements as saying that this was "[a] book for civilized people, not only to read—but to use as a weapon against the barbarians indicted in it." As late as the 1990s one prominent observer judged that this book "remains one of the great masterpieces of sociological reporting."[54] Betty recalled that this was the one time in their lives together that she was worried about Al: "As the riot started Al beat it out of the house and went to where it was going on. He was busily taking field notes. I did worry about him then. But he called home every hour indicating to me that he was still okay." Even during the McCarthy Era she saw no reason to worry about him "because we had nothing to be ashamed of since we never belonged to any organizations more subversive than the *ASA*."

Fraternities without Brotherhood is another example of clinical sociology.[55] A junior colleague of Al Lee's at Brooklyn College asked him why he was studying fraternities and Al replied that, although often overlooked, they were important social and political institutions. Although usually not considered integral parts of institutionalized racism, college sororities and fraternities in fact serve as training grounds for racial prejudice and discrimination. *Fraternities without Brotherhood* could have been written yesterday as a description of the racial and class discrimination of fraternities and sororities. The book was filled with a sense of urgency about the necessity for change, which is all the more depressing today, when we realize that after approximately four decades there has been little or no progress. The Lees produced this criticism as insiders for, while undergraduates, Al was a Sigma Chi and Betty a Kappa Kappa Gamma. The book notes that some campuses have forced chapters to sever ties with national fraternities to comply with university bans on discriminatory membership policies. At other times chapters have attempted to abide by universities' demands to end discrimination, only to be expelled from their national organizations. Most universities, however, do nothing but close their eyes to fraternity and sorority discrimination. A typical position was reported by the University of Missouri: "The University does not concern itself with the basis for membership in these organizations other than to require that members be students enrolled in the University."[56] At this writing this is still true.

In 1977 Al was cited by the Humanist Society of Metropolitan New York as a Humanist Fellow. It was noted that in the early 1950s Al formed and led the effort to secure funding for the National Committee on Fraternities in Education. Al was President of the organization; Noel Gist of Missouri University, vice-president. Al's book on fraternities came out of this effort as did articles in the *Christian Register* and the *Journal of Higher Education*.[57] In their 1974 Christmas newsletter, the Lees reported that Al had gone to Rochester, New York, the preceding February to support the contention of the city that such organizations should not be considered educational institutions and thus were not entitled to tax-free status.

ETHICS, POLITICS, AND MORALITY

Al Lee and School Integration

From 1967 to 1975 Al was a research consultant with the Metropolitan Applied Research Center in New York City, which was directed by the eminent African-American psychologist, Kenneth Clark. This association grew out of his earlier involvement with Clark in the effort to integrate American schools. Al was an expert social science witness used to help implement the Brown v. Topeka School Board Supreme Court case in 1954. Al merely said:

> I believe I first got acquainted with Ken through our mutual interest in the SPSSI. Then we both became members of the board of the New York Civil Liberties Union; that was in 1949–1956. I helped Ken on his statement that went into the hands of the Supreme Court. . . . I was asked by Thurgood Marshall to chair the NAACP committee of social science consultants. The committee's purpose was to provide consultants to school districts to help them implement the Brown directives. . . . I had no regular pay for any of the above.[58]

Al's contribution to the case is described by Clark as follows: "Contemporary social science interpretations of the nature of racial segregation indicates that it blocks communication and increases mutual hostility and suspicion; it reinforces prejudices and facilitates rather than inhibits outbreaks of racial violence."[59]

Clark also recalled: "I remember him as a most perceptive liberal. Always pleasant and emphatic, his sense of humor permeated his discussions with his colleagues, often bringing clarity to tangled discussions. In the early days after World War II, Al was one of the social scientists who conducted research and published articles on race relations in America."[60] We should remember, for example, that the Lees had reported in their book on Detroit that those living in integrated areas never rioted against their neighbors. Of Al's court testimony, Dr. Clark noted:

> I invited him to serve as an expert witness in the trial level cases on school segregation in Virginia, later to be known as the *Brown* case. I remember well, once Al was being cross examined by the lawyer for the State of Virginia; he asked Al if he was related to the distinguished southern general of the Civil War, General Robert E. Lee. Al answered by pointing out that while his family was originally from Virginia, they accepted the fact that General Lee's branch of the family was somehow related but considered of lower status. Those present in the court gasped, and then laughed at his response.[61]

The *Brown* decision in 1954 had dramatic consequences for school desegregation in the United States. "As the journalist James Reston commented in the *New York Times* with regard to the first decision, the 'court's opinion read more like an expert paper on sociology than a Supreme Court opinion.' "[62] "From this instance, it should be clear that sociological findings make their greatest positive impact upon public policy when they are simultaneously moving through educational, popular, and policy-influencing channels."[63] The Lees reasoned that:

> Sociological research, teaching, and counseling are contributing to this broader struggle both substantively and evaluatively. Substantively, sociologists continue to find and interpret evidence that verifies and emphasizes the contributions to social health of desegregation in all aspects of social life. On the evaluative side, sociologists produce articles and books that point time and again to contrasts between the alleged purposes of programs to improve employment or housing for the underprivileged and the actual consequences that follow.[64]

Thus research, teaching, and community service are all mutually reinforcing, and can all be evaluated on the basis of their relative contributions to the creation of a just society.

RELIGION, RACISM, AND REBELLION IN NORTHERN IRELAND

Terrorism in Northern Ireland, published in 1983, is another example of clinical sociology, as it explicitly addresses the common good through an examination of government policy.[65] The sectarian dispute in Northern Ireland between the Catholic and Protestant communities was of special interest to Betty and Al Lee as a prime example of how a racist ideology can be used to justify political oppression. The Lees became interested in Northern Ireland due to their Protestant "Scotch-Irish" backgrounds. As they note, the "Irish" are all Roman Catholics. These differences are precisely the way the lines of conflict are drawn in this small statelet. For this book, data were gathered from existing documents as well as from a total of ten trips to Ireland beginning in 1955, well before the onset of the recent wave of violence in 1969. According to the Lees, this book aimed at being neither anti-British nor anti-Irish, but rather "pro-human."[66] At this it succeeds, for it neither glorifies nor justifies Irish or British violence. As in the case of propaganda analysis during WWII, the Lees' effort to avoid taking either side in this violent conflict in Northern Ireland should not be interpreted as value neutrality. Because the Lees refused to support the violence of either the British or the Irish, this book did not wholly satisfy those who wish to take sides in this issue. Rather than justifying the violence of one side, this research tries to explain the origins of the continuing conflict and arrive at a just solution. To understand the contemporary conflict, it is essential to locate the dispute in history. The separation of the Church of England from Rome in 1534 under Henry VIII produced an Anglicanism that, as one historian has noted, "was from the beginning at once the most servile and the most efficient agent of tyranny."[67] With religious blessing for tyranny, the British systematically expropriated Irish lands.

The Lees distinguish between upper-class terror and lower-class terror. One example of the former is the British legal policy allowing imprisonment without trial. Another is systematic inequality through discrimination against Roman Catholics in housing and employment. For the working-class Protestant male, police and defense work has replaced shipbuilding as the primary employment in Northern Ireland. Thus there is also opportunity for "lower-class official terrorizing" by the police.[68] Numerous examples amply demonstrate that the police frequently have been violent, as in an infamous 1969 attack on unarmed civil rights demonstrators. Such attacks have generated Catholic support for the Irish Republican Army (IRA) and its own reign of terror, which the Lees also condemn.

The book discusses the popular support for the IRA hunger strikers in British prisons.[69] One mention of this support is that in 1981 an IRA prisoner, who was protesting through a hunger strike, was elected to Parliament shortly before his death. After approximately a thousand years of attempting to control the Irish, the British still do not understand that to discredit the IRA and its violence, they must cease their own brand of terror. The Lees could also have noted the "dirty protest," where IRA prisoners smear their fecal matter on the walls of their own cells to punish their British jailers. The dirty protest shows that the Irish excel at suffering and demonstrates the futility of the British use of coercive controls. Elsewhere the Lees have asked of war: "Do such unbelievable destructions of human lives accomplish the goals sought? It is possible that the mobilization and militarization of life did at least as much to nurture as to destroy authoritarianisms."[70] Their point is that the natives of India discovered long ago that nonviolence is far more effective than violence in neutralizing British colonialism.

Although most western writers describe the British as having the prototypical democratic government system, based on laws as opposed to force, the United Kingdom ironically has no written constitution or bill of rights. Until recently the British mass media was prohibited even from quoting any representative of the IRA. Whatever the aims of the British government, this policy was counterproductive, in that it served to keep both the British public and politicians generally ignorant of specific IRA goals in the conflict. The Lees note also that both Marx and Engles commented on the oppression of the Irish at the hands of the British. One example the Lees provide is the great famine of the 1840s, when so many Irish died and when many others emigrated to the United States. In reality, Ireland at this time had a food surplus, which was exported to enhance the wealth of the British merchants. The Lees' analysis is far from the usual descriptions of this great famine as purely a natural disaster.

In large part, the explanation for the continuing British savagery in Northern Ireland is found in the English aristocratic and authoritarian colonial controls, which were justified by British racist, anti-Irish stereotypes. Social scientists, the Lees note, have often provided legitimation for such controls. One splendid example of such fraudulent British legitimation listed by the Lees is the work of the famous British psychologist Cyril Burt. Burt was knighted by the crown for his research which, based on falsified data, allegedly found class and racial differences in innate abilities, thus supporting racial and class segregation in education. Such conscious distortion by social scientists in the name of segregated education is precisely the problem the Lees found in the work of sociologist James Coleman, which will be discussed in the following chapter.

The Lees' book on Northern Ireland has been widely reviewed. One 1984 review in Dublin praised the Lees for including upper-class government terrorism in their discussion and also praised them for condemning all terror not just IRA terrorism, as counterproductive.[71] A positive review in the *American Anthropologist* notes that in the Lees' view, "violence begets violence and is ultimately counterproductive."[72] But a *Social Forces* review notes: "Its tone is one of moral indignation. [The Lees] quite regularly find someone on whom [to] heap self-righteous abuse. Most of what [they] say is asserted without evidence."[73] Perhaps predictably, the book on Northern Ireland was not always well received in Britain. A reviewer in the British *Sociological Review* wrote that the: "book reviewed here is . . . the least satisfactory product of professional social science concerning Northern Ireland which this reviewer can remember reading. It is only with considerable misgivings that I review it at all."[74] Understandably, the reviewer particularly objected to the book's broad definition of terrorism, which includes the violence of the British army and of other law enforcement authorities. On the other hand, in the *Irish Literary Supplement* another reviewer disagreed, insisting that the book "has done a great service to the cause of peace—dynamic and continuing peace—in Northern Ireland."[75]

As noted earlier, in recognition of the significance of the Lees' research on Northern Ireland, the Irish Sociological Association made Betty and Al honorary members. To mark the occasion, the association's leaders asked Betty to present a keynote address at an annual dinner meeting in Dublin. The strength of their interest in Ireland is also reflected in the fact that they were asked to become officers of American Protestants for Truth about Ireland, which describes itself as "A Non-affiliated Corporation Advocating Peace through Justice, and Human Rights."[76] This organization produces it own regular publications and tries to get its message into other publications. The leaders of this organization feel that their reputation for objectivity is enhanced by stressing that this is a Protestant organization and not an American Roman Catholic organization dominated by knee-jerk Republicanism that demands a united Ireland. The organization's statement of purpose stresses "the need to investigate all sides of the issues and especially to listen to those who are suffering the greatest injustices." Their publications document the discrimination in employment against Roman Catholics, showing that Catholic unemployment is approximately twice that of Protestants; the indiscriminate use of plastic bullets by the British military forces; the unfair treatment of political prisoners in British prisons; and the summary execution of suspected IRA members by the British army. Special attention also has been given to the release in March 1991 of the "Birmingham Six," who served 16 years in prison for IRA terrorism they did not commit, on information trumped up by the British government.

Other testimonials regarding the Lees' book have come from both Protestants and Roman Catholics in Northern Ireland. A Roman Catholic Priest recalls: "I could not believe it, because I had given up all hope of ever finding people like that. I never read a treatment of the Northern Ireland situation like the Lees' book on Terrorism in Northern Ireland."[77] He continued: "The government and others were demanding that if you were a pacifist you had to prove it by condemning the enemies of the government and allowing the government the high moral ground. A peace movement, or pacifists themselves, could easily therefore be manipulated—and they were—to become an instrument of government rather than of justice."[78] A Unitarian: "I do know that Al has a delightful sense of humor and works amazingly well with other people. I can recall many occasions when he would find ways to resolve differences among a group and cause the group, itself, to find a mutually satisfactory solution. I haven't known his peer at this type of activity."[79] And finally, a Quaker comments: "Although I hope that I can see the arguments of both sides and can present a fair and reasoned case, I was born here and one belongs to one group or another. We are all 'ulster,' but some are Ulster/Irish, and some are Ulster/British. . . . So although I was born here my parents came in 1910 from London and Reading and so I am naturally Ulster/British, basically. . . . Al can take a more independent position. And I am grateful for him for bringing to Americans a fair and balanced report of the curious differences of this small piece of the world."[80]

MULTIVALENT MAN

This book, published in 1966, was a major watershed in the development in Betty and Al's career pulling together strands of their writing from over the previous three decades.[81] The Lees said that here they tried to address the question of how it is that people can behave in different ways in different groups without being seen as hypocritical. They also were impressed with the fact that the middle classes, who are often complete conformists, do not contribute as much to society as do the upper classes, or even the lower classes who sometimes rebel. According to this formulation, marginal people, such as those who are mobile—within a society or between societies—are free enough to make the greatest contributions. Elsewhere the Lees have noted: "Efforts to understand members of other groups do not necessarily require assimilation into them, but they do result in one's becoming somewhat cosmopolitan minded and somewhat marginal to one's own groups."[82] In the United States marginality is enhanced because there is not one ethnic tradition, but many, and there is an urban rootlessness. They acknowledged that Robert Park coined the term the "marginal man" and referred to the " 'emancipated Jew' historically and typically [as] the marginal man, the first cosmopolite and citizen of the world."[83] A person feels marginal by climbing or falling from one stratum to another, never feeling really at home in either. Geographical migration, intermarriage, and religious conversion also contribute to marginality. The following paragraphs illustrate the Lees' theoretical position:

> Society has a multiplicity of conflicting moral values. It is multivalent, and thus its members who mature within it and become more or less normal parts of it are also multivalent.[84]

> How many different sets of values are sanctioned within a society? How many different sets of values does each individual have etched upon his mind as he adapts himself to his life conditions? How do such contradictions persist in both culture and personality? How do we live with these contradictions?[85]

> We do not have to be very observant to discover that we do not have just one "social personality," but it requires unusual objectivity and the aid of others for us to come to a realization that we probably have at least as many social personalities as there are major types of groups aware of our existence.[86]

In modern society vocational valences are typically dominant. The book noted that psychiatrist Harry Stack Sullivan is one authority who recognized the diversity of values among various groups in the modern society.[87] Similarly, the Lees quote C. H. Cooley, who has described the period in early childhood development when the child learns "to be different things to different people, showing that he begins to apprehend personality and foresee its operation."[88]

Referring to Parsons' theory of social systems, the Lees stated: "Society as a going concern is much too complex and contradictory, much too dependent upon the illusion of 'system', for its arrangement to be considered analogous to the physical or biological arrangements called systems."[89] For example, physicians may suffer from conflicting feelings when faced with a terminally ill patient who has asked to be put to death, and how the physician deals with this depends on "his accumulation of values, experiences, feelings of loyalty, in other words of his multivalent sentiments."[90]

> The myth of social "system," so common in human cultures and in the philosophical formulations of intellectuals, has the sense of definite, methodological, and even logical plan or order. . . . This myth of social "system" gives individuals a sense of being integrated

into something stable and supportive. The "system" rarely lives up to the humanitarian promises made for it by its surrogates and its rationalizers, but it appears to sanction and to support statuses and relationships, including the current distribution of controls over social power.[91]

Those with more power often seek to defend the current "system," while the less privileged feel external to it. The Lees argue convincingly that those who hold the myth of a social system may rationalize the *status quo* as "healthy" and thus resist social change and ignore issues of human rights. Some theorists may even want to take us back to a *status quo ante* where the system was even more robust. According to the Lees, such theoretical conceptions are especially attractive to those elites controlling research funds. They quote approvingly from an analysis of Talcott Parsons' theory of society which claimed that Parsons had "a consistent tendency to gloss over the horrors of industrial society with bland phrases, thinly disguised cliches, and arrogance; and to abolish all individual values other than those which serve the 'total system.' "[92]

The Lees posit four types of cultural models: societal, small group, personal, and self models. The degree of influence from any of these may vary from situation to situation. Moreover, the societal morals in the U.S. are general and imprecise. The Lees claim that the self is largely covert and not recognized by the individual involved. For all these reasons the traditional image of the rational human actor is a myth. The Lees ask an appropriate question: "How do we live with these contradictions?"[93] There may be many conflicts and contradictions between societal morals and the mores of any particular group as seen in prostitution, riots, and white-collar crime. Parents, ministers of the gospel, and teachers as societal surrogates dominate the teaching of societal morals. And the mores of any particular group can be immoral in the wider society. The group member may respond: "Let's not be naive. It's time for you to learn what the score is."[94] "When an individual's behavior deviates too markedly from the norms of one or more of his groups, he may voluntarily find groups more comfortable for him or be forced to do so."[95]

The Lees quote sociologist Peter Berger, who uses the analogy of society as a puppet theater rather than an integrated system: "We locate ourselves in society," he says, "and thus recognize our own position as we hang from its subtle strings. For a moment we see ourselves as puppets indeed. But then we grasp a decisive difference between the puppet theater and our own drama. Unlike the puppets, we have the possibility of stopping our movements, looking up and perceiving the machinery by which we have been moved. In this act lies the first step towards freedom. And in this same act we find the conclusive justification of sociology as a humanistic discipline."[96]

In other words, people are not necessarily inert cogs in a system or machine, but rather have the capacity for reflection and independent action. The varieties of deviance in society "suggest vividly limitations upon morals as social controls."[97] According to the Lees, nonconformists at times keep society alive by helping it change. Mark Twain was an alienated critic of the existing system and was considered illegitimate by defenders of the establishment. The Lees quote Ralph Waldo Emerson: "Whoso would be a man, must be a nonconformist."[98] Correspondingly, they argue that a sociologist must not be hindered by the name of science or propriety from adding to existing knowledge.

Perhaps Betty and Al have been especially sensitive to the emancipating quality of marginality because they have experienced it first hand. Being active in religious groups and heavily involved in a very secular discipline surely has been an important basis for their own professional nonconformity. The Lees continually have sought to rise above and beyond their own group identities as white Protestants and explore the oppression of people of color by whites, Jews by Christians, and of Roman Catholics in Northern Ireland at the hands of the British government. As members of Greek-letter organizations they felt a special obligation to criticize the blatant racism of the fraternity and sorority system.

OTHER MONOGRAPHS

In *Sociology for Whom?*, published in 1978, the Lees observe that one thing many sociologists lack is intimate and varied field-clinical experiences.[99] In addition, sociologists should strive to make leaders represent "all the people's needs and desires . . . [and] amplify popular participation."[100] And the discipline needs to develop a sociology for all people to help them protect themselves from manipulation by those in power, reflecting their great faith in sociology's potential. The Lees note that, unfortunately, grants and contracts, rather than intellectual merit, increasingly are the measure of a scholar. For example, during the 1960s, Project Camelot, which had among its goals the prevention of insurgency and revolution in Chile, was defended by some leading social scientists. The Lees quote Irving L. Horowitz, who has noted that "many 'giants of the field' are involved in government contract work in one capacity or another. And few souls are in a position to tamper with the gods."[101] But Al often has tried to do just that.

The Lees comment on "sociological professionals . . . [who] learn to do 'research' that helps elites cope with rebels against the current 'social system.' . . . . [To such researchers] the 'system' is allegedly great, albeit wobbly, cannibalistic, and carelessly destructive of its own increasingly exhausted resources."[102] The Lees contrast positivism with the humanist view. Positivists look for natural laws (including biological determinants) that control human behavior, while the humanist celebrates and emphasizes the human potential for choice. The positivist is ethically neutral, unlike the humanist. Thus, according to the Lees, the divisions in social science are clear, precise and simple. The positivist is supportive of the *status quo*, while the humanist is dedicated to social change. Indeed, the Lees hoped for human liberation, but could not find an answer in Marxism, because they felt that human beings respond to more than merely material needs, relying as well on religion and other binding customs.

Sociology for People: Toward a Caring Profession, published in 1988, asks how sociology can aid the "rank-and-file people" and help emancipate them from the manipulation by elites.[103] Part of the answer lies with marginal people themselves: "Immigrants, blacks, and others forced to live in more than one culture, parvenus and others who have changed class level, migrants from country to city."[104] Marginality can contribute to greater creativity. Perhaps this is one reason the Lees have been so intent on increasing the participation of women and minorities in the American Sociological Association, as will be documented in the following chapter. One example of this marginality noted earlier in the Lees' study of the Detroit riot was when they had found that those living in racially integrated neighborhood did not riot. People did not attack their neighbors. The primary goal of the humanist sociologist, according to a quote from Herbert Blumer, should be "to lift the veils that cover group life. . . . The veils are not lifted by substituting, in whatever degree, preformed images for firsthand data."[105] Thus, participant observation is essential. Sociologists can and should inform people about how they are manipulated by the mass media. Humanist sociologists can sensitize people to the possibility and even desirability of change. Alvin Gouldner is quoted as referring to the value-free ideology as a "sign of professional senility."[106] The Lees "place the ASA code of ethics in a class with those of the medical, advertising, public relations, and legal professions. They are all facades."[107]

Often controversial, Al and Betty's work was not always favorably reviewed. Some feel the Lees' later writings were especially flawed. One reviewer claimed that in *Sociology for Whom?* "Lee fails the reader, not because he intermingles value judgments with science, but because he fails to do so in a way which is logically defensible. Professor Lee provides no evidence that he understands the issues of 'valuation'—the process of holding alternative value criteria up to logical scrutiny."[108] Even those sympathetic to the Lees' overall position did not always agree with their suggested solutions. For example, a fellow Association for Humanist Sociology member wrote: "I find myself largely in agreement with Lee's perspectives and goals, but I have difficulties with his discussion of strategies for social change. His position on this crucial issue seems vague and lacks substance. Propaganda analysis, which he puts in the center of his exploration of strategy, is certainly important; yet by itself, it is not an adequate strategy for social change."[109] And Goertzel observed:

> *Sociology for Whom* [originally published in 1978] was a populist manifesto, reflecting the mood of the radical sociologists of the 1960s and 1970s . . . [and] urged us to use our base in academia to serve as muckrakers and advocates for the oppressed and downtrodden. Lee was a dysutopian without a utopia. He condemned both American capitalism and Soviet communism, but he offered no alternative vision. He wanted sociologists to work closely with progressive movements, helping them to articulate their interests and empower themselves. . . . What I see as the negative side[s] of Al Lee's worldview [are] the self-righteousness and political correctness which led him to spearhead a drive to bring James Coleman up on ethics charges within the ASA. . . . I am glad that I did not personally join in that campaign. *Sociology for Whom*'s caustic tone reflected a period when radical and humanistic sociology was young and aggressive. . . . Too many radical and humanistic experiments have failed for me to be at all certain that they offer a viable alternative to market capitalism. Populist dysutopianism helped to energize us in the 1970s, but today I believe we need to be more modest and much more specific about what we can offer that is constructive.[110]

Even the best of scholars typically do not produce work of uniformly high quality and the true value of the Lees' best work can be fully appreciated by looking at their work that did not rise to that level. Perhaps predictably, there was a shift in the Lees' writing after Al's retirement. It became less analytical and predictably less responsive to colleagues' standards, and more programmatic and related to the Lees' interests in political organizing. There is no doubt that earlier books such as *Multivalent Man* or *Race Riot* were superior to later books such as *Sociology for Whom?*, *Sociology for People,* and *Toward*

Humanist Sociology, and the generally negative reviews of the three latter books reflect these differences. In spite of the admittedly uneven quality of their work, or perhaps because of it, their prominence and durability remain, largely through the associations they founded and thus the cultures they helped create.

BOOK REVIEWS

From the beginning of their careers the Lees were inveterate book reviewers, with nearly 300 published between 1930 and 1990 in both scholarly journals and a wide variety of general circulation magazines. They were ideal reviewers in that their strong and consistent intellectual commitments made their reviews clear and decisive. An example is found in a 1952 *ASR* review of a book by Morris Janowitz on neighborhood newspapers in cities. The review concludes: "The manipulative bias of Janowitz's study appears at many points but at no place more clearly than in his closing paragraph. 'It will become more and more apparent that the "big" mass media are less and less relevant for guiding the vast array of community-based activities required for national security.' "[111] Janowitz's hopes that the community press could fill this power vacuum in the interests of national security did not appeal to the Lees. Another review of a book by Edward Shils: "Shils' whipping boys are our 'intellectuals' and 'extremists,' and he calls 'populism' the most treacherous strain within our complicated cultural heritage."[112] These reviews of books written by prominent sociologists do not reflect the efforts of careerists interested in professional mobility, but of scholars with a genuine interest in influencing the course of intellectual debate both within and outside of the academy.

SUPPORT FOR VANCE PACKARD AND HIS POPULARIZATION OF SOCIOLOGY

If Betty and Al Lee were discontented with the thrust of American sociology, in journalism they found a kindred spirit who, like the Lees, was an irritant to the sociological establishment. During the 1950s and 1960s, journalist Vance Packard produced a series of books critical of the business and advertising industries. Among these were *The Hidden Persuaders* (1957), which analyzed the manipulation of the consumer and *The Status Seekers* (1959), which criticized class stratification and social climbing. Many prominent sociologists were outraged by this writer they considered to be an interloper who was pandering to the public and doing so on their professional turf. A review of *The Status Seekers* in the *ASR* by University of California sociologist William Petersen was typical: "Even more than their colleagues in related disciplines, American sociologists hold popularization in contempt."[113] With ironic arrogance he then complained that this left the field to those such as "Mr. Packard [who] is a journalist—a person, that is, with no necessary competence to discuss America's social structure."[114] Petersen offered up several quotes from *The Status Seekers* for special approbation including Packard's claim that in the United States there is "diminishing social mobility [where] democracy is still more of an ideal than a reality."[115] Petersen claimed that Packard had a "wooden style" of writing and thus was "no master" of journalism.[116] Given this general lack of ability, Petersen was at a loss to explain Packard's success, except to note that Packard was able to "simplify all concepts" and thereby appeal to a naive public.[117]

Other prominent professors joined in the criticism. A review by another University of California social scientist in the *American Anthropologist* also saw little of value in the book, but at least recognized that the source of the problem was social science's abdication of communication with the public: "Packard's book, unfortunately, is written in the tradition of the tabloid science feature writer. . . . The moral seems to be that unless professionals take it upon themselves to communicate with laymen, a layman may as well assume the role with results that not only further complicate the communication problem, but lead to the diffusion of error as well."[118]

Sociologist Seymour Martin Lipset was particularly distressed because of Packard's assertions that: "America is becoming much less equalitarian, that the democratic American way of life is being slowly eroded. The only trouble with this conclusion is that it is wrong."[119] Lipset claimed that such assertions were typical of " 'popular' books purporting to convey the findings of social science but misusing scientific evidence to construct a prejudiced and partisan case."[120] Lipset was incensed enough to conclude that while Packard was a member of the American Sociological Association, this was "no substitute for the introductory course in sociology which he gives no evidence of having taken."[121]

On the other hand, several years later a generally positive evaluation of Packard's work in *Trans-action* magazine noted that some of the criticism of writers who have attracted a popular audience is that none of them produce a " 'value-free' social science."[122] If this bothered other prominent sociologists, Al and Betty Lee were delighted with Packard's efforts. Al wrote to Packard after seeing Peterson's review to offer encouragement: "If it weren't for you, Whyte, Mills,

Sorokin, and a few others, sociologists could completely ignore social problems."[123] After seeing the *Trans-action* review Al wrote to Packard again:

> I am glad to see that sociologists are being forced to recognize the merits of your efforts to a greater extent than in the past. . . . But I would like to suggest a subject for one of your next books. Why don't you explore the wonderful world of university research—what contract research is doing to researchers, their research, and university education . . . under federal, state, city, and industrial subsidies? I get the impression that many of our social scientific colleagues will undertake to prove most anything for a fat budget.[124]

Packard's appeal to the public as well as his criticism of both manipulation by the mass media and of American social stratification could have been expected to strike responsive cords with the Lees. The outrage expressed by Peterson and Lipset undoubtedly only made Al more ready to spring to Packard's defense.

CONCLUSION: THE AUDIENCES FOR CLINICAL SOCIOLOGY

The research of the Lees is clearly consistent with C. Wright Mills' view that "the most admirable thinkers within the scholarly community . . . do not split their work from their lives. They seem to take both too seriously to allow such dissociation, and they want to use each for the enrichment of the other."[125] One of Mills' biographers has judged *Multivalent Man* to be a more significant exemplar of humanist sociology than even the writing of Mills, in great part because the Lees' book provided "one of the few confrontations with the functionalism of the mid-1960s."[126] One clear message of the book is that freedom is possible even in mass society.

All the research discussed in this chapter seems to have had two audiences; social science professionals *and* the general public. The Lees have authored numerous book reviews in a continuing effort to communicate with colleagues as well as the public. In the instance of the conflict in Northern Ireland, we see that lay people who actually live with and in the conflict often appreciated the Lees' clinical sociology more than the professionals in the field. Moreover, if clinical sociology is appreciated by some, it is sometimes resented by others. As we will see in chapter 4, this same controversy is found in the Lees' involvement in universities and professional associations. Clinical sociology is founded squarely on the belief in the possibility and desirability of liberal reforms to achieve greater freedom and equality, even in the seemingly most trivial of social institutions such as fraternities and sororities. Propaganda is abhorred because it generally interferes with the exercise of individual freedom. Racism and racial segregation also conflict with the assumptions that human beings are equal, and interfere as well with freedom and the exercise of such equal rights. In Vance Packard the Lees found a kindred spirit—an opponent of media manipulation and inequality who directed his appeals to the general public. Finally, the Lees maintained that the use of violence to pursue domination or even to attempt to throw off political oppression always will be counterproductive, because violence only justifies more violence. While the nonviolent civil disobedience of the people of India overwhelmed the colonial British government many years ago, the British still are able to match the Irish bullet for bullet and still have a garrison of many thousands of troops in Northern Ireland with no sign of withdrawal on the horizon.

Through nearly 60 years of research, Al and Betty generally have funded their projects themselves. There are at least two justifications for doing so. Funding ones own research, however modestly, avoids external controls on the course of the investigation. It is difficult to imagine Al and Betty securing grant support for their writing on Northern Ireland. Moreover, by eschewing external support, one can move swiftly to deal with an issue once it becomes a problem, such as Al's prompt response to the outbreak of the 1943 Detroit race riot. Al knows, based on his experience as a journalist, that once a story breaks the investigator must be ready to move. Clearly, in such a case as this, there was insufficient time for grant proposal writing, grant submission, and review. As indicated above, for clinical sociology to have a maximum input into the solution of social problems, research must be completed and published in a timely fashion. In any case, if you are committed to your research you will gladly spend your own money on it. If the Lees have had disdain for the support of funding agencies, they recognized from the beginning that social science makes the greatest impact on social problems when buttressed by professional associations as the following chapter will demonstrate. They never envisioned their role to be that of isolated critics such as L.L. Bernard, C. Wright Mills, or Robert Lynd.

NOTES

1. *Detroit Collegian.* "Lee Elected." Wayne University (January 18, 1943): 1.

2. Stansfield Sargent. Letter to John F. Galliher (July 5, 1990).

3. Henry Pratt Fairchild. *Dictionary of Sociology* (New York: Philosophical Library, 1944).

4. Ibid.: 303.

5. Alfred McClung Lee. "The Clinical Study of Society." *American Sociological Review* 20 (December 1955): 648.

6. Alfred McClung Lee. "The Services of Clinical Sociology." *American Behavioral Scientist* 23 (March/April 1979): 488.

7. Ibid.: 489.

8. Ibid.: 490.

9. Alfred McClung Lee. *Toward Humanist Sociology* (Englewood Cliffs, N.J.: Prentice-Hall, Inc., 1973).

10. Ibid.: 54.

11. Alfred McClung Lee and Elizabeth Briant Lee. *The Fine Art of Propaganda* (New York: Harcourt Brace and Company, 1939): 22.

12. Ibid.: 52.

13. Ibid.: 102.

14. Ibid.: 86.

15. Ibid.: 88.

16. *Newsweek*, "Swaggart's One-Edged Sword" (January 9, 1984): 65.

17. Russell I. Thackrey. Review. *Journalism Quarterly* (December 1939): 377–78.

18. H. A. Overstreet. Review. *The Saturday Review* (October 7, 1939): 14.

19. John Chamberlain. "How Propaganda Works." *The New Republic* (September 20, 1939): 192–93.

20. *The Communist*. Review. Vol. 18 (December 1939): 1167.

21. Kimball Young. Review. *American Sociological Review* 6 (February 1941): 118–19.

22. William White. Review. *The Quill Review* (July 1973): 10.

23. *New York Times*. "Propaganda Loses 2 Educators" (May 31, 1941): 13.

24. ———. "Dies Scrutinizes Propaganda Study" (February 23, 1941): 21.

25. ———. "Propaganda Study Instills Skepticism in 1,000,000 Pupils" (February 21, 1941): 1.

26. Alfred McClung Lee and Elizabeth Briant Lee. "An Influential Ghost: The Institute for Propaganda Analysis, 1936–1942." *Propaganda Review* (Winter 1988): 10–14.

27. *New York Times*. "No More Analysis" (November 15, 1941).

28. Alfred McClung Lee. *How to Understand Propaganda* (New York: Rinehart and Company, Inc., 1952): 27.

29. Alfred McClung Lee. "Depression, War, SPSSI, and SSSP." *Journal of Social Issues* 42 (1986): 65.

30. Barrington Moore, Jr. Letter to John F. Galliher (December 6, 1990).

31. Lee and Lee 1988 op. cit.: 11.

32. Alfred McClung Lee. "Sociological Theory in Public Opinion and Attitude Studies." *American Sociological Review* 12 (June 1947): 312–23.

33. ———. "Levels of Culture as Levels of Social Generalization." *American Sociological Review* 10 (August 1945): 485–95.

34. ———. "Attitudinal Multivalence in Relation to Culture and Personality." *American Journal of Sociology* 60 (November 1954): 297.

35. Talcott Parsons. *The Social System* (Glencoe, IL: The Free Press, 1951).

36. Alfred McClung Lee. "The Analysis of Propaganda: A Clinical Summary." *American Journal of Sociology* 51 (July 1945): 128.

37. Ibid.: 129.

38. Ibid.: 131.

39. Ibid.: 132.

40. Ibid.

41. Alfred McClung Lee. *Dry Propaganda: An Analysis of the New Prohibition Drive* (New York: Dryden Press, 1943), Mimeo.

42. Alfred McClung Lee and Norman Daymond Humphrey. *Race Riot* (New York: The Dryden Press, Inc., 1943).

43. Alfred McClung Lee. "Techniques of Social Reform: An Analysis of the New Prohibition Drive." *American Sociological Review* 9 (February 1944): 65–77.

44. Joseph R. Gusfield. *Symbolic Crusade: Status Politics and the American Temperance Movement* (Chicago: University of Chicago Press, 1963).

45. James H. Timberlake. *Prohibition and the Progressive Movement, 1900–1920* (Cambridge: Harvard University Press, 1966).

46. John J. Rumbarger. *Profits, Power and Prohibition: Alcohol Reform and the Industrializing of America, 1800–1930* (Albany, NY: State University Press of New York, 1989).

47. Ibid.

48. Gusfield op. cit.

49. David F. Musto. *The American Disease: Origins of Narcotic Control* (New Haven: Yale University Press, 1973).

50. Lee and Humphrey op. cit.

51. *Christian Science Monitor*. "To Prevent Race Riots." (November 20, 1943).

52. Kenneth Kaufman. "Two Books Discuss Race Problems We Face Today." *Chicago Tribune* (November 21, 1943).

53. Guy B. Johnson. Review. *Social Forces* 22 (March 1944): 339.

54. Irwin Deutscher. "Revisiting History: Hughes and Lee." *ASA Footnotes* 21 (January 1993): 7.

55. Alfred McClung Lee. *Fraternities without Brotherhood: A Study of Prejudice on the American Campus* (Boston: The Beacon Press, 1955).

56. Ibid.: 56.

57. Edwin H. Wilson. "Citation presented at the Humanist Dialogue" (New York City, May 16, 1977), American Humanist Association.

58. Alfred McClung Lee. Letter to John F. Galliher (September 12, 1990); see also Alfred McClung Lee. *Sociology for People: Toward a Caring Profession* (Syracuse, NY: Syracuse University Press, 1988).

59. Kenneth B. Clark. "The Social Scientist as an Expert Witness in Civil Rights Litigation." *Social Problems* 1 (June 1953): 7.

60. Kenneth B. Clark. Letter to John F. Galliher (September 25, 1990).

61. Ibid.

62. Lee 1988 op. cit.: 193.

63. Ibid.

64. Ibid.: 193–94.

65. Alfred McClung Lee. *Terrorism in Northern Ireland* (Bayside, NY: General Hall, Inc., 1983).

66. Ibid.: 2.

67. Ibid.: 44.

68. Ibid.: 144.

69. Ibid.

70. Ibid.: 80.

71. Rob Fairmichael. "Terrorism." DAWN (March 1984): 11.

72. Bruce Grindal. Review. *American Anthropologist* 87 (1985): 195.

73. Samuel Clark. Review. *Social Forces* 63 (June 1985): 1106.

74. Richard Jenkins. Review. *The Sociological Review* 33 (February 1985): 161–62.

75. Afif I. Tannous. "Understanding Terrorism: A Formula for Peace." *The Irish Literary Supplement* (1984).

76. Americans for Truth about Ireland. *APTI Newsletter* (Gwynedd, PA, September 1989).

77. Fr. Desmond Wilson. Letter to John F. Galliher (April 4, 1990).

78. Fr. Desmond Wilson. Letter to John F. Galliher (January 1991).

79. David Connolly. Letter to John F. Galliher (December 12, 1990).

80. Denis Barritt. Letter to John F. Galliher (November 22, 1990).

81. Alfred McClung Lee. *Multivalent Man* (New York: George Braziller, 1966).

82. Alfred McClung Lee. *Sociology for Whom?* 2nd ed. (Syracuse: NY: Syracuse University Press, 1986): 220.

83. Lee 1966 op. cit.: 273.

84. Ibid.: vii.

85. Ibid.: 42.

86. Ibid.: 7–8.

87. Ibid.: 70.

88. Ibid.: 78.

89. Ibid.: 34.

90. Ibid.: 107.

91. Ibid.: 209.

92. Ibid.: 352.

93. Ibid.: 42.

94. Ibid.: 62.

95. Ibid.: 68.

96. Ibid.: 309.

97. Ibid.: 50.

98. Ibid.: viii.

99. Alfred McClung Lee. *Sociology for Whom?* (New York: Oxford University Press, 1978).

100. Ibid.: 16.

101. Ibid.: 183.

102. Ibid.: 24.

103. Alfred McClung Lee. *Sociology for People: Toward a Caring Profession* (Syracuse: NY: Syracuse University Press, 1988): xvii.

104. Ibid.: 45.

105. Ibid.: x.

106. Ibid.: 20.

107. Ibid.: 30.

108. David M. Freeman. "Review Essay: Sociology and Public Policy—Challenge Unmet." *The Social Science Journal* 19 (January 1982): 123.

109. David Gil. "To Serve the People." *Contemporary Sociology* 8 (March 1979): 204.

110. Ted Goertzel. "Elizabeth Briant Lee and Alfred McClung Lee: A Tribute." Annual Meetings of the Association for Humanist Sociology, Ottawa, Canada (October 26, 1991).

111. Alfred McClung Lee. Review. *American Sociological Review* 17 (October 1952): 642.

112. ———. Review. *Social Problems* 4 (January 1957): 263.

113. William Petersen. Review of *The Status Seekers*. *American Sociological Review* 25 (February 1960): 124.

114. Ibid. 125.

115. Ibid.

116. William Petersen. "Reply to Mr. Packard." *American Sociological Review* 25 (June 1960): 409.

117. Ibid.

118. Raymond J. Murphy. Review of *The Status Seekers*, *American Anthropologist* 61 (December 1959): 1158–59.

119. Seymour Martin Lipset. Review of *The Status Seekers*. *The Reporter* 21 (July 1959): 31.

120. Ibid.

121. Ibid.: 33.

122. *Transaction*, "Is Vance Packard Necessary?" Volume 2 (January/February 1965): 14.

123. Alfred McClung Lee. Letter to Vance Packard (May 31, 1960).

124. Alfred McClung Lee, Letter to Vance Packard (February 2, 1965). Vance Packard Papers at the Pennsylvania State Library.

125. C. Wright Mills. *The Sociological Imagination* (New York: Grove Press, 1961): 195.

126. Joseph A. Scimecca. "An Analysis of Al Lee's *Multivalent Man*." Paper presented at the annual meetings of the Association for Humanist Sociology (Ottowa, Ontario, Canada, October 26, 1991).

Chapter 4

Clinical Sociology in Professional Associations, Universities, and the Discipline

EARLY COMMITTEE ACTIVITY IN THE ASS

From nearly the beginning of their careers, Al and Betty have been active in professional associations and frequently the center of controversy. Their commitment to the use of social science to promote human dignity, freedom, and equality, and especially Al's zealous pursuit of these ends, was often the source of the conflict. For example, from 1938 to 1943, undoubtedly on the strength of his background in journalism, Al was chosen to serve as chair of the ASS Committee on Public Relations. Betty served as a member. For the first two years of this assignment the annual reports were unexceptional. The reports merely noted the activities of the committee in publicizing the annual ASS convention and the amount of consequent press coverage. The 1940 report commented that: "The purpose of the Committee is not primarily to 'get space.' It is rather to interpret to the press those aspects of the Society's contributions which will give an understandable and a constructive impression of the work of sociologists."[1] In 1941, however, things began to heat up with the publication of the Supplementary Report of the Committee, which noted a controversial and critical address to the convention by Pitirim A. Sorokin. Sorokin's remarks later were expanded into *Fads and Foibles in Modern Sociology*.[2] Sorokin attacked the scientific pretensions of sociology, including its "quantrophrenia," its "cult of numerology," the "sham objectivism," and "obtuse jargon and sham-scientific slang."

From the beginning of his career Al Lee was willing to contradict very senior and powerful members of the profession. Al noted that several comments had been made to him "about the propriety of such

'destructive' publicity," all of which he ignored.[3] The 1941 report of
the committee contained an excerpt from an acerbic letter written to
Al by Howard P. Becker of the University of Wisconsin. "The Society
would have been far better off had no Public Relations Committee
been at work. I had no idea that you had 'released a press digest' of
Sorokin's speech. Such an error of judgment can be condoned by the
sufferers, but it certainly should not be defended by the perpetra-
tors."[4] Al's response also was reproduced in the committee report: "I
do not believe it would be wise for the American Sociological Society
to instruct its Public Relations Committee to assume powers of
censorship."[5] If Becker was distressed before, now that his letter to
Al had been published he was really angry. Thus in the April, 1942
ASR he shot back in a formal comment about the report of the
committee and in the process displayed his own arrogance. Becker
complained that his letter had been distributed to committee members
and published without his consent. "A scientific society is presumably
a professional body, with standards of relevance and significance
which cannot be appreciated by those who have not undergone the
requisite professional training. This being the case it would seem wise
to censor."[6]

Not all of the Lees' work on this committee provoked such heated
responses. Al later fondly recalled one of his experiences with this
committee on which he and Betty had served: "We were especially
happy to arrange very extensive international press coverage for
Edwin Sutherland's 1939 presidential address, 'White Collar
Criminality,' " critical as it was of the duplicity and greed of American corporate leaders.[7] Betty and Al admired the work of both
Sutherland and Sorokin, although they scarcely knew either of them.
In 1940, Al also served as the chair of the public relations committee
of the Eastern Sociological Society. From the beginning of their
careers the Lees have felt keenly the need to communicate sociology
to nonprofessional audiences.

ORGANIZATIONAL ACTIVISM BEGINS

The Lees recalled that many psychologists in 1930s and 1940s became
increasingly concerned with the development of the field along the
lines of mathematics and physics as well as the development of
widespread government sponsorship of research. Instead of this emphasis on quantification and sponsorship, the Lees saw a need for
increased attention to propaganda analysis, given the world's recent
experience with the Nazi propaganda machine.[8] The Society for the
Psychological Study of Social Issues [SPSSI] came into existence

during the 1930s as a reaction against leading social psychologists attempting to "scientize" their discipline. Many younger members of the profession desired to make their services broadly applicable and available in society, and attempted to combat the commercialization of their discipline.[9] The American Psychological Association, like the ASA, had become committed to rigorous investigation of noncontroversial issues. The SPSSI also was begun to "combat . . . the belittling of teaching, popular issues, and popularization."[10] The Lees also recalled that the "SPSSI's founders were alarmed by 'the attempted silencing of political dissenters by the government, its agencies, and by conservative businessmen who controlled many colleges and universities.' An SPSSI founder recalled: 'Fascism was a threatening reality in Europe and an alarming possibility in the United States'. . . . SPSSI was part of what might be called the propaganda analysis movement that had been gaining increasing academic attention ever since the end of World War I."[11] "SPSSI thus came into being as a 'group that might seek to create more job openings, . . . to facilitate research on pressing social problems, and to defend colleagues who seem to be victims of unfair treatment.' "[12] Thus substantive interests in propaganda, practical concerns with employment, and concerns about academic freedom all played a part in the founding of the SPSSI.

While Al was a charter member of SPSSI founded in 1936, Al and Betty early on were searching for a means to broaden the SPSSI mission, and Al recalled: "When I was a visiting professor at the University of Michigan in 1947–1948, I discussed with Daniel Katz and others there the needs of sociological social psychologists for an alternative organization, needs not wholly met by SPSSI."[13] The Lees continued: "Because the American Sociological Society (ASS) in the 1930s had come to resemble the APA in its restrictiveness and social values (or alleged "value-freeness"), many sociological social psychologists were attracted to SPSSI. I was one of them. . . . We were only sorry that SPSSI was not SSSI—a Society for the Study of Social Issues—in other words a more overtly interdisciplinary body."[14]

Being "fed up" with what they perceived as the entrepreneurial spirit of the ASA, the Lees valued their involvement with the SPSSI, but when this association resisted their efforts to become interdisciplinary, the Lees concluded that sociology should have its own alternative professional association.[15]

FOUNDING THE SOCIETY FOR THE STUDY OF SOCIAL PROBLEMS

Shortly after arriving at Brooklyn College in 1949, Al and Betty began plans to found the SSSP. Much later Al recalled: "I knew that the SSSP and AHS would be successful. I got my ideas from work in public relations when organizations need therapy. Professional groups sometimes need therapy." Certainly he felt that while the ASA needed therapy, it was probably beyond help. Betty and Al decided the SSSP was necessary during the depths of the McCarthyite furor that was especially intense during the early 1950s. "A description of SSSP that appears in early issues of its journal, *Social Problems*, includes among its objectives the 'improvement of the opportunities and working conditions of social scientists' and the 'protection of freedom of teaching, research and publication.' "[16] The SSSP was an effort "to bring sociological research and theorizing closer to pressing human concerns of the day."[17] Elsewhere the Lees have argued that "The Society for the Study of Social Problems came into existence in 1950–51 to help rescue sociology from the dehumanizing influences of abstract theorizing and of fancifully complex research methods."[18] Along with psychology and sociology, a similar rebellion occurred in anthropology. Referring to Samuel Stouffer's massive federally funded study of the military, the Lees were concerned that sociology increasingly was abandoning its historic concern with human welfare in favor of the management and control of citizens by government and other elites.[19] The Lees complained about the increasing "efforts to help control and manage soldiers, civilians, consumers and workers."[20] Social scientists thus became "the more obvious instruments of those in power."[21]

The paradox is that such consistent critics of professional organizations would be so active in them. Betty and Al were asked by the SSSP journal in 1976 to write their recollections of experiences in founding the association. They recalled that prior to founding the SSSP, as members of the ASS Press Relations Committee, the association's gatekeepers became alarmed by the public attention given to the criticism of business leaders found in Sutherland's 1939 presidential address "White Collar Criminality," and the criticism of the discipline found in Sorokin's ASS 1940 address. These were among their first signs of trouble in the ASS. Moreover, the Lees were troubled that while the Holocaust and WWII raged on the ASS gave no attention to either at its annual meetings or in its journal.

The Lees recognized the need for support from middlewesterners to ensure the success of their fledgling organization. They also recognized that a past ASS president such as Ernest Burgess would be a helpful addition. The files of Burgess, which are stored at the University of Chicago library, indicate that he had begun corresponding with Al Lee during the 1940s concerning their common interest in teaching about social problems. Burgess supported the concept of the

SSSP, became the chairperson of the organizing committee for 1950–51, and served two terms as SSSP president, all on the condition that others perform all the administrative detail. The initial organizing committee thus was composed of Burgess as chair, Arnold Rose as a member of the committee, and Al as secretary. As noted in Chapter 1, the Lees recalled L. L. Bernard's inability to keep *The American Sociologist* afloat,[22] and knew that the SSSP needed high-powered supporters. Another observer has noted that: "The same desire to legitimate SSSP affected the selection of *Social Problems* advisory editors, who were 'big names,' but often at SSSP's periphery."[23]

However, some prominent sociologists were not recruited and not really welcome. Betty and Al recognized that "even though Parsons had written on such social problems' topics as interethnic tensions, deviance, and the family and aging, they considered his work the antithesis of theirs."[24] In considering such establishment scholars, Arnold Rose claimed that "some of those who are engaged in the most utilitarian of studies for business and government are perhaps for that reason those who cry the loudest for 'basic research' and 'pure science.' "[25] Betty describes her role in the SSSP founding as follows:

> Al and I did everything together. Whatever Al did I was right there helping him do it. And there is an awful lot of work to do in setting up an organization and keeping it alive. The ASS was disturbed by it and didn't give us any support. Al wrote lots of letters and I helped him. I well remember that after a couple of years the SSSP budget was very low. Al and I sat at our kitchen table and talked about this. We had two boys to educate. Al said "I'll leave it up to you, do we or don't we give this organization any money to keep it going?" I decided we would put $100 into the organization which was quite a lot of money for us. If I hadn't done this the SSSP would not be alive today.

Jessie Bernard recalled that the SSSP was founded by those unhappy with the direction of the ASS and its refusal to take any stand on social issues, its elitism and cronyism, and its increasing service to business and industry.[26] By contrast, the SSSP was to be devoted to policy issues, and freedom of research, teaching, and publication.

> The actual leadership was in the hands of Alfred McClung Lee and Arnold Rose, who were not afraid to stand up to the conservative ASA elite. We embarrassed the ASA: it didn't know exactly how to deal with us. . . . [W]e scared the elite by threatening to give sociology a bad name by taking positions on issues. But we were

clearly in tune with the times. Before too many years had passed we became respectable. More's the pity, perhaps. The most elite members of the ASA not only joined, but became active. Became officers, in fact.[27]

When the SSSP was founded the rules stipulated that any five members of the association could nominate a candidate for any office.[28] Forty persons attended the first organizational meeting in September of 1951. There Burgess was elected chair, Al vice-chairperson, and Jessie Bernard secretary-treasurer. There were no dues the first year and only one dollar the second year, which helps explain why Betty and Al felt they had to provide their personal funds to keep it going. After Burgess' two terms as president, Al was the second president (1953–54), and by the end of Al's term, when Herbert Blumer was elected to be the third SSSP president, the association was off and running.[29]

Al Lee's presidential address in the October 1954 issue of *Social Problems* criticizes the research of those sociologists who would serve as technicians and who are bent on the use of statistics to further the manipulation of the masses through foundation-funded studies. The address quotes Daniel Bell, who referred to such research as "cowsociology," in that humans, like cows, are seen by such statistical researchers not as ends in themselves, but merely as means to an end.[30] According to Al's address, the legitimate use of sociology includes criticism of public policy, sociology for a liberal education, and a sociology "for everyman."[31] The SSSP presidential address represented Al's most forceful attack on statistical sociology. These themes would be renewed later in Al's presidential address to the ASA in 1976, titled "Sociology for Whom?"[32]

During the 1960s *Social Problems* published two addresses of SSSP presidents that are clearly consistent with the challenge of the Lees. In 1962, Alvin Gouldner's address, "Anti-Minotaur: The Myth of a Value-Free Sociology," attacked such sociology as being both heartless and disingenuous.[33] In 1967, Howard S. Becker's presidential address, "Whose Side are We On?" challenged sociologists to take the perspective of the underdog in their research.[34] These publications by leaders of this association indicate a good deal about the emerging values of both the association's leadership and rank-and-file members. Looking back on the early days of the SSSP, Gusfield recalled:

I think it must have been 1951 or 1952, in the very early years of SSSP, and Al had given a presidential address. A group of us who were then graduate students, mostly from the University of Chicago . . . were in a room discussing it and arguing about it, being led by

Gregory Stone. And those of you who knew Greg will remember his modes of arguing and talking were often quite loud. And the sound must have gone down every room in the hotel floor. . . . [W]e were talking a lot about Lee, and Lee's position on this, and Lee's position on that, and Greg was in some agreement, but mostly disagreement. And there came a knock at the door, it opened and in came this man who was obviously older than we were, and we asked, "Who are you?" He said "I'm Lee." We proceeded to have a wonderful evening of argument in which Al defended his position with vigor, but also gave you a sense that he was quite willing to treat people much younger than him as equal, and people who he could engage in argument without at the same time leaving one a sense that you were somehow the epitome of evil if you didn't agree with him.[35]

This reaction to junior faculty and graduate students was typical of the Lees.

Irwin Deutscher was another early SSSP member, considerably younger than the Lees, who recalled a sense of mission in the organization:

My earliest recollection of Al Lee was when I was a young Turk and was Secretary-Treasurer of the SSSP. Al created a democratic ethos—explicitly unlike the ASA elitism. Anyone could read a paper at the SSSP meetings. You didn't have to know someone at an elite university. I loved that as a young man. For a long time Al wanted to raise the association dues to have enough money for the legal defense of those involved in controversial research and teaching to protect them from McCarthyism. But I felt that in a democratic organization the dues should be kept as low as possible. Yet I didn't argue with him for I was in awe of him.[36]

Later Deutscher served as SSSP president and described the mission of the organization as "a censoring kind of conscience for criticism of sociology, by constantly pounding at the irrelevance of a great deal of contemporary reputable sociology. Such pounding worries them, the people who do that. They have to respond. They have to defend what they're doing and in doing that maybe they change it a little bit."[37]

Another early SSSP president went even further in describing the task of association members: "More than just talking about social problems and their analysis, it should include involving ourselves in the body politic. . . . I think we should be far bolder than we have ever been, than we are now."[38] Arnold Rose saw the SSSP as being of critical importance in opposing the elites who controlled the profession. In fact, Rose was sometimes referred to as "Mr. SSSP."[39] A later cohort felt the same way. Kai Erikson recalled: "I like to think of myself as part of the same spiritual generation as Howard Becker and Erving Goffman and people like that. I overlapped with them in Chicago, and most of them belonged to the SSSP."[40]

Early opposition to the ASA and value-free research faded, and in 1967 SSSP President Tumin "pleaded that sociologists not be partisans of any group and urged them to strive for objectivity."[41] Tumin asked: "Why, too, should ours be the discipline par excellence that puts 'fairness' and 'justice' and 'moral rectitude' at the center of our analyses of societies?"[42] It dismayed him that the discipline was "identified as the champions of Negroes, the youth, of underdeveloped nations, of the rights of women, of greater roles for the poor, of equal education for all."[43] Tumin feared that such identification would "endanger and damage our profession beyond easy repair."[44] The only legitimate obligation sociologists have is simply to "tell the truth."[45] And one observer noted that in 1969, SSSP president Albert Reiss urged sociologists not to bother with the direct study of social problems and instead to concentrate on mathematics and methodology.[46] Reiss especially urged that sociologists concentrate on the creation of social indicators that would increase the profession's ability in prediction.[47] Such is the fate of many nascent social movements; they broaden their appeal but at the price of the original organizational goals. The Lees lamented the fact that the SSSP had increased the number of names necessary for nominations and had become a "conservative and stable operation."[48]

But in spite of evidence of increasing conservatism in the SSSP, one member reasoned that since there was no chance of the ASA addressing critical social issues, the SSSP was the only hope, because "The SSSP has always been different. Its purpose is to analyze social problems, but with the point being to contribute to solutions. . . . It should suffice to say, on the one hand, that we have persisted as a progressive association, endowed with a tremendous plurality of perspectives, whereas many an 'alternative' association has collapsed."[49] Elsewhere, this member did note that "the SSSP has demonstrated a remarkably weak capacity for interacting with those social movements which have fought on the front lines of the social movements we analyze."[50]

A regular participant in SSSP annual meetings added that he still had high hopes for the SSSP: "The society in which we live and study and teach and write is in crisis. . . . I desire a greater sense of urgency from our annual meetings—an opportunity to be both disturbingly challenged and supportively encouraged to think critically and to act creatively; an opportunity, not simply to diagnose, but to learn better how to strategically counter the terrorist powers that dominate the material and imaginary landscape of contemporary North America."[51] Another long-time SSSP member, Joseph Gusfield noted that while he at one time had been very active in the ASA and had served on the ASA Council, he "drifted back into the SSSP in the late 1970s, largely out of the fervor of intellectual excitement going on."[52]

In 1978, Betty was nominated and ran unsuccessfully for President of the SSSP. Her candidate's statement notes the problems of poverty, sexism, racism, and the threat of nuclear annihilation, and promised that, if elected: "Willingly would I devote my efforts to helping SSSP increase its contribution toward the solution of the problems of humanity."[53] One illustration of how Betty's contributions to the SSSP have been minimized is reflected in a recent biography of Jessie Bernard.[54] The biography discussed Jessie Bernard's contributions to the association as its first secretary-treasurer, but makes no reference to the well-documented role of Betty as a SSSP co-founder.

In the early 1980s, the Lees wrote: "In the estimation of many, SSSP has both strengthened sociology—probably even saved undergraduate sociology—and given new life and direction to the ASA." They agreed with others that sociologists give no attention to "truly decisive events of our own age . . . [such as the] Nazi Holocaust, the bombing of Hiroshima, the Joseph McCarthy era, the Vietnam war, Selma, Attica, and Three Mile Island."[55] The Lees concluded that reformation of the ASA is probably impossible and thus there is a need for two distinct organizations: one a professional society and the other a scientific society, "with the control of the latter somehow entrusted to creative social scientists."[56] Thus, during the 1950s the Lees had begun to create a professional audience alternative to that of the ASA to which they and other social scientists could then respond.

It was not merely that people were nurtured by the SSSP, but that their ideas were nurtured as well. Labeling theory was given critical support and visibility in *Social Problems*, the new association's journal.[57] It is not a mere coincidence that labeling theory has focused on the behavior of superordinates, including government authorities, and on the influence of these behaviors on the lives of others. Later, Al desired to become ASA president, in part to influence the direction of that organization. Even later, as they saw the SSSP grow timid, middle-aged, ossified, and conventional, the Lees recognized a need for yet another professional organization. Paradoxically, neither Betty nor Al were ever the editors of any journal, including *Social Problems* or *Humanity and Society*, the journals of the associations which they founded. Those who came to lead the associations founded by the

Lees quickly developed a professional image of a journal incompatible with the Lees' vision which included politicizing the publication process. Indeed, approximately 20 years after the founding of the SSSP, the Lees expressed disappointment in the development of the association's journal: "It lacks controversy, variety, and fresh outlooks. . . . Why haven't sociologists through *Social Problems* portrayed the political-economic corruption of our society as an inherent concomitant of domestic and imperialistic plutocracy?"[58] Yet even without direct control by the Lees, the journals of the associations they founded reflected, even if in somewhat muted terms, the concern for injustice and human suffering so important to both Betty and Al.

Organizations and social movements mature over time. Skura has observed: "As they evolve, social movements often lose their initial sense of mission and become more concerned with self-maintenance. . . . To sustain itself, the movement needs resources, but to gain them it often must make accommodations."[59] One initial strategy in the SSSP was to involve prestigious sociologists in key roles on the editorial board of the journal.[60] In fact, the leaders of the SSSP often also held leadership positions in the ASA. And while one early SSSP president, Alfred Lindesmith, had hoped that *Social Problems* would not become just another sociology journal, he felt it devolved into one.[61] Indeed, another early president, Alvin Gouldner, was by 1976 ready to condemn the entire enterprise, claiming that its mission was now dead after having given the SSSP C. Wright Mills Research Award to Laud Humphreys for his research on sex performed by men in public places.[62] Recent calls challenging the SSSP to become more involved with its original mission of social justice and community activism show that the goals originally envisioned by the Lees are not dead after all. It should be noted also that the SSSP undoubtedly helped create the social conditions within which the AHS was founded. Without the hope of social change created by the mere existence of the SSSP, and its failure in the eyes of some to live up to such lofty goals, the idea of an association with yet even more visionary goals most likely would have been impossible to imagine.

In short, the Lees have been responsible for the creation of a subculture, including, but not limited to, the founding of the SSSP and the AHS. One close observer of Al's career argued that Al "was a major contributor to our field—more to the profession, however, than to the discipline. His essential role in the development of both the SSSP and the humanistic sociology organization, as well as his fairly successful efforts to democratize the ASA, places sociologists in his debt."[63]

AL AS A DEPARTMENT CHAIR

Al was chair at Wayne State University in Detroit prior to moving to Brooklyn College. A member of the Wayne State faculty noted: "The first time I heard about the Lees was when I joined the Wayne State University faculty. Al Lee had just departed after having served as the chair of sociology at Wayne. But he left a legacy of social activism such that the department members enthusiastically rescued me from my then [black-listed] 'status' as a victim of the McCarthy debacle in American life."[64]

Several of Al's Brooklyn College colleagues were interviewed and the comments immediately below are representative of their views. A long-time colleague and friend recalled those early days fondly: "The university president during the McCarthy era was a hard line anti-communist but Al stood up to him."[65] One of the many minority faculty members at Brooklyn College recalled: "Al was a fine administrator. He [was] imposing, fair minded, and clever. There was a scandal at Brooklyn College during the McCarthy Era with people being fired for their alleged communist leanings. The University president, Harry Gideonse, went on a witch hunt for communists on the faculty. Al had too much stature for the administration to punish him,"[66] despite the fact that Gideonse was: "a committed anti-Communist who, from the moment he took office in 1939, became embroiled with the radicals on his campus. This may have been deliberate for he believed that part of his mission to raise the prestige of Brooklyn College involved eradicating the popular image as a nest of Communists. Even so, he threw himself into the task with a ferocity that ultimately drew the criticism of the normally reticent ACLU."[67]

Another colleague gave a slightly different interpretation of Al's immunity from censure by the university president: "Although Al was department chair he did not get involved in college politics. He was involved outside. Al was a cosmopolitan rather than a local in Gouldner's terms. And Al was not around much. He lived in Connecticut and only came into town three days a week."[68] Thus, Al's immunity to administration punishment may have been a consequence of both his prominence and his orientation to issues larger than campus politics.

A junior faculty member at Brooklyn College from that period also acknowledged that "Al was fair, enthusiastic and helpful to younger faculty. He even supported my move to a better position at another university. Al had only one real enemy in the department, a social worker whom the university president promoted to dean."[69]

Another faculty member remembered: "I was just getting my Ph.D. when Al came to Brooklyn, but even so he treated me as a colleague and we often discussed our common interests in teaching introduction to sociology."[70] And a junior colleague who joined the Brooklyn College faculty as an assistant professor just prior to Al's retiring commented: "What impressed me at the time was that in the contacts we had, in spite of the discrepancy between his great knowledge and reputation and my lack of these attributes, he treated me (and other very junior colleagues) as equals."[71]

A female colleague noted Al's constant attempts to assist junior faculty:

> During the late 1950s I had conducted research on the exclusion of women from the profession. Al Lee knew of my research and told the *ASR* editor about it and the editor asked me to submit it and it was published in 1960.[72] *Social Problems* had a special issue on the Kinsey Report and I assisted the journal's editor to get out an edited book containing these and additional materials. Soon it became apparent to Al that I was much more than an assistant and Al insisted that the editor make me a co-editor of the book and not merely an assistant recognized in a footnote. But you had to know how to say "no" to Al, for he was very strong willed. For many years I worked as Al's deputy while he was chair of the department. Al was grooming me as the next chair. It was tough, but I refused to follow Al's suggestion that I succeed him.[73]

She later observed:

> Al is often thought of as an anti-bureaucrat and in many ways that is true for he certainly was opposed to hide-bound tradition, but on the other hand he founded bureaucracies like the SSSP, and the Association for Humanist Sociology. But more to the point he knew how to work in bureaucracy. He was a superb administrator. I had the opportunity to watch and learn, working with him as his deputy chair. He could be delicate and negotiate when it suited his purpose . . . [and] he understood budgets.[74]

She also remembered Al's attitudes toward racial justice:

> When I first met Al he made a great impression on me. It was in 1951 that I met him in his office and he asked me if I knew a black man who had a white wife at Northwestern who was being denied a degree. Al was extremely upset. Kimball Young was chair at Northwestern at the time and although he had left the Mormon church, apparently he didn't leave all his Mormonism behind. This showed me that as a chair Al had the right enemies and his heart was in the right place. In the early 1950s Brooklyn College was one of a very few places with black and women faculty members. One year

I was on the appointments committee. We had many applications but after having reviewed them Al declared that only one was worthwhile. He pulled out the vita of a Japanese-American woman who had been imprisoned in an internment camp during WWII and whose husband had served in the U.S. army during the war. The man had been seriously wounded in the war and his wife had previously been devoting herself to taking care of him.[75]

Other faculty at Brooklyn College also gave Al high marks for his recruitment efforts. One rated Al "the best chair I ever served under. He was largely responsible for recruiting a large number of blacks and women into the department during the 1950s at a time when it was difficult for black scholars to find employment except in the predominantly black colleges."[76] Perhaps as a legacy of Al's several terms as department chair, as late as 1990 it was reported that Brooklyn College was among a handful of graduate sociology departments with more than 35 percent female associate and full professors.[77]

One of his colleagues did admit however that "as a chair he was very decisive and generally had very good judgment, but he made a few mistakes in faculty appointments. His interest in people involved in social issues got in the way of judging quality. One guy he hired got letters only one line long which should have been a tipoff, but it wasn't."[78] She later recalled that Al's liberalism and humanitarianism created some humorous situations: "We had at one point in the department lost our beloved Sadie who was 'stolen' by a dean, and we got another secretary, a fine person but a poor typist who should have worn glasses but didn't, and was very inaccurate. . . . [S]o Al simply took the material away on the weekend and he would come back Monday morning with it typed."[79]

On occasion Al's ideology interfered with his professional activities in other ways. The first editor of the *Social Problems* journal recalled:

> Al asked me to start an SSSP newsletter prior to the journal. Only one issue was printed in December of 1952. I told Al that the association needed a journal. Although Al doubted that we had the financial resources for it, I found a low cost printer. Later when I moved to Brandeis I remained as editor and Brandeis helped support the journal, but by then Al felt the journal had become too independent. I'm a liberal but not worried about the establishment sociology of Harvard and Columbia as was Al. Al wanted the journal to reward the good guys and punish the bad guys. Thus there was some conflict about how much autonomy the editor should have from the publications committee. But I won out.[80]

Al's view of professional journals as primarily political vehicles was far from a fleeting fancy and would surface again. The irony is that had Al been successful in his efforts to control the direction of the journal it would not enjoy the prestige that it does today. In all of his activities in the Brooklyn sociology department we see Al's consistent attempts to serve the ends of racial, gender, and class justice. His relationships with minorities, women, and junior faculty were generally very supportive, and as we will see, at times very different from his associations with those in positions of authority where such nurturance was not required.

SOCIOLOGICAL ABSTRACTS

From 1961 until his death in 1992, Al served as a member of the board of directors of the *Sociological Abstracts* (*SA*), where he used his considerable business acumen on its behalf. He contacted libraries across the world attempting to sell subscriptions. He also solicited manuscripts from many foreign countries to be included in *SA's* abstracting service. He contacted those in other disciplines. He helped negotiate several National Science Foundation grants for *SA* from 1958–1965 to help get it started. He also assisted *SA* in attempting to get free operating quarters from a variety of universities including the CUNY system, the New School of Social Research, and Drew University. Aside from demonstrating his tremendous loyalty toward his friends, Al's long involvement in *SA* reflects his belief in assisting communication of the ideas of those who publish only in the relatively small circulation and relatively nonelite journals.

The founder of *SA*, gratefully acknowledged Al Lee's assistance with the NSF grant: "That was back in the late 1950s and early 1960s. In part he was guiding me through a maze of gate keepers who inhabited bureaucracies. . . . Several years later . . . [it] became clear that the quest for further funds would have hard going. It was Al who began to convince me gradually to bite the bullet and charge for subscriptions what we thought they were really worth. . . . Always vital, always a contributor, always a friend, in a word or two, he was my mentor and my shield."[81]

Elsewhere he recalled:

> I have known Al since 1953 when he offered me a job in the evening session at Brooklyn College. He also wanted to become part of what I was doing with *Sociological Abstracts*. So, I remained, between 1953 until 1962, a member of the department, and throughout those years I came to Al for advice, help, and succor. In a sense, he behaved like a mentor. After *SA* secured the NSF grant, Al continued his aid and

his abetting me in my activities. I liked the fact that Al never gave up; he was always a fighter for the things that he believed in and for him, *SA* was a bit of a fight vis-a-vis the sociological establishment. He had been fighting them for years. Although *SA* began at Columbia University, no one at Columbia was really interested enough to help *SA*.[82]

PROFESSIONAL OFFICE AND PUBLIC CRITICISM

Al used his work as SSSP representative to the ASA from 1963–1965 to publicize his criticism of ASA leadership and the direction in which he saw the organization going. He filed frequent reports, which were published in *Social Problems*. He had become concerned that the ASA president was assuming more power to appoint committee members than was allowed under the ASA constitution.[83] In the Winter 1963 report Al criticized the practice of the ASA presidents, who had been appointing the members of the committee on committees in apparent violation of ASA by-laws. The elected ASA council actually had the responsibility for such appointments. Allowing any president to make such appointments promoted the committee on committees to acting as the council and reduced the council to a rubber stamp of the president. A letter sent by the ASA president Everett Hughes to Lee was quoted in this report. Hughes responded to the criticism in part: "Yes, I appointed the Committee on Committees. It is the sort of action that would quite normally be taken by the president of any organization."[84] He defended his action on grounds of speed in decision making. The closing line of the letter reflects Hughes' pique: "Yours for constant vigilance, and for economy of effort baked in the same pie, Everett."

In the Spring 1963 issue, Al expressed his continuing concern about the ASA council's rubber-stamping of decisions made by the ASA leaders on the Executive Committee.[85] Later, Al discussed issues involved in the expense of moving the main ASA office to Washington D.C. and the hiring of a full time executive officer.[86] He argued that a scientific association had no need for a full-time executive officer nor for an office in Washington D.C. to help the association secure political influence and funding. These activities, he argued, were similar to those of trade organizations like the American Medical Association. This criticism of the professionalization of American sociology is consistent with the Lees' attacks on grants and statistical analysis. This anti-professionalism is very similar to that of L.L. Bernard's a generation earlier. Al ultimately reported that the SSSP was to lose its representation on the ASA council.[87] In all of this debate and controversy, Betty and Al seemed concerned with the changes taking place in the ASA as one significant portion of the professional audience of academic sociologists. Al and Betty consistently behaved as though the nature of professional associations made a difference in the pursuit and sharing of sociological knowledge.

In the Winter 1963 issue, Al also questioned action taken by the ASA council:

> At the request of the Eastern Sociological Society, the ASA was called upon to take "some positive action" in order to help offset "the growing loss of public statistics by race and color." The Council recommended to the general membership meeting the adoption of a motion calling upon and authorizing the Association to take the "positive action" of making formal representations to governmental officials (federal, state, and local) to restore or extend the collection of such statistics. . . . In the Council, I asked that my dissent be formally recorded in the minutes. . . . As physical anthropologists and psychologists have amply demonstrated, the social categories of "race" and "color" are so ill-defined and inconsistently used as to be meaningless to the scientific and misleading to the audiences of the racists who use such figures. . . . Far more significant than literacy or disease statistics concerning so-called "Negroes" or "colored" would be such statistics concerning significant socio-economic categories and groups regardless of "race" or "color."[88]

In the Spring 1963 report, Al Lee criticized the secrecy afforded by the incomplete minutes of the ASA council meetings and quoted a response from Talcott Parsons, the ASA council secretary who defended the practice of incomplete minutes. Parsons concluded: "I see no reason why a special exception should be made for your views."[89] Al recalled that at one point Parsons said to him, "Well, one thing I can say about you is that you are no gentleman."

An April 27, 1965, memo to ASA colleagues from Sylvia F. Fava of Brooklyn College, Barrington Moore, Jr. of Harvard, and Frank F. Lee of Northeastern urged others to join them in a write-in campaign to get Al's name on the 1965 ASA ballot to overcome its "unrepresentativeness:" "As the author of a series of careful analyses of the ASA problems, written as SSSP's ASA Council Representative, Alfred McC. Lee is the logical person to lead the slate. As SSSP organizer and officer and as three-time ASA Council member, Lee has done a great many things to democratize our major professional society. If he were its president, there would be constructive changes."[90] Another undated memo notes: "Alfred McClung Lee, during a long and distinguished career as teacher, officer of professional organizations and writer on professional and scholarly topics, has been an eloquent spokesman of those ideals which are of great concern to sociologists. He has advocated professional freedom, a broader participation of sociologists in professional affairs, and democratic procedures in professional and related organizations. As a candidate he represents the very same principles."

Several of Al's friends in 1966 also made an attempt to have him nominated as a candidate for ASA president. The list of supporters on the dittoed endorsement included Noel Gist, Elio Monachesi, John Mogey, Frank Hartung, and Sylvia Fava. That same year a letter from Leo Chall pledged his support to Al.[91] Al's avid supporters were spread across the country in academic institutions as diverse as the University of Minnesota, Missouri, Harvard, and Northeastern.

RETIREMENT: THE REAL WORK BEGINS

Al's retirement in 1971 marked the time when Al and Betty began the development of an explicit sociological humanism. Retirement seems to have created an intellectual environment for Al and Betty that gave them greater freedom, and certainly more time for writing. Yet even Al's retirement was not without controversy and conflict. For many years the Lee's sent out a photocopied Christmas letter to friends. The 1970 edition noted that during Al's last month of teaching at Brooklyn College a general student strike was triggered by the Vietnam war and that Al was involved in helping students finish course requirements in unorthodox ways. The 1972 Christmas letter noted that Al was forced to bring suit against the city of New York to collect his full pension. The 1974 letter listed 13 professional presentations that Betty and Al had made either jointly or individually. The 1986 letter mentioned that their "vacations" that year had consisted of trips to eight professional association conventions and the presentation of seven papers.

Shortly after Al retired from Brooklyn College he became a visiting scholar with an office and secretarial support at Drew University. Nothing originally was done for Betty until a female sociologist on the faculty complained about the disparity. Because the sociology department had no room for yet another person, the anthropology department took in Betty.

ASA PRESIDENCY

The 1973 *ASA Footnotes* noted: "Henceforth, as a result of the vote held in October, members will be able to augment the work of the

Committee on Nominations by adding names to the final official ballot through a petitioning process."⁹² At this time, with Betty and Al's full and energetic support, the ASA rules were altered so that only 100 names were needed for nomination for president. On the heels of this victory Leo Chall helped organize a write-in campaign for Al for the ASA Presidency (with the help of Herbert Blumer, Jessie Bernard, and Joseph Bensman, among others). Al won this election. A Brooklyn College colleague recalled:

> Al was upset with the Harvard-Columbia neglect of social problems. I had a post doc at Harvard 1961–1962 and attended Parsons' lectures. Parsons always took an incredible amount of time in his lectures to criticize his critics, especially Al Lee (but never by name). So to offset this Harvard-Columbia influence, in starting SSSP Al enlisted midwestern giants—Blumer, Burgess, Rose, and Znaniecki and junior members of the Brooklyn College sociology department. Al and Betty gave money, but Brooklyn College never helped the organization. When Al agreed to be a write-in candidate for ASA President, a group of us had a meeting at the graduate center in New York City. We all agreed to go through the ASA rolls and write everyone we knew.⁹³

The founder of the *Sociological Abstracts* recalled:

> Since I had to fight for the abstracts, I saw him as an ally. When he announced that he was going to run for the presidency of the ASA, I pulled out all the stops on my end. Al Bertrand (LSU chair) of the Southern Sociological Society was one of the sociologists who I thought was *persona grata*, and I gained some friendships among the chairpeople in the southern departments of sociology. I got on the telephone and proceeded to lobby for Al Lee. I think I made 200 calls. I don't know how effective the calls were, but we got him elected. . . . I had to do it, since Al got me into Brooklyn College, he got *SA* into Brooklyn College.⁹⁴

The contest involving Al and his opponents (James Short of Washington State and Hubert Blaylock of the University of Washington) drew 63 percent of ASA members, the largest percentage to ever vote in an ASA election.⁹⁵ It seems certain that the candidacy of such an anti-establishment scholar was aided by the widespread alienation generated by the war in Viet Nam. In any event, no similar candidate has been elected since that time. Gusfield has recalled that when Al was elected ASA president: "I remember the great consternation of many people. They thought this was a disaster second only to a nuclear attack."⁹⁶

Al Lee's inaugural address put all association members on notice that he was still a critic of the ASA "establishment." He presented his "ten point program" on which he had run for office. One point was to include the widest possible spectrum of ideas in the association. Another idea was to involve more women and minorities in the association [as Bernard had stressed before him] and to cease private meetings of the council that were revealed only by very brief and uninformative minutes. Another proposal was to elect members of the ASA council by regions. Still another was the support of freedom of research and teaching for dissenters. "Unless we fight for the dissenters, there is not much point in the effort at all."[97] Indeed, in the following chapter we will see that Al often has publicly defended junior radical or Marxist faculty when they were being dismissed by their universities—Fred Millar of George Mason University,[98] David Colfax of Washington University,[99] and Paul Nyden of the University of Pittsburgh.[100]

As the ASA President-elect Al was responsible for selecting a theme for the annual convention. His choice raised these questions: "What biases are prevalent among the profession's gate keepers to academic degrees, to employment, to promotion, to distribution of acclaim, grants, and prizes, to honorific lectureships, and to other kinds of professional preferment?"[101] While president, Al noted that he had served on the council on three previous occasions, twice for the Eastern Sociological Society and once for SSSP, and thus his experience with the council during his presidency was not all that new for him. He also emphasized a number of initiatives taken during his term in office, but leading the list was "program experimentation" with the highest participation ever recorded of women as session chairs.[102] In his "Report of the President" to the 1976 ASA council meeting he proposed a new periodical, the *Journal of Applied Sociology*,[103] which indeed was eventually begun by the ASA as the *Sociological Practice Review* in 1990.

Betty recalled Al's year as ASA president: "Al served as a member of the board and all that year he always voted opposite all the other members of the council. They are very conservative. They remind me of the new rich and they want to prove that they are real professionals." One issue that Al won involved the ASA censure on the administration of Simon Fraser University. Several years earlier the university had fired several faculty members whom they had accused of being radicals and attempted to blacklist them to prevent them from securing subsequent employment. In response the ASA had voted censure on the university administration. During Al's term on the council it was proposed that the censure be lifted. Al spoke against it and for once at least he prevailed.

Betty recalled that, in dealing with the staff of the ASA, Al also had his share of problems:

Alice Myers was the administrative officer of the ASA for many years. She was not at all helpful while Al was ASA president. On her own she appointed people to offices when Al as the elected president actually had the authority to do so. Al found this out by accident and she acknowledged what she had been doing all along. In her suite at the ASA convention hotel she hosted lavish receptions for past ASA presidents. We went to a couple of them but we could feel the hostility in the air and only once or twice did anyone even speak to us briefly. We were obviously outcasts.

This left few doubts in their minds about ASA leaders' tolerance for intellectual differences. Al agreed that his term in office, although fraught with problems, did provide a legacy:

Throughout my terms as president-elect, president, and past president of the ASA, I had to contend with persistent opposition—even sabotage—from the strongly pro-establishment Council and office staff. That I represented a majority of the ASA members did not appear to matter. . . . Many matters that the national office was supposed to refer to me were handled without my consultation or consent. Nevertheless the wisdom of the many proposals our group made at the time was such that a number of them had an influence on ASA practices then and later.[104]

For her part Alice Myers not surprisingly recalled: "I found Al Lee difficult to deal with while he was ASA President. He had all those political views—he set himself up as a spokesman for every radical, nonestablishment, nonconformist group. And those groups in turn set him up as a kind of God. Al tended to pull these people away from the ASA while others of us wanted to keep them in the organization."[105] This shows a willingness to abandon professional associations that he felt failed to meet the common good. We will demonstrate below that the Lees even began to feel that the SSSP was falling short of its original goals and thus another association was required.

In his ASA presidential address Al Lee observed: "This common emphasis upon quantrophrenia and other intellectual rituals turns away many persons who might develop into sensitive observers and literate recorders and interpreters of social behavior."[106] He viewed this dehumanizing type of sociology as actually serving the ruling elites. Sumner, Sorokin, and Mills—"All three were ritualistically canonized only after they were safely dead and their work bowdlerized or rationalized."[107] Al proposed organizational changes and chal-

lenged the ASA to bring minority groups and women more promi-
nently into the activities of the association and to convert the ASA
ethics committee into "an effective ethical guide."[108] Al also quoted
Irving L. Horowitz on elitism in research funding: "Sources of funds
for research tend to be exclusively concentrated in the upper classes,"
and added: "This infusion of government and corporate wealth makes
it difficult to bring about a countervailing pluralistic system of power
with respect to social science funding."[109]

A long-time Brooklyn College colleague gave a positive assessment of Al's organizational abilities:

> Al is a very unusual combination. Very liberal or even radical in his
> ideas, but highly organized. He has an ability to found and organize
> professional associations—SSSP, AHS and is active in many others.
> He is radical but able to function in organizations and set up budgets.
> As ASA president Al was responsible for permanent changes in the
> association—especially in the involvement of women in the associ-
> ation.[110]

Due to Al's efforts, sufficient signatures were collected to require a
referendum on the issue of election by regions. His reasoning was
that nomination and election of the ASA council and key committees
by region would increase the possibility of election of nonelites.[111]
The opposition was formidable: 16 of the 17 council members signed
the statement in opposition. In a somewhat surprising move, the
Sociologists for Women in Society also was opposed.[112] Later, Al
reported in a letter to Leo Chall his disappointment that the referendum failed by a 2 to 1 margin.[113]

During his tenure as ASA President, Al attempted to pass a
referendum for the election of ASA journal editors. On December 16,
1976 he informed Chall that he had collected 78 of the 300 signatures
required to force a referendum on the issue.[114] In May 1977, he
formally complained to fellow members of the ASA council that ASA
executive officer William Form had declared the resolution dead as of
January 24, 1977; Form had decided on his own that those collecting
such signatures should be allowed only three months for the process.[115] As early as 1974, as a member of the ASA council, Al had
suggested the election of editors and had received only one other vote
for the idea.[116] Although far from a mainstream idea, this proposal is
consistent with the view of Betty and Al that all knowledge is political
and value-laden. Ruth Hill Useem fondly recalled that she and Al
served together on the council as a team of two, with no support from
other members: "Al would say 'I'd like to move,' and nobody would
second his motion, and so finally my role was to say, 'I second that.'

We never passed one thing that Al moved, but he did change the council from meeting behind closed doors to a public meeting and from then on the council has had to be open."[117] Even after his term as ASA President, Al was not content to be a passive elder statesman, and in 1980 was elected to the nominations committee.[118]

VALUE-FREE SOCIOLOGY DURING THE 1970S: AL LEE AND JAMES COLEMAN

In a highly visible and controversial report James Coleman et al. allowed that "between 1968 and 1972, there was a sharp reduction in black-white segregation in the United States. . . . The average black child in 1972 went to a school that was 61% black (compared to 74% in 1968)"[119] The report also stated, however, that "the figures show that although segregation decreased in 16 of 22 cities, the proportion of white schoolmates increased in only 10 of these sixteen."[120] In the remaining cities the residential exodus of whites from the cities reduced the number of whites in the city school system available for integration. Thus, in some cities there was a more even dispersal of black students across all public schools, which reduced segregation, but also a shrinking proportion of white students. According to Coleman, the data demonstrated that whites fled the cities to avoid court-ordered integration, which he suggests they saw as an illegitimate exercise of authority by the courts: "Thus certain policy aims such as elimination of segregation among schools whatever its source may be appropriate for legislative action if it achieves certain desired consequences, but not appropriate for court action."[121]

Others were not so sure. In the years that followed Coleman's assessment, Farley took some exception to this interpretation of these obvious patterns in school enrollment: "It is impossible to conclude either that the school integration efforts and litigation of the past thirty years were successful or that they were failures."[122]

> To be sure, there tends to be an unusually large loss of white school enrollment during the year in which a city's schools are racially integrated. However, the loss of white enrollment attributable to white flight is small compared to the decline produced by long-run demographic trends such as the fall in the white birth rate, the aging of the white population of cities, and the continuing movement of whites away from older central cities. Cities in which judges have not issued integration orders, such as Chicago, New York, and Philadelphia, have lost white students at a rate comparable to cities involved in court-ordered integration.[123]

Thus, we see considerable divergence in interpretation of these enrollment figures.

Al threw himself into the dispute with zeal. It was clear to him
that Coleman's reports amounted to nothing less than purposeful
misstatement. In 1975, during his term as ASA president, Al Lee
raised questions with the ASA council and the ASA ethics committee
about Coleman's reported findings that busing for educational opportunity did not achieve its intended goals and in addition led to white
flight from the cities. The council rejected Al Lee's recommendation
of an investigation of Coleman as a violation of Coleman's right to
freedom of speech.[124] Indeed, there appeared to be an abundance of
outrage at the mere suggestion that the council should pursue an
investigation. At the time Lewis Killian was a council member and
felt he "was being asked to take part in an intellectual lynching."[125]
He recalled that Al had once attempted to have him censured by the
Eastern Sociological Society for having conducted research for the
Florida attorney general regarding local leaders' attitudes toward
problems involved in the enforcement of the Brown vs. Topeka
School Board decision.[126]

When the council refused to support Al's charges, Al attacked
them as well: "The Council is an ideologically self-perpetuating body
that represents on the whole the same military industrial interests. . . .
They are people far more interested in the entrepreneurial games of
grants and contracts for corporations, governmental agencies, and
foundations than they are in building a humane scientific discipline of
sociology of service to people."[127] In any case, it was clear to the
Lees that the *ASA Footnotes* opened considerable space for Coleman
supporters to attack Al Lee, but not nearly so much for those
members who opposed Coleman.[128]

Coleman realized that his report that school desegregation in large
cities was contributing to white flight would anger those interested in
civil rights.[129] He was correct. In January of 1976, in a letter to Al Lee,
the noted African-American psychologist Kenneth Clark observed
that "Coleman himself was aware that his findings did not support his
anti-busing public statements."[130] Elsewhere Dr. Clark reported:
"The study, by Dr. James S. Coleman of the University of Chicago,
maintaining that busing efforts in the country's 20 largest cities
between 1968 and 1972 had caused white flight and thus intensified
racial imbalance in the schools, was called statistically unfounded,
morally tainted and the object of distortion by the press."[131]

At this point some background information should be considered.
In 1966, Coleman had published a well-known report dealing with
racial segregation in public education titled *Equality of Educational*

Opportunity, which made him a widely recognized expert in this area.[132] This report concluded that "the average white student's achievement is less affected by the strength or weakness of his school's facilities, curricula, and teachers than is the average minority pupil's."[133] "The report stated also that "if a minority pupil from a home without much educational strength is put with schoolmates with strong educational backgrounds, his achievement is likely to increase."[134] "Coleman concluded that "the test performance of Negro children in integrated schools indicates positive effects of integration."[135] Coleman later changed his mind about the generally positive contributions of government policies aimed at achieving racial balance.

A withering critique of Coleman's later research was provided by Pettigrew and Green.[136] They discuss events that began in April 1975 and continued through December 1975. During this time, Coleman granted many interviews with the press, appeared on television, authored several articles in magazines, submitted affidavits in school-desegregation cases, and testified before the U. S. Congress as well as before the Massachusetts legislature.[137] Pettigrew and Green concluded: "We are not discussing, then, a single research study and the policy interpretations to be drawn from its findings. Rather, we are reviewing an unprecedented campaign by a sociologist to influence public policy."[138] Moreover, Pettigrew and Green insisted that the research which was conducted in a demographic vacuum ignored the fact that white flight from the cities had been going on long before court-ordered busing had begun. They insisted also that Coleman used only aggregate data to understand individual actions: "Not one white parent was asked by Coleman if his or her child was removed from the public schools because of school desegregation."[139] The critique went on to state that "Coleman committed the classic ecological fallacy, inferring individual motives from broad-gauged aggregate data."[140]

The first paper Coleman wrote based on his 1970s busing research was "moderate" in tone, but his comments to the press "offered blunt and far-ranging opposition to federal court orders that required extensive urban desegregation."[141] To the *Boston Globe* he asserted that "a whole generation of young legal talent thinks it can transform the society by winning court cases. That's enormously subversive of the whole political process in the United States."[142] In the *National Observer*, Coleman added that the courts were "the worst of all possible instruments for carrying out a very sensitive activity like integrating schools."[143] These comments by Coleman were big news, because they appeared to represent a major and surprising reversal of position by a nationally known figure regarding the ultimate results of government policies aimed at racial integration of schools. These conclusions fit nicely into the conservative mood of many white voters and their increasing opposition to school busing.

Critics of Coleman's research noted that he had neglected to consider many variables that might influence "white flight," and questioned as well the ethics of communicating research results in the way he did. A *New York Times* writer checked all the 20 cities studied by Coleman and "could find no court-ordered busing, rezoning or any other kind of coerced integration in any of the cities during the 1969–1970 period."[144] Coleman even admitted to the *Times* reporter that he had not studied busing. Given this criticism, a second draft was produced by Coleman and discussed at an August 4 meeting in Washington, D.C. involving Coleman and several of his critics. It was observed that his research was not about busing, integration, school achievement, disruption, or court orders. Coleman's work dealt only with the relationship between school desegregation and changes in white enrollment in urban public schools. His studies ignored a variety of predictor variables and "instead chose to test the narrow question of whether the racial desegregation of urban schools leads to a loss of white students."[145] Coleman's research ignored the demographic context and long history of white flight from the center cities. On August 15, Notre Dame University held a symposium on white flight and school desegregation, at which time Coleman produced yet a third draft of his paper. At this point, one critic noted that "whites are moving out of central cities for many other reasons. We have shown that cities whose schools were integrated between 1967 and 1972 did not lose white students at a higher rate than cities whose schools remained segregated."[146]

Pettigrew and Green noted that: "All told, over an eight-month period, Coleman presented five editions of his paper (plus a thirty-nine-page erratum edition) containing three contrasting analyses of his data. Although Coleman's research was constantly changing, his expressed views remained substantially the same."[147] According to Pettigrew and Green: "It is the persistent confusion of political opinions with new research findings in an intense media campaign which concerns us—not the exercise of Coleman's right to express his views."[148] So it appears that this allegedly value-free social scientist was not so value-free after all, just as had been true of Sutherland, Parsons and Lundberg before him. Pettigrew and Green conclude that: "When Coleman argues that metropolitan remedies and extensive busing for desegregation are wrong because they limit individual rights, he is speaking largely of white rights, and, in effect, of a white right to discriminate."[149] They state also that "Coleman's argument is remarkably similar to the position of the nineteenth-century Social Darwinists; 'Statcways cannot change folkways' was their dogma, and this reasoning is embedded in the 1896 Supreme Court decision in Plessy v. Ferguson which affirmed the legitimacy of 'separate-but-equal' public facilities."[150] The article further noted that, in fact, opinion surveys have shown that positive shifts in racial attitudes of white Americans have occurred after racial desegregation has been achieved by court order.

Others recognized that it is false to assume that the use of statistical techniques would automatically take care of value questions, as an officer of the fledgling AHS noted: "By suggesting that sociologists themselves have a responsibility for the consequences of their findings, Professor Lee has done a great service to our discipline, which must move in the direction of greater ethical and moral awareness of the implications of its findings."[151] Yet Al seemed inconsistent to some by attempting to denounce Coleman, considering the Lees' well-known support for political dissenters, as well as their insistence that social science research be relevant to public policy. Indeed, in a May 7, 1979 press release sociologist/priest Fr. Andrew Greeley threw the waning moral weight of the Roman Catholic church into the fray, siding with Coleman, and against Al Lee.[152]

After considering the opposition of the ASA to Al Lee's complaint, Kenneth Clark wrote to Al: "This type of behavior would not only be discouraged but would be severely punished if found in undergraduate or in graduate students or in young post-doctoral research assistants in either the social or physical sciences. Such behavior is even more intolerable when found in an established scientist."[153] In spite of such reasoning, ultimately it was reported in the minutes of the third meeting of the 1976 ASA council that the council had decided, with only one dissenting vote, to oppose Al Lee's request for an investigation by the ASA ethics committee, and proclaimed: "The Council reaffirms Professor Coleman's right of freedom of expression and conscience."[154] The lasting impression on the Lees was that this action clearly demonstrated a preference for protecting individual professional freedom, at least for association insiders, as opposed to preventing collective harm to minority people.

But more than mere misrepresentations: "Coleman continued to make unfortunate *ad hominem* attacks on his critics."[155] Looking back on the dispute over a decade later Al Lee still believed that "Freedom of expression does not mean freedom from criticism."[156] Like Parsons before him, Coleman ultimately was elected ASA president, indicating little lasting concern among those most active in the ASA regarding this case and the issues raised in this controversy. This demonstrates again how important countervailing professional organizations such as the SSSP and AHS continued to be. From the Lees' perspective the primary thing that was so damaging about the entire Coleman episode was the impact upon the audience of nonsociologists. In their view, Coleman had skillfully misrepresented his research findings and had done so in a fashion to discredit the entire effort of metropolitan school desegregation begun by the Lees and others in the Brown versus Topeka Supreme Court case.

Yet one prominent sociologist expressed support for both Coleman and the value-free tradition: "Coleman has shifted his policy recommendations from compulsory busing to voluntary busing for one reason: because his research convinced him that compulsory busing leads not to greater integration but to greater segregation."[157] For his part Coleman also remained convinced of the straightforwardness of his results and recalled the details of this controversy vividly. In response to this controversy the ASA planned a special plenary session to discuss the issue: "The ASA Convention, in which there was a plenary session, filled to standing room only, [was] occasioned by a sequence of events that began with an attempt by Alfred McClung Lee, the president of ASA, to have me censured for research showing that city-wide busing had produced extensive white flight in cities where it had been used as a desegregation tool."[158]

Recalling what was for him "a tortured period of intellectual isolation," Coleman noted that "I still have the posters that were plastered at the entrance to the ballroom and behind the podium, covered with Nazi swastikas, epithets, and my name."[159] Clearly Coleman holds Al Lee responsible, for this "sequence of events" began with Al's attempted censure. In the next decade a similar conflict was engaged challenging Coleman's findings that Catholic schools "produced higher achievement than public schools"[160]— another contradiction of conventional wisdom. Coleman argued that the profession must fight against all research taboos, revealingly illustrating his point (and his political predispositions) by mentioning his support for investigations into the biological causes of crime. In reflecting on these events Coleman asked: "How can the discipline . . . so structure itself that it does not erect norms against research that challenges the conventional wisdom? Or more pointedly, how can the discipline structure itself so as not to violate academic freedom, as it has done in the past?"[161]

Coleman was genuinely hurt by what he believed to be the intrusion of political interests into issues of scientific fact.[162] So stunned was he by the criticism of his work that he dropped his membership in the ASA for a number of years. Assuming the position of proponents of value-free sociology before him, he argued that the social scientist must remain unfettered and not held responsible for even obvious misinterpretations, no matter how onerous the policy implications occasioned by such mistakes. Coleman apparently believed, just as Tumin before him, that if sociology became "identified as the champions of Negros"[163] it would become impossible to "tell the truth."[164]

Increased understanding of the underlying basis for this dispute between James Coleman and the Lees requires consideration of their divergent views regarding the audiences required for social science research. Coleman argued that as a consequence of social structural changes after World War II the participant observation research of the Chicago school, which emphasized urban social problems, and was so much admired by the Lees, was no longer relevant to significant audiences and lost its preeminence for this reason.[165] This decline was not so much a matter of personal choice among sociologists, but according to Coleman's unusually sanguine assessment occurred because "urban life had become somewhat more ordered, cities had become habitable."[166] To the extent that this was true there was now less need of, and demand for, Chicago sociology. Coleman further contended that after World War II continuing social-structural changes were responsible for ushering in the era of "empirical sociology" personified by the work of Paul Lazarsfeld.[167] In this environment market research and investigations of public opinion at the behest of groups such as "national manufacturers" were the order of the day.[168] Now the challenge was to answer questions such as "What made people buy a certain good?"[169] Throughout these changes in the focus of mainstream sociology the Lees continued to claim that the primary audience for social science research should be the general public, and that this remained a matter of personal choice not dictated by natural market forces or social structure. Both Coleman and the Lees agreed, however, as Buxton and Turner have claimed, that the issue of the audiences of sociological research is of critical significance.[170]

STARTING THE ASSOCIATION FOR HUMANIST SOCIOLOGY

If it is highly unusual for scholars to start a new professional association, it is even more unusual to start two. Surely it would be more common to spend a lifetime merely nurturing the original organization. Al reasoned differently: "Several of us became aware of the need for a more value-oriented society than the SSSP had become. This resulted in [the late] Charles P. C. Flynn, Elizabeth, and I forming the Association for Humanist Sociology."[171] Betty and Al felt that professional associations and their journals quickly experience a type of aging process and become overly careful, professional, and conservative. A long-time friend explained the reasoning:

> I once asked Al why he was instrumental in starting and developing so many major associations. He simply said that after a few years most associations become too focused and then are dominated by the few at the expense of the many. Al and Betty expect the association they are involved with to maintain a core of humanist and communal values and practices. When individuals begin to reify their associations, then it seems to Al and Betty that it is time to start a new association. . . . Betty and Al made many different contributions to AHS from monetary to spiritual. However, their greatest contribution was their constant presence and availability.[172]

Betty recalled that she and Al felt a sense of mission in starting yet another organization: "We felt we needed to start the AHS because while those in the SSSP studied social problems they increasingly did so by writing stiff articles for publication. That is good so far as it goes, but you need to do more and try to figure out ways of alleviating the situation. The AHS will never be as big as the SSSP because it is usually not in the nature of people attracted to academic life to be activists as well as sociologists." And an early AHS member noted:

> I believe it was in 1976 that Al, Betty, and ten other sociologists met at the home of Charles Flynn to discuss the formation of the AHS. . . . Al and Betty Lee, however, were clearly the *inspiration* for the founding of the AHS. Al's longstanding humanistic concerns reflected in his work (e.g., his early study of the discriminatory character of college fraternities, his work on propaganda, etc.). . . . Al also contributed immensely to the content of the AHS constitution and By-Laws. [We] met in Chuck Flynn's kitchen in Miami, Ohio, to discuss the founding of the new association. Al felt a new association was needed because the SSSP was getting too stodgy and a new association was needed to address more humanistic type questions. Al insisted that the name be humanist and not humanistic even though this resulted in a noun modifying a noun. Flynn did a lot of the early work on details such as getting out a newsletter.[173]

Another sociologist has recalled that she stood up during an ASA business meeting to voice frustration with the association.[174] After the meeting she was approached by an "older gentleman who introduced himself as Al Lee. He explained that he and Betty Lee had been organizing an alternative [association], the AHS, and asked if I would be interested. . . . I became active in the AHS. . . . The AHS meetings were qualitatively different from the other professional meetings and its membership was intensely loyal."[175]

A testimonial came from another early AHS member:

> I had basically dropped out. I was not attending the ASA or SSSP meetings or even joining the associations and receiving journals. I attended the initial organizational meeting with cautious optimism, that there may be other sociologists wanting to combine activism and advocacy with their professional work. It was a small and diverse group who attended, and I was pleased that a Marxist perspective was not hegemonic among the new members or leaders. I began to see a possibility for reclaiming a strand of radical sociology as my intellectual home.[176]

While the Lees helped the group develop a constitution, a journal, and a philosophy based on their long experience in building organizations, "they did not demand that we do things their way, and they listened to other points of view,"[177] except of course for Al's insistence on the name for the new association.

But there were other interpretations of the Lees' influence. Because Al and Betty were so much more experienced and skilled in the task of founding and organizing an association than the other early AHS members, Al in particular sometimes appeared to be domineering by merely wanting what was best for the association. An early AHS member recalled these concerns: "Early in the association's history, I sometimes felt he considered the AHS to be "his" group, and its members to be "his" followers. After all, he had a long, well-known association with its goals and purposes, and he was more than central to its foundation. He held strong, well-founded opinions and sometimes bristled a little at others' ideas (especially—and justifiably—if the ideas were less than well done)."[178] This same person remembered that in 1975–76, Al had gone through stormy relations with the ASA council and around that time Charles Flynn contacted him. A small group led by the Lees and Flynn set up an interest table on humanist sociology during the 1976 ASA meetings. In October, 1977, Al and Betty invited Chuck Flynn and a few others to convene at their New Jersey home to write the constitution and by-laws of the AHS.

> As time went by, however, the political identity (as separate from their intellectual identity) of the Lees as "the" founders (and hence the power behind the AHS) faded with the natural growth of other natural constituencies gained as a by-product of the wider variety of new members who were not directly recruited by the Lees. For a very important phase of inception and development, the success of

the Lees in serving as famous founding intellectuals was the corner-
stone of the foundation of the AHS. Many who know them—or
knew of them—could more easily accept the tenets of an organization which they were known to have been identified with from
the start. Within perhaps five years, their political influence faded
"naturally," as a result of political movements within the association
itself. Their intellectual role as founders, however, was never dimin-
ished.[179]

In 1985, the president of the AHS described the philosophy of
the association:

> The philosophy of the Association is one in which humanists view
> people not merely as products of social forces but also as shapers of
> social life, capable of creating social orders in which everyone's
> potential can unfold. Accordingly, humanist sociologists study so-
> cial life with a value commitment to advance that possibility through
> scholarship and practice. Members of the AHS consider that social
> scientists have an ethical responsibility to contribute actively through
> their scholarly activity to improvements in the quality of human life
> as well as to increase understanding of social reality.[180]

The published statement of purpose of the association printed on its
membership form is: "We intend to be an active support network for
sociologists committed to humanist values, as they practice sociology
in institutions often hostile to such an approach. We strive to inspire,
support and learn from one another as we make our humanist practice
more conscious and skillful." The society also routinely publishes in
its journal a short statement on its history: "The Association arose
out of growing disenchantment with conventional sociology, and a
need for a more clearly value committed emphasis in sociological
work. We came together in 1976, not out of shared politics or similar
'schools' of sociology, which were, and are still, richly varied, but
out of common concern for 'real life' problems of peace, equality and
social justice."[181] Moreover, in the association's journal "authors of
articles will be asked to include information as to the primary moral
and/or value commitments, as well as their commitments to any
particular sociological paradigm . . . [and] 'domain assumptions' that
undergird their analyses."[182]

Recently, Betty has noted some confusion in others' perceptions
of the goals of the AHS:

> Some have tried to identify the AHS with a sectarian religious
> humanism, such as represented by the American Humanist Associa-
> tion, but AHS presidents and editors have brought a stimulating
> range of viewpoints to their leadership in the organization. The

humanist sociologists with whom we like to associate come from a range of disciplinary and religious backgrounds. These include people who might be labeled Jews, Roman Catholics, Muslims, Protestants, Agnostics, Atheists, or whatever but whose concerns are similarly dedicated to an open and hopeful search for human problems, questions, answers, and strategies.[183]

A Brooklyn College colleague recalled Al's total commitment to the organization: "I was approached by Al and Sid Aronson, who was chairman of our department from 1975 to 1978, to take charge of the business end of the organization, which would be housed at Brooklyn College. I agreed, and for a couple of years Al and I worked together closely on planning an annual meeting, the newsletter, membership recruiting, and financing. During that period I was struck by the energy that Al devoted to the Association."[184]

Yet the tension reflected in Al's proposal to elect ASA editors, and also found in the early days of the SSSP journal, developed here as well. An early editor of the AHS journal recalled: "Al and Betty wanted to make the AHS journal as inclusive as possible, but when I became editor I attempted to change that and it got more professional."[185]

PARTICIPATION IN OTHER ASSOCIATIONS

Al and Betty Lee were at the founding meeting of the Clinical Sociology Association in San Francisco in 1978, and have been active in the organization from the beginning. (It was renamed the Sociological Practice Association in 1986.) And Al is one of very few sociologist members of the Association for Humanistic Psychology. The Lees also were important to humanist social scientists in yet other disciplines. For example, the founder of the Society for Humanistic Anthropology notes, "I first met Al Lee through correspondence in 1976, when along with humanistically leaning colleagues in anthropology, I as editor initiated a new journal, *Anthropology and Humanism Quarterly*, and a professional association, the Society for Humanistic Anthropology. Al Lee was the first paid subscriber to the journal! Since that time, we have shared much correspondence about intellectual and personal life."[186] To Al he confided: "You know, Al, whatever I have written over the last fifteen years which I regard to be of value, were things I first shared with you. You have been my mentor."[187] And he continued: "In no small way, the success of the journal and the Society for Humanistic Anthropology may be attributed to Al Lee's continued support and guidance. Throughout the years, as I sought to define humanistic anthropology, I relied upon Al for direction. And Al's advice was immediately forthcoming; and it was always good advice: thoroughgoing, critical, compassionate and encouraging."[188]

He published portions of Al's ASA inaugural remarks in his new journal in 1976, and asked Al to become a member of the editorial board. Al in turn invited him to make an address to the AHS annual meeting.

As a veteran of the process of starting new journals, Al suggested that the editor of *Anthropology and Humanism* contact libraries regarding subscriptions due to the premium subscription rates they pay; Al also recommended that the editor solicit authors for manuscript submissions. Al suggested that the humanist anthropologists exchange advertisements with the humanist psychologists and sociologists as a way of picking up new members and suggested also that *Sociological Abstracts* be consulted, since inclusion there would give the journal greater visibility across disciplines.

CONCLUSION: PROFESSIONAL AUDIENCES FOR CLINICAL SOCIOLOGY

This chapter demonstrates the Lees' assumptions about the significance of professional audiences of academic sociologists. Al and Betty have always behaved as though the nature of professional associations makes a difference in the pursuit and sharing of sociological knowledge. The Lees did all they could to encourage the development of democratic practices in established associations; when this failed, they began their own associations. They felt the SSSP was especially necessary to overcome the political oppression associated with the 1950s, which the ASA ignored and thereby encouraged. And just as they were not satisfied with the ASA, they became frustrated with what they saw as the conservative trend in the SSSP and therefore founded the AHS. According to the Lees, social scientists need professional associations to foster the development of democratic ideology. As a department chair Al Lee also did what he could to encourage the development of color-blind hiring practices long before it was required by law.

The Lees have frequently pursued innovative if unpopular ideas, such as the election of journal editors or the attempts to have prominent members of the discipline censured by professional associations. Indeed, by recognizing the potential influence of sociologists among the general public vis-a-vis the conflicts involving James Coleman and Lewis Killian, it was clear that Al Lee saw no room in the discipline for opposition to the Brown versus Topeka School Board decision with which he had assisted. The Lees always believed that for social science to be effective it must address all its audiences and, as the following chapter demonstrates, teaching became in their view an essential arm of clinical sociology.

NOTES

1. Alfred McClung Lee. "Report of the Committee on Public Relations." *American Sociological Review* 6 (February 1941): 96.

2. Pitirim Sorokin. *Fads and Foibles in Modern Sociology* (Chicago: Henry Regnery, 1956).

3. Alfred McClung Lee. "Supplementary Report of the Public Relations Committee." *American Sociological Review* 6 (April 1941): 260.

4. ———. "Report of the Committee on Public Relations." *American Sociological Review* 7 (February 1942): 90–91.

5. Ibid.: 91.

6. Howard Becker. "Comment on the Public Relations Committee Report." *American Sociological Review* 7 (April 1942): 230.

7. Alfred McClung Lee. "Random Notes on Radicalism in Sociology." *The Insurgent Sociologist* (Winter 1973): 23.

8. ———. "Depression, War, SPSSI, and SSSP." *Journal of Social Issues* 42 (1986): 61–69.

9. Ibid.

10. Elizabeth Briant Lee and Alfred McClung Lee. " The Continuing Values of SSSP." *SSSP Newsletter* 19 (Winter 1988): 4.

11. Alfred McClung Lee. "Steps Taken Toward Liberating Sociologists." *Critical Sociology* 15 (Summer 1988): 50.

12. Ibid.: 49–50.

13. Lee 1986 op. cit.: 66.

14. ———. *Sociology for People: Toward a Caring Profession* (Syracuse: Syracuse University Press, 1988): 200.

15. Lee and Lee 1988 op. cit.

16. Lee. *Critical Sociology*. op. cit.: 51.

17. ———. *Toward Humanist Sociology* (Englewood Cliffs, N.J.: Prentice Hall, Inc., 1973): 134.

18. Lee. *Sociology for People*. op. cit.: 12.

19. Robert C. Bannister. *Jessie Bernard: The Making of a Feminist* (New Brunswick, NJ: Rutgers University Press, 1991): 135.

20. Elizabeth Briant Lee and Alfred McClung Lee. "The Society for the Study of Social Problems: Parental Recollections and Hopes." *Social Problems* 24 (October 1976): 5.

21. Ibid.

22. Ibid.

23. Barry Skura. "Constraints on a Reform Movement: Relationships between SSSP and ASA, 1951–1970." *Social Problems* 24 (October 1976): 21.

24. Ibid.: 17.

25. Ibid.: 18.

26. Jessie Bernard. "My Four Revolutions: An Autobiographical History of the ASA." *American Journal of Sociology* 78 (January 1973): 773–91.

27. Ibid.: 774.

28. Lee. *The Insurgent Sociologist.* op. cit.

29. Lee and Lee. 1976 op. cit.

30. Alfred McClung Lee. "Sociologists in an Integrating Society: Significance and Satisfaction in Sociological Work." *Social Problems* 2 (October 1954): 61.

31. Ibid.: 58.

32. Alfred McClung Lee. "Sociology for Whom?" *American Sociological Review* 41 (December 1976): 925–36.

33. Alvin W. Gouldner. "Anti-Minotaur: The Myth of a Value-free Sociology." *Social Problems* 9 (Winter 1962): 199–213.

34. Howard S. Becker. "Whose Side are We On?" *Social Problems* (Winter 1967): 239–47.

35. Joseph R. Gusfield. "Tribute Session: Remembering Alfred McClung Lee." Annual Meetings of the Society for the Study of Social Problems, Pittsburgh, PA (August 20, 1992); *SSSP Newsletter* (Fall 1992): 14.

36. Irwin Deutscher. Interview (February 22, 1993).

37. ———. "Comments and Suggestions." *Social Problems* 24 (October 1976): 85.

38. Byron Fox. "Comments and Suggestions." *Social Problems* 24 (October 1976): 40.

39. Skura op. cit.: 21.

40. Kai Erikson. "Comments and Suggestions." *Social Problems* 24 (October 1976): 48.

41. Skura op. cit.: 25.

42. Melvin M. Tumin. "In Dispraise of Loyalty." *Social Problems* 15 (Winter 1968): 270.

43. Ibid.: 274.

44. Ibid.: 277.

45. Ibid.

46. Skura op. cit.

47. Albert J. Reiss, Jr. "Putting Sociology in Policy." *Social Problems* 17 (Winter 1970): 289–94.

48. Lee. *The Insurgent Sociologist.* op. cit.: 23.

49. Richard A. Dello Buono. "From Critique to Constructive Action: Concrete Steps toward a More Progressive SSSP." *The American Sociologist* 21 (Winter 1990): 338.

50. Ibid.: 341.

51. Stephen Pfohl. "Re-forming the SSSP: Questions of Praxis." *The American Sociologist* 21 (Winter 1990): 332–33.

52. Gusfield op. cit.

53. Elizabeth Briant Lee. "Candidate's Statement." Society for the Study of Social Problems (April 1978).

54. Bannister op. cit.

55. Alfred McClung Lee. "How Can the American Sociological Association Become More Useful?" *The American Sociologist* 16 (May 1981): 94–95.

56. Ibid.: 96.

57. Malcolm Spector. "Labeling Theory in *Social Problems*: A Young Journal Launches a New Theory." *Social Problems* 24 (October 1976): 69–75.

58. Lee and Lee op. cit.: 13.

59. Skura op. cit.: 15.

60. Ibid.

61. Alfred R. Lindesmith. "Comments and Suggestions." *Social Problems* 24 (October 1976): 87.

62. Alvin W. Gouldner. "Comments and Suggestions." *Social Problems* 24 (October 1976): 40–41.

63. Bernard N. Meltzer. Letter to John F. Galliher (March 15, 1993).

64. Thomas Ford Hoult. Letter to John F. Galliher (n.d.).

65. Sidney Aronson. Interview (February 13, 1991).

66. Setsuko Nishi. Interview (February 13, 1991).

67. Ellen W. Schrecker. *No Ivory Tower: McCarthyism and the Universities* (New York: Oxford University Press, 1986): 168.

68. S. M. Miller. Interview (February 13, 1991).

69. Jerome Himelhoch. Interview (January 28, 1991).

70. Miller op. cit.

71. Daniel Claster. Letter to John F. Galliher (December 8, 1990).

72. Sylvia F. Fava. "The Profession: Reports and Opinion." *American Sociological Review* 25 (April 1960): 271–76.

73. Sylvia Fava. Interview (March, 7, 1991).

74. Sylvia Fava. "Tribute Session: Remembering Alfred McClung Lee." Annual Meetings of the Society for the Study of Social Problems, Pittsburgh, PA, (August 20, 1992); *SSSP Newsletter* (Fall 1992): 10–11.

75. Fava 1991 op. cit.

76. Aronson op. cit.

77. *ASA Footnotes*. "Status of Women Faculty in Graduate Departments: 1973 and 1988." Vol. 18 (December 1990): 3

78. Fava 1991 op. cit.

79. ———. 1992 op. cit.

80. Himelhoch op cit.

81. Leo Chall. "Tribute Session: Remembering Alfred McClung Lee." Annual Meetings of the Society for the Study of Social Problems, Pittsburgh, PA, (August, 20, 1992); *SSSP Newsletter* 23 (Fall 1992): 11–12.

82. ———. Interview (July 28, 1990).

83. Alfred McClung Lee. "The 1962 Meetings of the ASA Council: A Report from the SSSP Delegate." *Social Problems* 10 (Winter 1963): 293–97.

84. Ibid.: 294.

85. Alfred McClung Lee. "The Special January 12, 1963 Meeting of the ASA Council: Comments by the SSSP Representative." *Social Problems* 10 (Spring 1963): 409–11.

86. Alfred McClung Lee. "Annual Report for 1962–63 of the SSSP Representative to the ASA Council." *Social Problems* 11 (Winter 1964): 319–21; "Annual Report for 1963–64 of the SSSP Representative to the ASA Council." *Social Problems* 12 (Winter 1965): 356–60.

87. Ibid. 1965.

88. Lee (Winter 1963) op. cit.: 293–94.

89. Lee (Spring 1963) op. cit.: 410.

90. Sylvia F. Fava, Barrington Moore, Jr., Frank F. Lee. Mimeo. (April 27, 1965).

91. Leo Chall. Letter to Alfred McClung Lee (April 16, 1966).

92. *ASA Footnotes*. "Nominations Opened and Canadians Internationalized as Members Vote to Revise By-Laws." Vol. 1 (December 1973): 8.

93. Aronson op. cit.

94. Leo Chall. Letter to John F. Galliher (December 14, 1990).

95. John F. Glass. "Portrait of a President." *Association for Humanist Psychology Newsletter* (December 1975): 1, 11.

96. Gusfield op. cit.

97. Alfred McClung Lee. "Inaugural remarks by ASA President

Alfred McClung Lee before ASA Business Meeting, August 28, 1975." *ASA Footnotes* (January 1976): 1.

98. *Broadside*. "Al Lee Speaks on Academic Freedom." (George Mason University, Fairfax, Virginia, October 31, 1977): 2.

99. *St. Louis Post-Dispatch*. "Sociologist and 3 Witnesses Won't Testify in Tenure Case" (October 12, 1971): 3.

100. *The Pitt News*. "Lee Voices Nyden Support" (October 27, 1976): 1, 3.

101. *ASA Footnotes*. "President-elect Lee States Theme for 1976 Program." Vol. 3 (August 1975): 3.

102. *ASA Footnotes*. "Valedictory: A Report of the Year 1975–1976." Vol. 4 (August 1976): 1.

103. *ASA Footnotes*. "Minutes of the 1976 Council Meeting." Vol. 4 (December 1976): 4.

104. Lee. "Steps Taken Toward Liberating Sociologists." 1988 op. cit.: 56.

105. Alice F. Myers. Interview (February 22, 1993).

106. Alfred McClung Lee. "Sociology for Whom?" 1976 op. cit.: 927.

107. Ibid.: 926.

108. Ibid.: 934.

109. Ibid.: 926.

110. Sylvia Fava 1991 op. cit.

111. *ASA Footnotes*. "In Favor of Referendum Proposals" (April 1976): 1.

112. Steering Committee, Sociologists for Women in Society. "Letter to the Editor." *ASA Footnotes* 4 (May 1976): 2.

113. Alfred McClung Lee. Letter to Leo Chall (September 14, 1976).

114. ———. Letter to Leo Chall (December 16, 1976).

115. ———. Letter to ASA Council Members (May 16, 1977).

116. ———. Letter to Leo Chall (December 16, 1974).

117. Ruth Hill Useem. "Tribute Session: Remembering Alfred McClung Lee." Annual Meetings of the Society for the Study of Social Problems, Pittsburgh, PA (August 20, 1992); *SSSP Newsletter* 23 (Fall 1992): 15.

118. ———. Letter to Leo Chall (June 6, 1980).

119. James S. Coleman, Sara D. Kelly, and John A. Moore. *Trends in School Segregation, 1968–73* (Washington, D.C.: The Urban Institute, August 1975): 27.

120. Ibid.: 39.

121. Ibid.: 5.

122. Reynolds Farley. *Blacks and Whites: Narrowing the Gap?* (Cambridge, MA: Harvard University Press, 1984): 32.

123. Ibid.: 24.

124. *ASA Footnotes.* "Minutes of the Third Meeting of the 1976 ASA Council" (May 1976). Vol. 4: 8–9.

125. Lewis M. Killian. *Black and White: Reflections of a White Southern Sociologist* (Dix Hills, N.Y.: General Hall, Inc., 1994): 191.

126. Ibid.; Lewis M. Killian. "Working for the Segregationist Establishment." *Journal of Applied Behavioral Science* 25 (1989): 487–98.

127. Alfred McClung Lee. "The Nyden Case: A Alumnus Revisits Pitt." *The Insurgent Sociologist* 7 (Winter 1977): 71.

128. ———. *Sociology for Whom?* 2nd ed. (Syracuse, NY: Syracuse University Press, 1986): 192.

129. James Coleman. Letter to the Editor. *ASA Footnotes* 4 (November 1976): 4.

130. Kenneth Clark. Letter to Alfred McClung Lee (January 21, 1976).

131. *New York Times.* "Clark Group Assails New Coleman Study" (June 25, 1975): 49.

132. James S. Coleman, Ernest Campbell, Carol Hobson, James McPartland, Alexander Mood, Frederic Weinfeld, and Robert York. *Equality of Educational Opportunity* (Washington, D.C.: United States Government Printing Office, 1966).

133. Ibid.: 21.

134. Ibid.: 22.

135. Ibid.: 28.

136. Thomas F. Pettigrew and Robert L. Green. "School Desegregation in Large Cities: A Critique of the Coleman 'White Flight' Thesis." *Harvard Educational Review* 46 (February 1976): 1–53.

137. Ibid.: 2; Killian 1994 op. cit.

138. Ibid.: 2.

139. Ibid.: 5.

140. Ibid.: 19.

141. Ibid.: 8.

142. Ibid.

143. Ibid.: 9.

144. *New York Times.* "Coleman Concedes Views Exceed New Racial Data" (July 11, 1975): 1, 7.

145. Pettigrew and Green op. cit.: 18.

146. Ibid.: 24.

147. Ibid.: 50.

148. Ibid.: 51.

149. Ibid.: 48.

150. Ibid.: 46.

151. Charles P. Flynn. "Letter to the Editor." *ASA Footnotes* 4 (November 1976): 4.

152. Fr. Andrew Greeley. Statement to the Press (May 7, 1979).

153. Clark op. cit.

154. *ASA Footnotes*. "Minutes of the Third Meeting of the ASA Council." Vol. 4 (May 1976): 9.

155. Pettigrew and Green, op. cit.: 43.

156. Alfred McClung Lee. "More on Coleman." *ASA Footnotes* 17 (May 1989): 8.

157. Jackson Toby. Letter to the Editor. *ASA Footnotes* 4 (August 1976): 7.

158. James S. Coleman. "For the Record: Response to the Sociology of Education Award," *Academic Questions* 2 (Summer 1989): 76. First printed in the official newsletter of the ASA's Section on Sociology and Education, (Autumn 1988).

159. Ibid.

160. Ibid.: 77.

161. Ibid.

162. James S. Coleman. Letter to John F. Galliher (February 15, 1993).

163. Tumin op. cit.: 270.

164. Ibid.: 277.

165. James S. Coleman. "The Role of Social Policy Research in Society and in Sociology." *The American Sociologist* 18 (Summer 1987): 127–33.

166. Ibid.: 128.

167. Ibid.: 129.

168. Ibid.: 130.

169. Ibid.

170. William Buxton and Stephen P. Turner. "From Education to Expertise: Sociology as a 'Profession.' " *Sociology and Its Publics: The Forms and Fates of Disciplinary Organization*. Terence C. Halliday and Morris Janowitz, eds. (Chicago: University of Chicago Press, 1992): 373–407.

171. Lee. *Sociology for People* op. cit.: 202.

172. Richard H. Wells. Letter to John F. Galliher (January 9, 1991).

173. Stuart Hills. Letter to John F. Galliher (December 4, 1990).

174. Lynda Ann Ewen. "Coming Home: A Sociological Journey." *Radical Sociologists and the Movement: Experiences, Lessons, and Legacies*. Martin Oppenheimer, Martin J. Murray, and Rhonda F. Levine, eds., (Philadelphia: Temple University Press, 1991): 140–57.

175. Ibid.: 154.

176. Victoria Rader. Letter to John F. Galliher (n.d.).

177. Ibid.

178. Jon Darling. Letter to John F. Galliher (January 2, 1991).

179. Ibid.

180. Stuart Hills. "Association for Humanist Sociology." *ASA Footnotes* 13 (October 1985): 11.

181. *Humanity and Society*. Vol. 8 (November 1984).

182. Charles P. Flynn. *The Humanist Sociology Newsletter* 1 (Summer 1976): 2.

183. Elizabeth Briant Lee. "Efforts toward the Broadening of Sociology." Sociology Department Panel on the Future of Sociology, Drew University (May 2, 1991).

184. Daniel Claster op. cit.

185. Jerold Starr. Interview (February, 6, 1991).

186. Bruce T. Grindal. Letter to John F. Galliher (March 22, 1990).

187. ———. Letter to Alfred McClung Lee (October 23, 1990).

188. ———. Letter to John F. Galliher (January 11, 1991).

Chapter 5

Branching Out: Academic Freedom and Teaching Clinical Sociology

THE SIGNIFICANCE OF TEACHING

The significance of the teaching role and the defense of academic freedom have always been high priorities to the Lees. And it is easy to demonstrate how the Lees' activities in professional associations influenced teaching and instruction. The reader will recall that part of the motivation for founding the SPSSI in the 1930s was a reaction to the American Psychological Association belittling teaching.[1] Even if something of an exaggeration, there is some truth to the claim that the SSSP for its part "probably even saved undergraduate sociology."[2] Certainly the *Social Problems* journal has published a sociology accessible to undergraduate students.

The Lees reviewed various methods of introducing students to sociology.[3] One style is the "philosophically" oriented course. They feel this tactic often confuses the introductory student. Another style is the "technically" oriented course, rushing students directly to the study of research methods. Yet another is the "chamber of horrors," emphasizing human suffering in all its various forms, including poor, handicapped, and prison populations. Unfortunately students in such courses often get no idea of the broader social context that creates such problems. The best alternative is to show how people can help shape their own society and not continually be its victims. This option shows the role of conflict and compromise and the part sociologists can play, as for example in helping to facilitate racial desegregation. The great impact that sociology had on the Brown versus Topeka school board decision demonstrates that the boundaries between teaching, research, and sociological practice are analytical distinctions at best.

In Al's SSSP presidential address various categories of sociology were listed. They include: "1. trivia; 2. technology for management and manipulation; 3. criticisms and proposed modifications of public policy; 4. sociology for liberal education; 5. sociology for every-man."[4] According to the Lees, most sociology is found in one of the first two categories; while the last three are the only ones worth pursuing, and all three of these involve some type of teaching. Al and Betty noted that in the area of interethnic and race relations, the world has been made better by the thousands of students who have taken sociology, anthropology, and psychology courses. They recognized that: "You can insist that all sociology of any consequence is for specialists",[5] but they argued this unnecessarily limits sociology's impact. And with this in mind they also noted that sociology has rarely been published in *Time*, *The Atlantic Monthly*, or *The Saturday Review* and this may lead one to ask if sociology really has anything important to say to non-sociologists. Certainly there are few professional rewards for this type of writing and publication. In any case, Betty and Al took their own implicit advice and published widely in mass circulation publications, as is reflected in the appendix's list of the Lee's publications.

As indicated in the Introduction, Al and Betty have spent all of their professional lives at "teaching institutions," rather than any of the leading research universities. In the various part-time positions Betty has held over the years, she has taught Introduction to Sociology, Marriage and Family, Women's Careers, and Criminology. Al's teaching assignments were somewhat more varied. While at the University of Kansas in the school of journalism he taught courses on The Newspaper in Society, Feature Writing; and in the Kansas sociology department, Culture and Personality, as well as Marriage and the Family. At Wayne State and New York University he was responsible for Introduction to Sociology, Propaganda Analysis, Public Relations, and Methods of Social Science Research. At Brooklyn College, his courses were Research Methods, Culture and Personality, and Public Opinion and Propaganda.

Most of Al's teaching career was spent at Brooklyn College. This is an institution which earlier in the century educated the children of European, working-class immigrants, the majority of whom were Jewish.[6] Later in the 20th century Brooklyn College became a major vehicle for the education of African Americans. The other university where Al spent nearly a decade of his career was Wayne State, also catering to the urban working classes. Such institutions seemed ideally suited to the populist sympathies of the Lees.

ON PROTECTING ACADEMIC FREEDOM

During the height of McCarthyism in April, 1951, Al urged in a public memo that other sociologists join him in the ACLU fight to protect American freedoms. That same year, in the *Nation*, he argued that the decline in competing daily newspapers leads inevitably to an orthodoxy and ultimate loss of American freedoms.[7] The *Boston Post* headline declared on May 23, 1952, "Sees U.S. Building Iron Curtain of Own." The article noted that:

> The 127th annual six-day conference of the American Unitarian Association opened . . . and Dr. Alfred McClung Lee, professor of sociology at Brooklyn College, who was elected president [of the Unitarian Fellowship for Social Justice], declared the United States is "building an iron curtain around itself." He said scientists, "or anyone else who is suspect," cannot get into or out of this country to visit other lands for important work. He suggested . . . repeal of the McCarran Act involving security. At the time he said it is becoming "increasingly precarious" to follow the "pacifist teachings of Jesus," and added that "these days of the hush-hush and the crawl-crawl are days when an oppressive pall of orthodoxy threatens America's heritage of civil liberty."[8]

Sometime during the early 1950s, at the height of the McCarthy era, Al gave an impassioned speech from hand-written notes to a Brooklyn College faculty meeting. Showing his subtle humor, he asked that the faculty not suppress any student organization because of "off-campus connections. . . . Let us continue to permit our students to play and work at being Republicans and Communists, Democrats and Socialists. Former archconservative students of mine are now successful insurance salesmen, telephone executives, and bank clerks. They are much better citizens for their days of political irresponsibility. . . . Let us not carry out Communist predictions that we are afraid to depend upon our own democratic procedures."

In the 1953 Report of the ASA Committee on Standards and Ethics in Research Practice, Al Lee, as committee chair, perhaps thinking of the African-American student at Northwestern, noted that the ASA needed a new committee to look into the "rights and needs of graduate students."[9] The ASA Code of Ethics, originally adopted in 1968, did not include any consideration of teaching.[10] The ASA continued to ignore such calls and even a decade later the ASA Code of Ethics still had not taken account of student needs. The ASA ignored this problem even though graduate students are especially vulnerable because, unlike most undergraduates, their whole careers are controlled by a particular department and, moreover, graduate students, being fewer in number, are more visible targets. Illustrations of abuse of the teaching role are not difficult to cite. Sexual harassment and expropriation of a student's work are but two. The reason illustrations are so easy to cite is that, as teachers, sociologists always have special authority that can be abused. The reason teaching was ignored is clear from the historical record. The code originally was adopted to protect the association and its members from external government controls on research activity.[11] Yet the code's rules, which originally were applied to research, logically can be extended to teaching. Integrity in research clearly should apply to teaching, respect for the privacy and dignity of research subjects should extend to students, and the honest presentation of research findings applies equally well to class lectures.

Oppenheimer *et al.*[12] have noted that the price of survival for radical sociologists, either students or professors, has been withdrawal from active political practice. But many who did so nonetheless were purged by their departments. A prime example is found at the University of Pittsburgh. A resolution passed by the membership in attendance at the ASA annual business meeting in 1976 demanded that the University of Pittsburgh award Paul Nyden a new contract.[13] At the insistence of then ASA President Lee, the Committee on Freedom of Research and Teaching appointed by the ASA Council investigated the situation at the University of Pittsburgh where a highly productive but radical professor had just been denied tenure. But the association committee sided with the University administration in finding no violations of academic freedom and held instead that ASA President Lee had acted "irresponsibly in making statements to the press [on behalf of the ASA] that were inaccurate and biased."[14] As for the charge of bias, at least part of the problem was that the majority on the ASA committee apparently felt uncomfortable with the characterizations of the University of Pittsburgh sociology department made by Al Lee as the association's president and spokesperson. In the press Al had referred to the firing of Nyden as "very sophisticated McCarthyism."[15] Al also was quoted as saying, "Their department has a reputation of senior faculty members doing research for special interest groups—big industry, the Army, the Navy."[16] Another paper noted that Al felt the sociology department denied Nyden tenure "so they could have a 'more homogeneous' department and not endanger their chances of receiving government and business research grants."[17] Al made these charges in an address given on the University of Pittsburgh campus during the controversy; he also bitterly criticized the ASA Council for its failure to support Paul Nyden.[18]

Al was also involved in defending junior faculty facing dismissal at Washington University and at George Mason University. Al travelled to Washington University in 1971 to testify at a university hearing on behalf of David Colfax.[19] He also went to George Mason

University in 1977 and spoke on behalf of Fred Millar. Al observed that the university tenure system "traps especially those with fresh ideas, the non-conformists, the critics of social abuses so entrenched in our society, the opponents of racism."[20] Another faculty member at George Mason recalled:

> Al flew down a few years ago, when a colleague and friend of mine—and an AHS member—was being fired from my department for his activism on campus. Al testified about his scholarship on his behalf. He had taken the time to read my colleague's materials and he was incredibly articulate in his review. I remember that we were not even able to compensate Al for plane fare, but he was glad to be of help in what is one other small part of the struggle in our field, the wholesale firing and denial of tenure to people who rock the boat.[21]

Paul Nyden recalled the furor at Pitt and said:

> Looking back on it the University of Pittsburgh really did me a favor. I am happier now as an investigative reporter for a newspaper. During the fight against Pitt, Al's support was personally very important to me. I felt I was treated unfairly by Pitt and Al's support helped me psychologically to move on with my life. He came to Pittsburgh three times at his own expense, once he spoke at a program organized about the case, another time before the university senate hearing board. Richard Cloward and Herbert Gans also spoke there and the board decided 6–0 that I should have my contract renewed. The board seemed impressed with Al who after all was both a Pitt alum and ASA president. In 1977 there was a court hearing and Al came back once again to testify at the trial. After the hearing Pitt offered me $50,000 to drop the case. Al recommended that I accept it and I would not have if Al had not advised me to do so.[22]

In a SSSP session organized as a memorial to Al, Nyden added, choking with emotion:

> Al then helped me make the transition from being a professor to becoming a reporter. . . . Every year I write scores of articles detailing the environmental, safety, and tax violations by the Appalachian coal barons. I was never able to really repay Al for his trips to Pittsburgh, for his professional advice over the years, for his many phone calls. I hope that my work is able to help to make the world better, a little bit, for its people, for its environment. . . . I imagine that is the only repayment that Al ever expected.[23]

EVALUATING OTHER TEACHING PROGRAMS

In 1979 Al Lee was asked to participate in an outside review committee charged with evaluating the sociology faculty and course offerings at Rutgers University. After visiting Rutgers, the committee was charged with issuing their recommendations along with a final report. For reasons that will become clear immediately below, Al could not agree with the other members of the committee and submitted a minority report. This episode demonstrates that Al's strong convictions and his assertive, even abrasive personality often were not easy for others to accept.

Al recalled that others on the committee felt that an increased emphasis on instruction in statistics and survey research, and perhaps a decreased emphasis on Marxism, with its typical problems of objectivity, would serve the department and its students well. The unusual emphasis on Marxism was a consequence of the creation in the 1960s of Livingston College at Rutgers, which was intentionally designed to be a nontraditional department attractive to both minority and liberal white students.[24] Irving Louis Horowitz was Livingstone College's first chair. Unlike Al, the three other sociologists on the committee saw the issue as one of a balance which would reflect the emphasis that the discipline places on various specialties. On its face these recommendations would seem straightforward and noncontroversial to most sociologists. Al, on the other hand, saw the issue as being one of academic freedom. Although not a Marxist, Al Lee parted company with many in the discipline on the matters of statistics, survey research, and objectivity that was also eschewed by most Marxists. Indeed, Al Lee could not have agreed with these recommendations less.[25] He disagreed with the existing plan to disband the predominantly Marxist political sociology specialty in spite of "student interest" and "outside recognition," as well as with the plan to develop a new area in " 'Comparative Social and Political Development'. . . aimed [in his view] at providing technicians for the state department and for multinational corporations."[26] He disagreed with the idea of separating the evening classes offered by the University College from the remainder of the university. Al concluded: "Rutgers has a uniquely valuable setup in its variety of college orientations to sociology. I hope very much that this variety of viewpoints is not destroyed through the integration and homogenization of the sociology offerings into one over-all department."[27] These developments presumably would have involved the domination of all points of view by the more traditional sociologists on the New Brunswick campus. In spite of Al Lee's protestations, Livingston college soon lost its autonomy.[28]

A Rutgers' faculty member sympathetic to Marxist analysis interpreted the events in the following way:

We all knew Al would make a fair review of the Rutgers program. With the evaluation, we thought that the establishment sociologists would go after non-establishment sociologists on Rutgers' various campuses. The administration did not want any possibility of Livingston College and the University College joining forces since we had so much in common. Livingston College was started as a cultural experiment in education, was urban oriented, and had a minority emphasis, and originally attracted a lot of minorities and radicals both among faculty and students. So did the University College which was composed mainly of older students who had to work full time and go to school part time at night. The administration's idea was to keep the University College in its place by isolating it from the rest of the university.[29]

It is impossible to imagine Al voting with the committee majority, whatever the intellectual balance in the sociology program or the quality of the Marxists at Rutgers. Al did not even consider negotiating a compromise with the committee majority, but instead planned from the beginning to file a minority report. Long before the differences of opinion regarding the Rutgers program, the Lees referred to "irritating nonconformism,"[30] and also noted: "It is often assumed that everyone knows what we mean by academic freedom. . . . But by taking into consideration the whole web of social controls operative on any given campus at any given time just what is it? Sincere and competent men often disagree on this in specific instances."[31] And so it was at Rutgers.

TEACHING OUTSIDE THE CLASSROOM:
FOREIGN TEACHING ASSIGNMENTS

Al was a UNESCO Professor in 1957–58, with the assignment of organizing and directing a center for sociological research at the Catholic University of the Sacred Heart in Milan, Italy. He and Betty started out by spending the summer of 1957 at the University for Foreigners in Perugia, Italy, in order to improve their knowledge of Italian. They lived with an Italian family who could not speak English, and attended classes in Italian. As a result, they both were able to give talks in Italian. Al supervised a staff of two people, one of whom later became his successor. The program specialized in communication problems and initiated some research projects. Al's lectures were later published in Italian as a book: *La Sociologia delle Comunicazioni* (The Sociology of Communication).[32]

In 1960–61, during a senior Fulbright lectureship, the educational office of the U.S. embassy arranged speaking engagements for both

Betty and Al in a variety of Italian cities and universities, as they had in 1957–58. Al's lectures that year were published under the title *Che Cos'e' la Propaganda?* (What Sort of Thing is Propaganda?).[33] In 1966–67 they both were American Specialist Lecturers for the U.S. Department of State. Their lectures began in Pakistan, then to India, Syria, Lebanon, Italy, Austria, Belgium, and Iceland. There were many lectures arranged for both Betty and Al, this time all in English except in Italy. In all, they spent five months travelling through nine foreign countries delivering a series of lectures on numerous topics. Betty was to deliver lectures on American women, family problems, and teenagers. Al spoke on race and racism, public opinion research, and public relations. In 1988 Betty travelled to the Soviet Union with a group of 30 professional women organized by People to People to meet with their counterparts there. Betty recalled: "We had a fascinating group and we enjoyed one another's company very much. We were of all sorts." The group included three black women, clergy people, graduate students, social workers, deans, and even a college president.

TEACHING IN THE MASS MEDIA: SOCIOLOGY FOR "EVERYMAN"

Teaching in the mass media, aimed at the general public, was a long-term objective of the Lees. This teaching is only analytically distinguishable from their research in clinical sociology, which also has as its primary aim communication with the general public. As noted in Chapter 3, from the earliest part of their careers the Lees have recognized book reviews to be of critical importance. Beginning with a book review published in 1934 in the New Haven *Journal Courier*, they wrote numerous reviews every year until Al's death. Many appeared in scholarly journals, but an approximately equal number were published in magazines read by the general public.

The Lees wrote a review of a book by Robert Park published in *The Humanist* which reads in part: "Easy facades of symbols and methods borrowed from the physical and biological sciences did not attract Park. . . . They dress up inadequate and inaccurate observations and make them look impressive. . . . Much of the contemporary graduate training in sociology is likely to isolate young social scientists from just such fundamental contributions as Park made."[34] *The Humanist* published another review by the Lees of a book by Florian Znaniecki: "Znaniecki has always exhibited a devotion to science in service of humanity. . . . he believes men of knowledge have a responsibility for the values they serve. Znaniecki has not joined the groups which are perverting what they label sociology into a manipulative technology and have, as part of this profitable process, become assimilated members of the business community."[35] Even in positive reviews, critical commentary was present.

The Lees wrote an essay for *The Humanist* which was critical of mass classroom teaching techniques built around large lecture classes, noncontroversial textbooks, and multiple choice tests.[36] Another *Humanist* article by the Lees contains the following: "The one game is the ancient scholastic flight from reality into the juggling of terms and theories. The other is a flight from reality into the world of complicated formulas and statistical indexes, the filtrate of computation machines." On the other hand, the Lees note that fieldwork is ignored by such writers. But some social scientists "really want a humanistic grasp of human affairs . . . and what might be done to help people cope with the present's disastrous tendencies."[37]

In 1943, the *Detroit Evening Times* started a "Clinic of Wartime Problems" to deal with the economic dislocations, family and other problems brought on by war. The paper recruited 12 eminent local professionals from a variety of fields including religion, law, psychology, social work, and sociology. Al was the chosen expert in sociology. The idea was that readers would be encouraged to address their questions to specific experts and then, as with any advice column, their question would be published anonymously and then answered.[38] As a member of the clinic's roster of professionals, Al offered advice on a wide range of topics including alcoholism, infidelity, and occupational choice. For example, he advised a wife not to rely on rumors of her husband's alleged infidelity. He advised a worker to look for a secure position rather than highly paid but unstable work in the war industry, and advised another to attempt to persuade an alcoholic spouse to seek assistance from Alcoholics Anonymous.

The *Detroit Free Press* noted in 1947 that Al's research had revealed "many similarities in communists, [and] klansmen,"[39] reflecting the Lees' long rejection of the undemocratic excesses of either the political left or right. An earlier article in the *Pittsburgh Courier* quoted Al, who made the following charges against American physicians: "First, the medical profession has promoted or permitted itself to be a party to the promotion of intergroup, interracial and inter-religious tensions by setting up quota systems in medical schools, by barring certain races and religions from representation among its employees or even patients of many hospitals, and by being party to that crowning and unscientific indignity to the American Negro, the jim-crowed blood bank and plasma supply."[40]

Al served for many years (1950–1988) as Vice Chairperson of the Public Affairs Committee, Inc. This was a not-for-profit organization begun in 1935 whose goal was to produce concise and readable material for the general public based on scientific evidence.[41] The organization itself had no political agenda and its officers served without pay. It produced pamphlets at a modest cost designed to educate the public on a variety of topics, including epilepsy, a parental guide to educating children about sex, abortion, and smoking and cancer, which the tobacco industry vigorously opposed. The Committee also published a pamphlet by the Lees titled "Race Riots Aren't Necessary" which grew out of their research on the 1943 Detroit race riot.[42] The pamphlet begins with the use of prestige association by drawing on a long quote from Marshall Field's book (which, of course, Al had written) condemning racial discrimination. The Lees emphasize here that there are a number of "danger signals" which can lead to such riots, including demagogic groups such as the Ku Klux Klan, police racism and bias, job discrimination, and inadequate ghetto housing. The pamphlet reads as though it could have been written yesterday.

Perhaps the Committee's best known report was designed to attack the false and unscientific Nazi racial doctrine. The pamphlet, written by anthropologists Ruth Benedict and Gene Weltfish, was titled "The Races of Mankind."[43] The pamphlet's documented assertions included: 1) human blood has identical characteristics across all races, 2) there is no evidence of a relationship between race and intelligence, and 3) Jews represent a religious and not a distinct racial group. Al recalled that such evidence as this sparked an immediate attack from a southern white member of Congress who claimed that the organization's pamphlets were sold in communist bookstores. There was also an attack on the editor of the pamphlets during the McCarthy era that claimed he had associated with subversive people or organizations. As always, Al quickly rose to the occasion and helped convince the other organizational leaders that they could survive these attacks. The organization existed until 1988. Al's involvement in the Institute for Propaganda Analysis, discussed in Chapter 3, with its emphasis on public education as a defense against propaganda, is also a prime example of teaching sociology for "everyman." All of these instructional activities show how closely intertwined the relationship is between teaching and research in clinical sociology.

AL'S CLASSROOM TEACHING AND ADVISING

Some sense of Al Lee as a teacher can be seen in his letters to a former graduate student before, during, and after he was one of Al's advisees.

A letter confides that the eminent sociologist Erving Goffman gives the impression that people are almost "acting."[44] "This glosses over the tremendously subtle elements of habituation and of emotional involvement." Goffman's idea of the presentation of self did not completely capture the Lees' notion of multivalence, or the intermingling of conflicting social pressures. Another letter described the meetings of the Eastern Sociological Society, where two senior sociologists "gave terribly reactionary talks. [One] explained that no one was responsible for the dropping of the atomic bomb on Japan. [Another] righteously explained how value-free his 'scientific' work is."[45]

On the other hand, the thinking of self-proclaimed radicals never completely captured the precise position of Betty and Al Lee. For example, in another letter Al described Alvin Gouldner's book, *The Coming Crisis of Western Sociology*, as "overblown [because] the extent to which the Marxist sociologists and the Western sociologists are involved in the same business under nominally different ideological umbrellas was abundantly obvious."[46] A decade prior to the disintegration of eastern European dictatorships and the destruction of the Berlin Wall, Al clearly saw the limitations of communism: "But I do not think that the blueprint for an ideal society offered by Marx or the Marxians is tenable, that is as a final answer. . . . I think fantasies are useful in human affairs, but they are rarely achieved, and they have to be geared to a changing scene. They need to be rewritten from time to time. Soviet communism made a contribution, but who would want to live in the Soviet Union today if he did not have to?"[47] The erection and eventual destruction of the Berlin wall nicely illustrates his point.

In Al's eyes Asian communism fared no better. "Maoist communism also made a great contribution, but it, too, has now crystallized or is crystallizing and is probably becoming repressive." Al Lee recognized this long before the internationally televised government crushing of the nonviolent student rebellion during the summer of 1989. Yet according to another of Al's letters, even the most vicious government assault is ultimately doomed to failure when opposed by passive resistance. "Nonviolent confrontations terrify the establishment. Violent confrontations are duck soup for the establishment. The latter justify any form of violence against the 'terrorists.' "[48]

Two former journalism students at the University of Kansas remembered Al vividly:

> We do recall an incident in one of the classes, which as we look back on it, revealed where he stood on at least one issue. This was in the

1930s when the American Newspaper Guild was in its infancy. He told the class that he supposed they all expected to become editors or occupy other important posts in the newspaper business, but he warned them that most would end up as reporters and other lower level workers. He advised them to learn where their interests lie and urged them to join the Guild. We recall that a few students walked out.[49]

Another Kansas University student who worked with Al in preparing his dissertation for publication recalled that: "[Al's] course in journalism was stimulating and terribly iconoclastic. I believe he had worked as assistant to the publisher of one the Pittsburgh papers and this together with such behavior as that of Hearst and others had given him a wry picture of the press which was not exactly what the Kansas newspaper publishers or the university administration had in mind when they invited him there."[50]

One of Al's former advisees recalled that he

became a graduate student at Brooklyn College in 1963, when Parsonianism was all the rage. An instructor of mine when I was an undergraduate in an Industrial Sociology course tried to brainwash me with it. I underwent an apprenticeship with Al. Al is the master of a wisdom school and about life. He taught me how to look at society on the hoof as a participant observer. In truth he was not a dynamic lecturer, but he paid attention to students and was a good listener. He was low key, soft spoken and not flashy. He did have a dry sense of humor. Al liked students and was accessible to them. I made a habit of seeing him before and after class and the benefit of these sessions was incalculable. My father was a union organizer and a leftist. Al was the only person in college who represented this tradition.[51]

Another student recalled this same easy familarity with Al Lee at a local campus hangout: "After our classes at Brooklyn College, a group of us would often go with Al to Wolfies."[52]

Another graduate student advisee recalled:

As a teacher he was inspirational. Very cosmopolitan. He had a wide view of things. An international perspective, including Ireland. He was skeptical of the broadcast medium. As a citizen he was a man of the left and he let this influence his work without making him an ideologue. It was not so much that he was didactic—he encouraged students to be critical. Robert Park was one of his heros. Like Park, Al felt sociologists must go out into the world and check things out for themselves. Although he came from Yale he was tuned into Herb Blumer and Chicago sociology. He urged me to go to the University of Minnesota to absorb the Chicago tradition. He handed me off to Arnold Rose at the University of Minnesota.[53]

At the first meeting of the Society for the Study of Symbolic Interaction in San Francisco in 1975, Al made a short address which concluded with his consistently strong defense of observations from fieldwork: "I contend that there is no substitute for studying what people actually do. What they say about what they think or do is a long jump from actual action."

Yet another of Al's graduate student advisees recalled that:

Al's approach to methods was very qualitative. He wanted students to conduct participant observation studies. I did one paper on adolescents who played street games like stick ball. Al was not entirely happy with my initial analysis which was very psychological since I had been a psychology undergraduate major. My masters' thesis committee was chaired by Al and my thesis was another participant observation study, this time based on my experiences as an employee working in the hotels in the Catskill resort area. When making a decision of where to go on to study symbolic interaction at the Ph.D. level, Al suggested that I go to Minnesota since the City University graduate program had not yet been started. Al's emphasis on qualitative sociology influenced me. The Lees' vision of C. Wright Mills' sociological imagination was humanistic sociology. Over the years of seeing Al at professional meetings I never felt any transition from student to faculty status. The Lees' assumed an intellectual equality with students. They assumed students were merely short on experience but not on ability.[54]

A junior colleague at Brooklyn College: "One thing I should mention is the continuing support Al has given to young people, particularly former graduate students. Al has also been very influential in helping other younger colleagues to get their work published."[55] Kenneth Skelton's introduction to Al's ASA presidential address also describes Al as a teacher: "When you find him with a former student at association meetings they will be in a quiet corner with Al more likely to be listening than talking with his wonderfully quizzical face ready to put a question which, when it comes, comes in a soft voice alive with interest."[56] The founder of the *Sociological Abstracts* recalled his early glimpse of Al's easy acceptance of graduate students as colleagues in the teaching enterprise:

My first contact with Al Lee was on the telephone. He called me. He asked if I would like to teach an evening session of Introductory Sociology at Brooklyn College. . . . During [a later] conversation I sort of remonstrated that I was not sure I could handle it, after all I was just a first-year graduate student at Columbia, and was not seasoned enough to undertake the teaching of sociology. Al said "all you have to do is keep two textbook chapters ahead of your students. . . . He said with a wide smile that "It would only be fitting to have some intellectual distance between yourself and your students."[57]

But not everyone gave positive evaluations of Al as a teacher. A former student at Wayne State recalled that he "reacted negatively to Al's sociological theory courses" due to Al's disregard for almost all prominent sociologists, since in Al's courses during the early 1940s "Mark Twain received equal or greater attention than most American sociologists (with the exception of Sumner)."[58] Even "more disillusioning than the foregoing, however, was his conduct relating to my Master's thesis (in 1944)."[59] Not only did not Al approve of the topic, he also pointed out that the proposed advisor for the project was a "loser; after all . . . was a mere associate professor, while Al ('thirteen years younger') was a full professor and chair. Finally, he cautioned me that my oral defense would encounter devastating challenges from him. Throughout the project, he reminded me of these points, and he nastily impugned [my advisor's] judgment and motives during a conference of the three of us."[60]

However, after all of this, Al's comments during the actual thesis defense were subdued and even gracious.[61] This student went on to earn a Ph.D. and in following Al's career he observed: "My experiences left a residue and made me ambivalent toward him, even though I approved what he was attempting to do with the ASA."[62]

Disenchantment with Graduate Teaching

Al's decision to retire was due in part to his frustration with the graduate program at the City University. In 1969 he wrote to the executive officer of the Sociology Ph.D. program at the graduate center.[63] He protested about his being scheduled to teach a seminar when he had previously resigned from all participation in the program. He reiterated his reasons for this action. The program was not designed to serve the people of the city of New York, but rather to train technicians with no knowledge of ethnic relations, poverty, and violence. It was geared to the interests of those who could award grants rather than to the people as a whole. He also noted that until then, no candidate had ever been graduated from the program and that the vast majority of students attended only part time. He suggested that the program could be revitalized by concentrating on recruiting and training underprivileged students from the city to address in their specialties the problems of violence and racism. Early the next year he wrote to the president of Brooklyn College, observing that the graduate program, originally intended to strengthen the individual undergraduate colleges, actually served as a drain on them.[64] He complained that faculty got double teaching credit for courses taught in the graduate center, that the Brooklyn College faculty presently had no formal participation in the program, and that the center was increasingly hiring its own faculty. He therefore recommended that, given the prominence of many faculty in the Brooklyn College sociology department, the president consider allowing Brooklyn College to organize its own Ph.D. program independent of the graduate center. So great was Al's frustration that within a few months he retired from Brooklyn College.

At least part of the origins of his frustration was opposition from colleagues on other campuses of the CUNY system in his efforts to promote the interests of his friends at Brooklyn College. The first executive officer of the sociology Ph.D. program at the CUNY graduate center, who served from 1965 to 1969, recalled that Al was: "domineering and a difficult person to deal with."[65] The next executive officer of the sociology program added:

> Although on a personal level Al could be gracious and charming, when it came to campus politics he could be a tiger. The first executive officer of the sociology program, who served until 1969, was a lovely guy but he could not stand up to Al, and Al filled the leadership vacuum. He had a great influence over the previous director. At the time I believed that Al hoped that Brooklyn College would dominate the CUNY graduate sociology program and eventually take it over. But at a higher administrative level a decision was made that all campuses would contribute. When I took over as Executive Officer from 1969–1976 there was an executive committee in place with representatives from all the campuses in the CUNY system, not just Brooklyn College, but the others such as Queens, Hunter, and City College. Al attempted to bulldoze me and the executive committee, but it didn't work. Soon Al decided to retire and out of deference to him I went to his retirement party at Brooklyn College. At the party he made a speech where he lambasted me personally.[66]

A senior member of the graduate center sociology faculty at the time, who did not wish to be identified, described how and why this change was implemented: "Although I never had a personal run-in with Al Lee, I was part of a group at the graduate center who sought to alter the governance procedure. This effort took the form of electing an executive committee in a democratic manner—an action that Al supported. However, this action resulted in reducing his control over the program."[67]

The second director of the graduate center's sociology program that had such conflict with Al also recalled that sometime during the late 1960s there was a boycott of Al's seminar at the graduate center because of his domineering manner.[68] Al's graduate center colleague quoted immediately above also recalled the strike: "In the classroom, as in all his activities, you were either for him or against him. One semester only one graduate student signed up for his course."[69] This unusual rejection by students and defeat at the hands of colleagues help explain Al's withdrawal from the graduate program and retirement from Brooklyn College.

CRITICAL EVALUATION

While Betty Lee was always described as a caring, courteous and friendly person, the same of course cannot be said for Al. As even his best friends concede, there may have been occasional errors of judgment. One of the Lees' long-time friends brings balance to the assessment of Al Lee's personal characteristics: "Al was not a saint, and I think we should not paint him as such. He had, I would say the faults of his virtues. Al was passionate, he was very committed, and he had many enemies. . . . [In the ASA] He had many powerful enemies."[70]

Another associate clearly remembered the early days of the SSSP and noted that Al's incessant and strident demands could be wearying. "By the mid-fifties I had become Secretary-Treasurer of the SSSP. . . . I recall Al Lee's awesome warnings on the state of the discipline and the world. . . . I liked and respected Al Lee (most of the time) during all those decades."[71] Many of Al's closest friends have often used similar words when speaking of him. Elsewhere this long-time associate admitted: "Al could have been more helpful during his years on the ASA Council if he had been a little less self-righteous. He lost on every single issue that he raised because he raised so many issues rather than picking his issues more carefully and selecting those he could win."[72]

There is no doubt that Al Lee could be self-righteous, irascible and difficult, since for him so many issues were reducible to matters of principle. The ASA Executive Officer who served while Al was the association President evaluated Al's contributions: "The enterprise of social science needs pluralism and Al added to that pluralism. Yet Al was so ideologically committed that ironically he didn't appreciate pluralism since he reduced all intellectual differences to political differences. He would have been a much bigger man if he had a wider world view. Al never really made a dent in the dominant professional ideology—intellectually or organizationally—even though he always seemed to feel that revolutionary change was imminent."[73]

Another critic of the Lees expanded on their failures: "The Lees also tended to assert that 'true values' were self-evident, that those who disagreed were wrong. . . . What civilization needs is non-coercive, non-destructive means of negotiating, discussing, compromising. . . . Measure the Lees against that."[74] This writer concluded that the subtitle for this biography should be "Believing is Seeing."[75]

In short, Al was the prototypical moral entrepreneur. According to Becker the moral entrepreneur "operates with an absolute ethic; what he sees is truly and totally evil with no qualification. Any means is justified to do away with it. The crusader is fervent and righteous, often self righteous. . . . they typically believe that their mission is a holy one. . . . The crusader is not only interested in seeing to it that other people do what he thinks is right, . . . he may feel that his reform will prevent certain kinds of exploitation of one person by another.[76]

Whether moral entrepreneurs locate themselves on the right, left or political center, and whether they are opposed to rum or racism, their intensity and zealotry is often difficult for others with more modest motivations to abide.

Any contradictions in the Lees' careers can be explained by this unusual and passionate commitment to humanity, friends, and family. Al Lee was gentle and abrasive, open- and closed-minded, forgiving and contentious. In reality, all these assessments are largely correct, because "there was [generally] a totally different Betty and Al in their dealings with the friendless and powerless (including graduate students), than with the highly placed and powerful. With the former they could be forgiving and patient; with the latter they could become unyielding adversaries. Indeed, the multifaceted nature of human relationships was the central thesis of their writing."[77]

TEXTBOOKS

During Al Lee's long teaching career at Wayne State and Brooklyn College he and Betty devoted considerable energy to writing textbooks. As noted earlier, though not always published in both their names, these books were always the product of their collaboration.

In *Principles of Sociology*, an anthology published in 1946, they wrote: "The more definite and accepted the class system may be, the greater will be the power of rationalizations that the 'wise men' know what is 'best' for the rest of us. The basis for this 'wisdom' may be divine revelation, personal age, heredity status, conquest, or scholarship. But whatever the basis, so long as popular compulsion upon those in control is lacking, it is an aristocratic or pseudoaristocratic conception, with all the limitations that that implies."[78]

In spite of this critical comment, overall this is a mainstream collection of essays contributed by several prominent figures. This collaboration gives some reflection of the Lees' stature even as early as 1946, and was actually a second edition of a book previously published in 1939 under the editorship of Robert E. Park. This revised edition contained new sections by the Lees and Norman Daymond Humphrey. Part I on social problems was by Humphrey, Part II on human ecology by A.B. Hollingshead, Part III on race and culture was by Edward B. Reuter, Part IV on collective behavior was by Herbert Blumer, Part V on institutions was by Everett Cherrington Hughes, and Part VI on socialization was by the Lees. Here, the Lees note:

> But the way-breakers for social change, whether gradual or drastic, are social deviants. They are those sufficiently aggressive and heedless to defy the overwhelming social forces making for uniformity and the maintenance of the status quo. They are the social manipulators of change just as the successful dominators of society are the social manipulators of stability. . . . And the chief characteristic of such manipulators or agitators of change is that they are—to established and satisfied members of society—unreasonable.[79]

Some of Al's associates, both promoters and detractors, undoubtedly would have described him in precisely these terms. The Lees further note that the temptation is for the authorities to censor such agitators for change, but the costs to the entire society are immeasurable. Al's publisher's file from Barnes and Noble contains the following from Professor Tamotsu Shibutani of the University of California at Santa Barbara: "The sections on Human Ecology, Collective Behavior, and Social Institutions are among the finest ever written."[80] The book was dedicated to the memory of Robert Ezra Park, whom the Lees described as a "Great and Inspiring Stimulator of Sociological Research."

Social Problems in America was published in 1949 with Betty acknowledged as coeditor. The second edition was published in 1955 and Betty noted: "Al was too busy to help with this edition. He was preoccupied with being the Brooklyn College department chair. So on the second edition my name was moved from second to first." The various sections of the reader cover such issues as the nature of social problems, social disorganization, societal change, changing land and energy resources, the physically ill and handicapped, the delinquent and criminal, class, status, race, depressions, drought, riots, and wars. Contributions were taken from the works of W. G. Sumner on the impossibility of preventing war by preparing for war due to the ever-present and futile arms race, Edwin Sutherland on white collar criminality, L. L. Bernard on the inevitability of revolutions, C. Wright Mills on social pathologists, and a reprinted Public Affairs Pamphlet by Arthur M. Schlesinger, Jr., "What About Communism," defending equal rights for those identified as communists in America, plus two pieces by the Lees, "Freedom of the Press" and "Discrimination in College Fraternities and Sororities." The first of the Lees' articles demonstrates the diminishing competition among daily newspapers in America and the devastating implications for freedom of the press when such freedoms are exercised only by monopolies. In the introduction, Betty and Al noted:

> Social problems, some insist, are the business of "applied" sociology, and sociological problems are the proper sphere of interest for "pure" or "scientific" sociology. . . . [But] only through seeing and understanding actual instances of white-collar criminality, unemployment, despair, poverty, panic, and riot can the sociologist bring . . . theories into some degree of correspondence with social realities. Only by studying the accumulated generalizations of other investigators can the specific instances of crime, poverty, or panic come into some more adequate perspective.[81]

In short, social problems are clearly an appropriate concern for all sociologists.

Readings in Sociology, published in 1951, included articles by Talcott Parsons and George Lundberg, as well as articles by the Lees. The Parsons' article analyzes the structure and function of the family which give it stability. This article is used uncritically and may reflect the Lees' unique views and personal experience of the family as an institution distinct from all others. One article by the Lees describes the construction of an opinion poll and the interest of pollsters in prediction of behavior (reprinted from the *ASR* "A Sociological Appraisal of Opinion Polls and Predictions"). Another article analyzes the use of propaganda and was reprinted from the *AJS* ("The Analysis of Propaganda: A Clinical Summary"). A final Lee article reprinted in this collection originally appeared in the *ASR* ("Subsidies for Sociological Research"), and was used as a counterpoint to a selection by Lundberg from his 1947 book "Can Science Save Us?" Lundberg claimed that society was doomed without setting policy based on the scientific method. But that "[s]cience, as such, is nonmoral. There is nothing in scientific work, as such, which dictates to what ends the products of science shall be used. . . . *As scientists, it is their business to determine reliably the immediate and remote costs and consequences of alternate possible courses of action.*"[82] Lundberg compares the scientist with the physician who can tell the patient any likely positive or negative consequences of refusing an operation, but cannot decide for the patient that the operation should be done. According to Lundberg, "Any scientist who pretends that science authorizes him to make the latter statement [involving values] is a fraud and a menace."[83] Lundberg concludes: "My point is that no science tells us *what to do* with the knowledge that constitutes science."[84] The Lees countered, however, that such value-free research is impossible: "A 'perfectly open mind' in sociology is at least as valuable to society as is its equivalent in physical science, but it is a much more difficult accomplishment even under ideal conditions and especially when the situation is complicated by the fact of a donor's grant renewal always around the corner. At the least, it requires a patient, understanding, or deceased donor."[85] The Lees also warn:

> To the extent that the system of special interest subsidies for research becomes imbedded in academic departments of sociology, commercial incentives will replace teaching and academic research objectives for student majors. The orientation of future teachers, researchers, and textbook writers may thus be expected to veer toward emphases upon data and theories useful primarily in managerial manipulations and only secondarily, if at all, in the development of a scientific sociology of service broadly to mankind—to the manipulated as well as to the manipulators.[86]

Thus, even as early as 1951 we see clear signs of movement away from establishment sociology.

How to Understand Propaganda, published in 1952, is essentially an exposition, in textbook form, of the techniques propagandists use to control people's thoughts and beliefs, including the scapegoating of racial and ethnic groups. "As a device, propaganda offers many opportunities to the antisocial and venal, but it is also difficult to visualize a mass society in terms of present possibilities without tremendous dependence on propaganda."[87] The Lees note that during the reign of the Tom Pendergast machine in Kansas City, the influential *Kansas City Star* newspaper could have directly attacked the machine and its other respectable and powerful allies, but it did not use its powerful potential for positive propaganda. From the pages of great literature the Lees locate a case of propaganda in the character of Humpty-Dumpty in *Through the Looking Glass*. In the story the egg demanded that he define words as he pleased. Humpty Dumpty saw the issue in these terms: "which is to be master—that's all."[88] The Lees asked rhetorically: "How can we be less puppets and more the rational human beings the traditions of democracy idealize?"[89] The answer they soon provide is: "We can refuse to be stampeded by anyone for any cause."[90]

Social Darwinism is referred to as a prime example of propaganda and a "hard pellet of doctrine."[91] According to Adolf Hitler in *Mein Kampf*, "All propaganda has to limit itself only to a very few points and to use them as slogans until even the very last man is able to imagine what is intended by such a word."[92] Propagandists' use of the media is illustrated by the late U.S. Senator Joseph McCarthy, who attempted to associate other Americans with communism through simple name-calling in the press and guilt by association. This anticommunist propaganda ironically generated such tension in the United States that government policy became largely a reflection of Soviet policy. The Lees quote Archibald MacLeish: "American foreign policy was a mirror image of Russian foreign policy; whatever the Russians did, we did the reverse."[93] Hysterical propaganda also resulted in the mass internment of Americans of Japanese ancestry during WWII without their being charged with any actual disloyalty or crimes.

This book also dealt with conflicts in social rules that had become a trademark of the Lees, and noted that there are inconsistencies among societal, group, intimate, and personal norms. A well-adjusted person "represses awareness of such contradictions. . . . Cliches help: Can't be a Boy Scout all my life!"[94] "Behind the facade of an institution defined by morals, the mores set the basic rules in terms of which an institution and its functionaries 'really work.' "[95] These inconsistencies allow one "to cut corners on morals." The book was widely and positively reviewed in publications as diverse as the *Annals of the American Academy of Political and Social Science*, the *Christian Science Monitor, The Humanist,* and the *St. Louis Post Dispatch.*

Public Opinion and Propaganda appeared in 1954, edited by Al Lee, as well as by Daniel Katz, Dorwin Cartwright, and Samuel Eldersveld, all of the University of Michigan.[96] Reprinted in this collection is the Lees' essay, "Freedom of the Press," which deals with the diminishing competition among daily newspapers in America, as well as another paper, "Social Determinants of Public Opinions," which deals with the conflicts in values among different groups. The idea of the latter essay is that a person may belong to groups in conflict; the ways in which these conflicts are mediated by the society, small groups, and self concepts of actors is essential to an understanding of human behavior. The book's foreword indicates that this edited collection originated in 1947 from discussion among those in the SPSSI. The book's sections include: The Role of Public Opinion in a Democracy, the Mass Media, and the Nature of Propaganda and the Propagandist. The list of contributors reads like a Whos Who in social psychology and political sociology, including among others Floyd and Gordon Allport, Herbert Blumer, Bernard Berlson, Kimball Young, Louis Guttman, S.M. Lipset, Philip Hauser, Alex Inkeles, Edward Shils, Morris Janowitz, and Paul Lazarsfeld. The book became a classic in the field. That Al Lee coedited this collection suggests something of his stature in the field at that time.

Marriage and the Family, published in 1961, is a standard textbook dealing with topics such as love and courtship, children and the family, adoption and divorce, and global overpopulation. This is a traditional book written by a husband and wife who enjoyed a very traditional relationship of fidelity and mutual commitment. Here the Lees assert: "Compared with the family, no other arrangement succeeds so well in rearing children and in giving adults a modicum of stability and psychological security. . . . We now realize that healthy conditions of family living offer the best environment in which to avoid or cope with some of the maladjustments that require the services of pediatricians, family physicians, psychiatrists, special teachers, clergymen, social caseworkers, policemen, and lawyers."[97] Children become multivalent in part because of the unique influence of the individual family. In later writing the feminist commitment of the Lees shows through in a discussion of the family. Positive family influences include increasing education, falling birth rates, and use of the pill, and other contraceptive devices.[98]

In *Toward Humanist Sociology*, published in 1973, the challenge is made for social science to strive for the widest possible dissemination of knowledge so people can control their own lives and their own society; this challenge goes against the traditional dissemination of such knowledge only among elites. The Lees argued that by lifting the veils that cover the truth, we can see that we all are hypocrites and products of the multivalence and contradictions of modern society. "Human values find vivid expression in youths' revolt against war and depersonalization, in black impatience with racism, hypocrisy, and exploitation, in female rebellion against traditional sex roles and male sexism."[99] While alienation implies some defect in socialization, the Lees feel alienation from a corrupt society provides special opportunities rather than problems. Indeed, they preferred to use the term *marginality* rather than alienation and emphasized that there can be increased sensitivity through marginality. Some who have been cut loose from a group's culture find it can be very stimulating and are thus capable of perceptions denied to others.

The Lees note three myths common in modern society. It is commonly believed that there can be "peace through war,"[100] "freedom through subservience,"[101] and "education through rote learning."[102] The Lees observe that in point of fact the "winners" of WWII lost six-sevenths of the total number of people who perished in the conflict. Wars merely preserve inequality and delay needed social change: "The great challenge of social science is the development and wide dissemination of social wisdom and social action techniques that will enable more and more people to participate in the control and guidance of their groups and their society."[103] Yet the Lees acknowledge that "[i]t is also granted that technicianism may equip many other sociologists for employment by social manipulators."[104] Such technicians typically "regard those oriented solely or principally toward innovation and revision as irresponsible, negative, and, of course, unscientific, biased, or perhaps value-laden."[105] The Lees caution that in studying deviant behavior the sociologist, above all, "needs to approach the deviant curiously and perceptively, not blinded by popular stereotypes."[106] The Lees assert that the best defense against propaganda is a true liberal education, but not training as a technician. Certainly not all contemporary sociologists earned their special scorn. Humanist sociologists included C. Wright Mills, Peter Berger, and Robert Bierstedt. And other humanist writers listed were Upton Sinclair, Sinclair Lewis, and Henry L. Mencken.

One example of humanist sociology mentioned is found in the work of the Italian Danilo Dolci. Originally trained as an architect, he began what he considered his real education by working with a Christian group that was caring for a large number of boys and girls left homeless by WWII. By 1952, however, he felt new challenges were required and he moved to a horribly economically depressed fishing village in Sicily. The Lees noted that: "Dolci wanted to help western Sicilians to find ways to obtain more jobs, adequate irrigation, better health facilities, better opportunities for their young, and better living conditions."[107] Dolci faced either indifference or opposition from the Mafia, the church, and business leaders. He encouraged the poor to organize, and he argued: "The struggle must be nonviolent—taking the form of active or passive strikes; refusal to cooperate on what is deemed to be harmful; protests and public demonstrations."[108] The life and work of Danilo Dolci is held up by the Lees as an ideal means of making sociology useful to the community and a sure path "toward Humanist Sociology."

Reviews of the book were very diverse and not always complimentary. One review correctly predicted that "chances are that Lee's small but provocative volume will make no friends on either the more radical or conservative sides of the discipline."[109] A 1977 review in *Contemporary Sociology* misspelled the title and evaluated the book in one short paragraph as follows: "Its publisher claims that *Toward Humanistic Sociology* is an introductory textbook. I'm not sure what it is, but it is not an introductory text. Lee does say a number of things that are worth saying, but most of them have been said earlier and better by C. Wright Mills in *The Sociological Imagination*."[110] Earlier, a Marxist scholar, Albert Szymanski, reviewed the book for *Social Forces*:

> *Toward Humanist Sociology* is a poorly organized, rambling polemic against the main currents of contemporary American sociology, against some aspects of American society. . . . Lee fails in both his social criticism and concrete proposals. In his treatment of American society he often sounds more like a conservative than a radical. He argues, for example, that the number one enemy facing us is not "vested interests" but rather our life-long conditioning which has produced the "tyranny of our minds" over us. . . . He criticizes both minority movements in the U.S. and the Irish freedom movement as tribalistic, argues that oppressed groups ought to find alternatives to using violence. . . . It is not a question of a choice between "power" or "man" in the abstract, but a question of whether to side with one or the other of the great social forces of our time— monopoly capitalism/imperialism or the oppressed groups and their movements. . . . It is the "vested interests," specifically the forces of monopoly capitalism, that are responsible for the body of current social ills: racism, sexism, imperialism, pollution, alienation, lack of democracy, etc. Not the "tyranny of our minds," as suggested by Lee.[111]

This criticism bears a striking resemblance to the 1930s' review of *The Fine Art of Propaganda* that appeared in *The Communist*. Both reviews were critical of the Lees' minimization of the significance of capitalism in the creation of social problems. Marxists such as Syzmanski see the use of violence by oppressed minorities not only as morally justified, but also as essential in the pursuit of freedom. The Lees questioned the use of violence on both grounds. As they noted of WWII: "Military action did not save the lives of six million Jews, Poles, and others in the Nazi concentration camps."[112] This implicit criticism of the Allies' war effort shows both a consistent commitment to nonviolence and an unusual willingness to champion exceedingly unpopular views. Perhaps the Lees' long commitment to nonviolence made explicit recognition of the institutionalized economic inequality of capitalism more difficult for them due to the type of response possibly required to change such institutions.

CONCLUSION: Teaching Audiences about Clinical Sociology

For the Lees, teaching is clinical sociology in action. While teaching played a critical role in the careers of the Lees (as it does for most sociologists), scholars who are typically the subjects of biographies are associated with elite universities where teaching almost never rises to such a level of importance. The Lees have argued that teaching about race relations undoubtedly has made a difference in racism in the United States. Violations of academic freedom are to be opposed not only because they are unjust, but also because they make the practice of clinical sociology in the classroom impossible. Teaching viewed in this sense includes publication in many nonprofessional sources. In this way, clinical sociology blurs the boundary between research and community service on the one hand, and research and teaching on the other. Therefore, the usual distinctions between and priorities given to the various audiences of academic sociology—professionals, students, and the general public—are blurred as well. It is in these terms of total commitment to teaching or instruction, rather than crass commercialism, that we can best understand the Lees' heavy commitment to publication of textbooks and readers. In their view only the collection of information through first-hand participant observation provides the information upon which quality teaching, innovative research and effective reforms can be based. In addition, social policy should ideally be based upon democratic participation by an informed and educated public, rather than consultation and grants from government or foundations. Sociology, they claimed, could be the vehicle for informing and educating the public. The Lees have long been critical of communism, for they have supported the relative gradualism of legal reform as opposed to massive violent revolution. Moreover, according to their view, the economic determinism of some Marxism provides an oversimplified view of the modern world.

If the Lees' political views were not extreme, they were nonetheless passionately held. This was so much the case that at least some students felt that Al's intensity left no grounds for an open exchange of ideas. Just as one observer has noted that there were two Erving Goffmans in the classroom, one sensitive and concerned and one controlling and indifferent,[113] there were clearly two Al Lees. If he believed that your motives were pure, Al Lee could be warm, supportive and approachable. This seems to have been the typical case with students who worked under his supervision. On the other hand, with those he felt he had reason to distrust, or with whom he disagreed, it apparently became a matter of high moral principle to engage in personal conflict.

NOTES

1. Elizabeth Briant Lee and Alfred McClung Lee. "The Continuing Values of SSSP." *SSSP Newsletter* 19 (1988): 4–5.

2. Alfred McClung Lee. "How Can the American Sociological Association Become More Useful?" *The American Sociologist* 16 (May 1981): 94.

3. ———. *Sociology for People: Toward a Caring Profession* (Syracuse, NY: Syracuse University Press 1988).

4. ———. "Sociologists in an Integrating Society: Significance and Satisfaction in Sociological Work." *Social Problems* 2 (October 1954): 58.

5. Ibid.: 64.

6. Thomas Evans Coulton. *A City College in Action: Struggle and Achievement at Brooklyn College 1930–1955* (New York: Harper & Brothers Publishers, 1955).

7. Alfred McClung Lee. "The Pall of Orthodoxy." *The Nation* (August 11, 1951): 110–111.

8. *Boston Post.* "Sees U.S. Building Iron Curtain of Own" (May 23, 1952).

9. Alfred McClung Lee. "Report of the Committee on Standards and Ethics in Research Practice." *American Sociological Review* 18 (December 1953): 684.

10. "Toward a Code of Ethics for Sociologists." *The American Sociologist* 3 (November 1968): 316–318.

11. John F. Galliher. "The Protection of Human Subjects: A Reexamination of the Professional Code of Ethics." *The American Sociologist* 8 (August 1973): 93–100.

12. Martin Oppenheimer, Martin J. Murray and Rhonda F. Levine. "Introduction: The Movement and the Academy." *Radical Sociologists and the Movement: Experiences, Legacies, and Lessons.* Martin Oppenheimer, Martin J. Murray and Rhonda F. Levine, eds. (Philadelphia: Temple University Press, 1991).

13. *Pittsburgh Press.* "Marxist Professor Fired by Pitt Gets Backing of Sociology Group" (September 4, 1976): 2.

14. ASA Committee on Freedom of Research and Teaching. "Report of the Committee on Freedom of Research and Teaching of the American Sociological Association on the Case of Dr. Paul J. Nyden and the Department of Sociology, University of Pittsburgh" (March 4, 1977).

15. *Pittsburgh Press.* " 'McCarthyism' Blamed in Pitt Firings" (October 26, 1976).

16. *Pittsburgh Post-Gazette.* "Sociologists Rap Pitt Prof's Firing" (September 4, 1976). Section D: 1.

17. *The Pitt News.* "Lee Voices Nyden Support" (October 27, 1976): 1,3.

18. Alfred McClung Lee. Address given October 25, 1976. Reprinted in *The Insurgent Sociologist* 7 (Winter 1977): 70–73.

19. *St. Louis Post-Dispatch.* "Sociologist and 3 Witnesses Won't Testify in Tenure Case" (October 12, 1971): 3.

20. *Broadside.* "Al Lee Speaks on Academic Freedom." George Mason University, Fairfax, Virginia (October 31, 1977): 2.

21. Victoria Rader. Letter to John F. Galliher (n.d.).

22. Interview (February 6, 1991).

23. Paul Nyden. "Tribute Session: Remembering Alfred McClung Lee." Annual Meetings of the Society for the Study of Social Problems, Pittsburgh, PA (August 20, 1992): *SSSP Newsletter* 23 (Fall 1992): 13–14.

24. Martin Oppenheimer. "Pages from a Journal of the Middle Left." *Radical Sociologists and the Movement: Experiences, Lessons, and Legacies.* Martin Oppenheimer, Martin J. Murray and Rhonda F. Levine, eds. (Philadelphia: Temple University Press 1991): 113–27.

25. Alfred McClung Lee. "Memo Concerning Visit to Rutgers University Sociology Departments, April 31 to May 1, 1979" (June 4, 1979).

26. Ibid.: 2.

27. Ibid.: 4.

28. Oppenheimer. "Pages from a Journal of the Middle Left." op. cit.

29. John Leggett. Interview (June 12, 1991).

30. Alfred McClung Lee. *Multivalent Man* (New York: George Braziller, 1966): 318.

31. Ibid.: 315.

32. Alfred McClung Lee. *La Sociologia delle Comunicazoni* (Torino: Casa Editrice Taylor, 1960).

33. ———. *Che Cos 'e' la Propaganda?* (Torino: Casa Editrice Taylor, 1961).

34. ———. "Big News." *The Humanist* (1952): 191.

35. ———. "Blueprint for One World." *The Humanist* (1952): 241.

36. ———. "In the College Boom, What is Going to Give?" *The Humanist* 17 (September/October 1957): 269–75.

37. ———. "Humanist Strength: Reality." *The Humanist* (January/February 1980): 7.

38. *Detroit Evening Times.* "Times Founds Clinic of Wartime Problems" (February 14, 1943): 1, 15.

39. *Detroit Free Press.* "Study of Hate Reveals Many Similarities in Communists, Klansmen" (February 23, 1947).

40. *Pittsburgh Courier.* "Charges White Physicians Supporting Racial Hatred" (January 27, 1945).

41. Maxwell Stewart. "20th Century Pamphleteering—The History of the Public Affairs Committee" (New York: Public Affairs Committee, Inc., 1975).

42. Alfred McClung Lee. "Race Riots Aren't Necessary." *Public Affairs Pamphlet* No. 17 (1945).

43. Ruth Benedict and Gene Weltfish. *The Races of Mankind* (New York: Public Affairs Committee, Inc., 1943).

44. Alfred McClung Lee. Letter to Glenn Jacobs (April 6, 1966).

45. ———. Letter to Glenn Jacobs (March 3, 1982).

46. ———. Letter to Glenn Jacobs (October 28, 1970).

47. ———. Letter to Glenn Jacobs (December 3, 1979).

48. Ibid.

49. Samuel and Freda Sass. Letter to John F. Galliher (n.d.).

50. John Malone. Letter to John F. Galliher (March 17, 1990).

51. Glenn Jacobs. Interview (September 12, 1990).

52. Morton Wagenfeld. Letter to John F. Galliher (March 20, 1990).

53. Harvey Farberman. Interview (February 12, 1991).

54. Mark Hutter. Interview (February 12, 1991).

55. Daniel Claster. Letter to John F. Galliher (December 8, 1990).

56. Kenneth Skelton. "Introduction for Alfred McClung Lee's ASA Presidential Address" (August 30, 1976).

57. Leo Chall. "Tribute Session: Remembering Alfred McClung Lee." Annual Meetings of the Society for the Study of Social Problems, Pittsburgh, PA (August 20, 1992); *SSSP Newsletter* 23 (Fall 1992): 11.

58. Bernard N. Meltzer. Letter to John F. Galliher (March 15, 1993).

59. Ibid.

60. Ibid.

61. Ibid.

62. Bernard Meltzer. Interview (March 10, 1993).
63. Alfred McClung Lee. Letter to Professor Benjamin B. Ringer (October 11, 1969).
64. ———. Letter to Brooklyn College President John W. Kneller (February 23, 1970).
65. Interview. Milton Barron (April 18, 1993).
66. Benjamin Ringer. Interview (March 23, 1993).
67. Letter to John F. Galliher (April 27, 1993).
68. Ringer op. cit.
69. Letter to John F. Galliher (April 27, 1993).
70. Sylvia Fava. "Tribute Session: Remembering Alfred McClung Lee." Annual Meetings of the Society for the Study of Social Problems, Pittsburgh, PA (August 20, 1992); *SSSP Newsletter* 23 (Fall 1992): 11.
71. Irwin Deutscher. "Revisiting History: Hughes and Al Lee," *ASA Footnotes* (January 1993): 7.
72. Irwin Deutscher. Interview (February 22, 1993).
73. Otto N. Larsen. Interview (February 22, 1993).
74. Anonymous review of the Lees' joint-biography manuscript, in the possession of John F. Galliher (n.d).
75. Ibid.
76. Howard S. Becker. *Outsiders: Studies in the Sociology of Deviance* (New York: The Free Press of Glencoe, 1963): 148.
77. John F. Galliher. [Obituary] "Alfred McClung Lee: 1906–1992." *ASA Footnotes* 20 (August 1992): 14.
78. Alfred McClung Lee, (ed.) *New Outline of the Principles of Sociology* (New York: Barnes and Noble, Inc., 1946): 337.
79. Ibid.: 338–39.
80. T. Shibutani. Barnes and Noble advertisement (September, 1962).
81. Elizabeth Briant Lee and Alfred McClung Lee, eds. *Social Problems in America: A Source Book* (New York: Holt, Rinehart and Winston, Inc., 1955): v.
82. Alfred McClung Lee. *Readings in Sociology* (New York: Barnes and Noble, Inc., 1951): 402.
83. Ibid.: 403.
84. Ibid.: 404.
85. Ibid.: 409–410.
86. Ibid.: 410–411.
87. Alfred McClung Lee. *How to Understand Propaganda* (New York: Rinehart and Company, Inc., 1952): 7.
88. Ibid.: 47.
89. Ibid.: 257.

90. Ibid.: 267.

91. Ibid.: 14.

92. Ibid.: 17.

93. Ibid.: 56.

94. Ibid.: 191–92.

95. Ibid.: 191.

96. Daniel Katz, Dorwin Cartwright, Samuel Eldersveld, and Alfred McClung Lee, eds. *Public Opinion and Propaganda.* Edited for the Society for the Psychological Study of Social Issues (New York: Holt, Rinehart and Winston, 1952).

97. Alfred McClung Lee and Elizabeth Briant Lee. *Marriage and the Family* (New York: Barnes and Noble, 1961): 55.

98. Alfred McClung Lee. *Toward Humanist Sociology* (Englewood Cliffs, N.J.: Prentice-Hall, Inc., 1973): 73.

99. Ibid.: 3.

100. Ibid.: 11.

101. Ibid.: 14.

102. Ibid.: 12.

103. Ibid.: 6.

104. Ibid.: 36.

105. Ibid.: 107.

106. Ibid.: 169.

107. Ibid.: 42.

108. Ibid.: 43.

109. Joseph A. Amato. Review. *Annals of the American Academy of Political and Social Science* 416 (November 1974): 256.

110. David Arnold. Review. *Contemporary Sociology* 6 (March 1977): 266.

111. Albert Szymanski. Review. *Social Forces* 52 (June 1974): 585.

112. Lee 1973 op. cit.: 80.

113. Gary T. Marx. "Role Models and Role Distance." *Theory and Society* 13 (1984): 649–62.

Chapter 6

Conclusion

COMMITMENT

For some time sociologists have been intrigued by the nature of human commitment to both ideas and to a course of action.[1] What is beyond dispute is that the Lees displayed an early and continuing commitment to each other, to their sons, and to a sociology that could serve the community. The Lees' personal files show how their profession and their family are intimately tied together. For example, notes on annual SSSP meetings were intermingled with records of their sons' progress in college and marriages. As noted earlier, their sons registered as conscientious objectors, continuing their parents' commitment to pacifism. Al commented that in rearing their two boys that he and Betty hoped they had "aided them to feel that no human problem—even the terminal one—is without some degree of remedy or relief."

Robert Bellah *et al.* have shown how most Americans lack even a language to describe their commitments, focused as they typically are on individual success.[2] In this individualistic context it is difficult or impossible to consider distributive justice or human rights; indeed, there are no longer any "objectifiable criteria of right and wrong, good or evil."[3] And real love of others—which requires a sharing of one's self—is impossible in the context of rampant individualism found in modern America. In this situation there can be no sense of community or "shared commitment to the good."[4] What has happened to modern America predictably is reflected in much of modern American sociology. The Lees fought against these trends all their lives. In Chapter 2 we noted that a long-time friend described the Lees as follows: "I suggest that this concept of commitment may provide the theme which may guide the exposition of their careers."[5]

The Lees have been a moral force in the discipline by seeing clearly their obligations to the larger community. Their research has been directed toward fighting bigotry and pretenses of moral superiority. The societal problems Al and Betty addressed include racism and religious hatred. As two very young and untenured sociologists they selected the racist propaganda of Fr. Charles Coughlin as their initial problem for clinical analysis. They later played a part in the Brown versus Topeka School Board decision. They steadfastly resisted the professionalization of sociology. With no separation between their personal lives and the profession, the ethical mandate to fight false pretenses, inhumanity, and racism clearly extended into sociology.

Teaching, both within and outside the classroom, was every bit as important to the Lees as was research activity. Indeed, to the clinical sociologist the distinction between teaching and research is meaningless, for sociological findings must be communicated to have an impact upon social policy. Throughout their careers the Lees have been active in publishing in nonsociological magazines and in the press. Al played a key role in the *Detroit Evening News* Wartime Clinic, the Institute for Propaganda Analysis, and the Public Affairs Committee, all of which sought to bring a reasoned analysis of current issues to the community. Al was a long-term champion of academic freedom, and defended this freedom by supporting diversity in graduate education. He indicated that he retired from his university teaching post when he saw a clear rigidity developing.

ORIGINS OF IDEAS ON FREEDOM, EQUALITY, METHODOLOGY, AND PUBLIC POLICY

As young adults maturing during the great depression of the 1930s, the Lees' backgrounds—especially Al's—were privileged, compared to others of their generation. For example, both attended private universities, while many young people at that time had no opportunity to receive university training. As with many other educated, Anglo-Saxon Christians and earlier generations of sociologists, the Lees' ideals reflected the tenants of the Christian faith: equality, peace and hope in the possibility of incremental social reform. As Vidich and Lyman observed for early Christian sociologists, the Lees "perceived the new discipline of sociology as both social science and a source of moral regeneration."[6] Betty and Al Lee have been affiliated since birth with religious organizations, first as a Baptist and an Episcopalian respectively, and later as both Quakers and Unitarians. And to a greater degree than most other sociologists, Betty and Al Lee built their careers and their personal lives on the values of their families of birth. Indeed, many sociologists reject the values of their families rather than spending a lifetime celebrating these values.

The academic origins of the Lees' ideas are also easy to trace. To Sumner the Lees attribute their lasting commitment to human freedom. Communism thus was never attractive to them. Mills also expressed a skepticism of communism, which seemed to the Lees to provide at best equality at the cost of freedom. In Sorokin and Blumer the Lees found firm support for their attacks on scientific pretenses and scientism, and in Park they found a journalist-sociologist expressing both a concern with racial injustice and a commitment to communication with the general public. Bernard and Mills provided a model for criticism of the discipline and professional associations which had ceased to contribute to human freedom and equality. The influence of Robert Lynd's pioneering book *Knowledge for What?* is readily apparent in the Lees' book *Sociology for Whom?* as well as in Al's ASA presidential address. Like Robert Lynd, the Lees have been keenly aware of the contradictions in American society. And like Lynd, they felt that sociology and sociologists must take a stand on social issues and become forces for social justice to fight inequality and war.

Small provides a model for mixing sociology and religion, yet one that is not entirely applicable in an increasingly secular twentieth century. In a totally secular profession the Lees have been very circumspect in the use of their religious beliefs and affiliations. Yet for the Lees, personal ethics led to theoretical and methodological assumptions and to community action. A frequent criticism of left-leaning academics is that while their intellectual contributions are real, their influence is limited, in that they fail to translate their ideas into any public forum, safely ensconced as they are within the walls of academe. Oppenheimer et al. argue that this criticism does not apply uniformly.[7] Certainly not to the Lees. In the tradition of Sutherland and Mills, the criticism of societal elites is continued and focused on the use of propaganda by these groups as a primary means of social control. Beginning their careers as they did in the early twentieth century, as the menace of Hitler and National Socialism became apparent, these young scholars could have been expected to appreciate and emphasize the power of propaganda.

THE ORGANIZATIONAL LEGACY OF THE LEES

Whatever impact the Lees have had on contemporary sociology, it has been accomplished without their having an institutional base at a leading American university. Their careers represent one aspect of the counter-mainstream tradition in sociology during the 40 years after

World War II. The Lees consistently positioned themselves against the dominant forces in the discipline, with Al only briefly achieving a position in the profession's establishment as ASA president. Without the support of dominant organizations, the Lees created their own institutions, the SSSP and AHS. Betty and Al have been pragmatic master-builders of organizations, not just isolated idealists. When existing professional associations did not adequately address social issues, the Lees formed their own associations. Along with founding the SSSP and the AHS, they had a major role in founding the Clinical Sociological Association. They have consistently attacked the "professionalism" of the ASA. As ASA president, Al succeeded in increasing the involvement of women and minorities in the affairs of the association, even with little or no cooperation from the association council or association staff.

The SSSP maintained the earlier concerns of the Chicago sociology department with fieldwork research on social problems and with symbolic interactionism, at a time Chicago sociology was being battered on the one hand by structural functionalism and on the other by quantitative sociology.[8] Reflective of this emphasis is the fact that half of SSSP presidents during the first twenty years of the association's existence were either Chicago graduates or trained by Chicago graduates. Ernest Burgess was the first president, followed in order by Al Lee, Herb Blumer, and Arnold Rose. Burgess, Rose, and Blumer were Chicago products. The fifth president was Mabel Elliott, and since then over 25 percent of the association's presidents have been women.

Significant parts of this cultural fabric of the associations founded by the Lees are journals which by their very existence mandate a particular type of social science. The influence of the SSSP journal *Social Problems* is secure, being among the most frequently cited in the discipline.[9] To some degree, Al Lee, as department chair at Wayne State and Brooklyn College, also has altered the culture of both institutions' sociology departments. One obvious way this occurred at Brooklyn was through his impact on hiring practices. Al's involvement with both the Institute for Propaganda Analysis and the Public Affairs Committee shows a close integration between research, teaching, and community service, as does his involvement with Kenneth Clark in the Brown versus Topeka Supreme Court case. Thus it is impossible to isolate the Lees' impact on universities, professional associations, the teaching mission, and community service, as well as on writing and research, because they have devoted their lives to an integration of all of these activities.

CONFLICT, CONTRADICTIONS AND MARGINALITY

Al was a proficient organizer as well as a moral crusader, never uncomfortable in launching attacks against the profession's elites such as Hughes, Parsons and Coleman. All of this activity required a considerable self-confidence which in turn may have been a consequence of Al's relatively privileged childhood background. Both his father and his grandfather were attorneys in an era when a college education was a rarity. Seemingly in conflict with his populist sentiments, as an adult Al felt at home as a member of New York City's Yale Club, where his correspondence indicates he sometimes entertained friends. In addition, between 1961 and 1983 Betty and Al lived in a large house (pictured in the front of the book) in the posh New York City suburb of Short Hills, New Jersey. Al's social class background was such that he apparently did not feel out of place in such environs nor looking eyeball to eyeball with senior professors at America's most elite universities.

The Lees' view of society emphasized, and even celebrated, contradictions, conflicts, and discontinuities, including the marginal individual. According to the Lees' vision of modern society, human beings, by being multivalent, are thereby free of the tyranny of custom and tradition. To understand this world of conflict and contradictions, the Lees argued that fieldwork and actual participant observation were essential. Nowhere is this emphasis on direct fieldwork better reflected than in the Lees' book on the Detroit race riot. The Lees also maintained that human beings are by their very nature equal and thus public policy should be designed to encourage freedom for all citizens, as opposed to freedom for some at the expense of tyranny for others. In their view, teaching, research, and professional associations should be harnessed together as vehicles for achieving such freedom and equality; and all should be judged by their contribution to community service. Thus, the Lees' ideas, like the ideas of the late Dr. Martin Luther King, Jr., represented the mainstream of American support for social justice, and were not radical in the sense of wishing to destroy American institutions. Given the Lee's centrality in the American political spectrum, it is initially surprising that sociologists of their type are so unusual in contemporary sociology. Within the discipline of sociology they are truly the deviant or "marginal" people they have often described in their writings, who by virtue of their marginality are relatively free from the grip of social structure and thus can see clearly the oppression that surrounds them.

Yet in championing the cause of freedom as he saw it, Al often ran afoul of others. For example, his attempts to protect the principle of academic freedom at the University of Pittsburgh, Washington University, George Mason University, and at Rutgers University undoubtedly irritated faculty who felt he was interfering with the legitimate exercise of their professional judgment in matters such as professional evaluation and tenure decisions. Certainly, Al was an irritant to many during his tenure as ASA president, in his work as SSSP representative on the ASA council, and as chair of the ASA press relations committee. His disputes with Parsons and Hughes regarding the future course of the ASA probably have seemed to many within the discipline as unnecessary; one prominent sociologist called these activities the work of a "crank." However, Al did not fight merely for the sake of fighting. He was vitally concerned with the lack of democracy and accountability of ASA leadership and with what he and Betty saw as its tendency to mimic trade organizations of medicine and law rather than striving to lead a community of scholars. It is for this reason that Al opposed the hiring of a full-time executive director and the moving of the ASA offices nearer the seat of political power and funding agencies in Washington, D.C.

CRITICAL EVALUATION: CREDIBILITY, PROMINENCE
AND DURABILITY

The work of the Lees has been attacked from the left as well as from the right. Theirs were liberal-reformist ideas, which critics over the years have observed fail to strike at the heart of social problems. Earlier we noted that a review of *The Fine Art of Propaganda* claimed that the Lees' analysis did "not understand the class nature of fascism."[10] Similarly, a review of *Toward Humanist Sociology* observed that the Lees' position was more akin to conservatism than radicalism, in that they argued that the major problem creating poverty, racism and sexism was propaganda and the "tyranny of our minds" rather than monopoly capitalism.[11] Thus, if the essential problem is located in the propagandizing of the individual, then the ideal solution, according to the Lees, was education of the individual, which would enable people to protect themselves against propaganda.

There is no doubt that Al and Betty's writing largely ignored economic forces in society, as many of their critics have observed. Whatever the merits of the Lees' analysis, surely the permanent African-American underclass are victims of more than merely propaganda. The material source of the misery of victims of poverty did not receive adequate attention from the Lees. Analysis of powerful economic forces was beyond the scope of their research and perhaps also inconsistent with their commitment to pacifism and peaceful reform as the appropriate avenue for social change. Without attributing any particular caution to the Lees, it can also be said that this gap in their research may well have helped protect them from the purges of intellectuals during the McCarthy Era.

The Lees' individualistic analysis is not totally dissimilar from Sumner's individualism. Sumner emphasized the relationship of the individual to society and illustrated this claim by arguing that workers would lose their freedom if government attempted to offer them legal protection against their employers. This similarity may help explain the kinship the Lees felt for Sumner's work, even though they helped to lay the foundation for the U.S. Supreme Court decision ending legal segregation of public schools. Irony is heaped upon irony, in that this same individualism is found in the work of some of those the Lees criticized, such as that of James Coleman, which emphasized the futility of government policies to end educational segregation. He drew their fire at least in part because of his criticism of the efforts of the courts in school integration. Coleman's and Sumner's reservations about government attempts at social change seem more consistent with individualism than does the Lees' passionate support for policies aimed at the legal integration of schools.

The Lees' objections to Marxism were clearly shared by their long-time nemesis Talcott Parsons. Given the Lees' individualistic perspective and criticism of Marxist thought, they were curious standard-bearers for the left wing of American sociology. It appears that they filled this role primarily on the strength of their character, personalities, and organizational skills rather than the nature of their theoretical and political predispositions. On a more general level, the Lees' leadership of the sociological left actually reflected the poverty of radical thought in American sociology.[12] Indeed, radical intellectual life has had a tenuous existence in the United States.[13] What passed for radical thought has often failed to provide thoroughgoing structural analysis and criticism, as aptly illustrated in the work and lives of the Lees.

Social critics are often ignored by sociologists at the leading graduate departments. Mills, Lynd, and Gouldner had little direct involvement in graduate training and none trained a group of graduate students to carry on their intellectual tradition. As a consequence, Gouldner's name especially seems to be disappearing from the literature scarcely a decade after his death. L. L. Bernard and Sutherland were both social critics, but Bernard also criticized the profession and, perhaps predictably, he and his journal have been largely forgotten.[14] Sutherland, on the other hand, has become a professional icon and his ideas are widely remembered over half a century after his death.

Among his primary ideas that are remembered is his passionate defense of sociology.[15] The Lees have been critics of the profession, but have worked from within organizations by creating their own associations and thus have been more difficult for the establishment to ignore.

A friend volunteered: "The thing that has always impressed me most about Al is his almost instinctive support for the underdog,"[16] and a Unitarian friend noted that: "Al was always a 'committee of one' whenever he served—pressing hard for 'minority' positions."[17] The Lees insisted that sociology cannot be value free and that it must be dedicated to improving human welfare. Consequently, "[t]he Lees have been considered radicals, or at least hotheaded and impatient, or not properly 'scientific'. . . . For its concern with social issues and its focus on ethical matters and public interest, SPSSI used to be called the 'conscience' of the American Psychological Association. I sometimes wonder if the Lees aren't regarded as the conscience of the ASA?"[18]

Yet it is arguable that as an outside evaluator Al could have been more effective in protecting his friends in the Livingston College at Rutgers University had he been willing to compromise. If he had negotiated with the other members of the committee charged with evaluating the university's sociology offerings, he most likely would have had a significant impact on the final committee report. As it was, the report of the committee majority suggesting a reduced emphasis on Marxism went forward unchanged. In addition, had Al compromised and negotiated with those leading the CUNY sociology Ph.D. program, he most likely would have had a more lasting impact (and presence) there as well. Finally, a more patient critic of James Coleman's behavior could possibly have been more effective in engaging a serious consideration of the political, empirical, and ethical issues involved. And to add to this complexity, Al's relationships with graduate students, at times went sour (as at Wayne State and in his last years at the New York City Graduate Center), due to his passionately held positions that sometimes were translated into dogmatism. Those students with whom he got along the best and to whom he offered support and encouragement were *his* students, who appreciated his sense of mission and view of the discipline. Students who did not choose to be a disciple could not count on such consideration. Indeed, Al had the "faults of his virtues."

Consciences can be difficult to deal with, whether one's own or those of others, and Al's frequently has been difficult for many others. Yet what revisionist historians have done for history, in demanding that institutionalized oppression be recognized, Betty and Al Lee have attempted to do for sociology. Al especially was always vigilant and always ready, in the view of some too ready, to enter the fray against what he considered to be the forces of evil. Kenneth Clark summed up Al Lee's life in this way:

> For Al being white did not mean superiority. On the contrary, he believed that anyone who associated color and lightness with superiority needed education, needed to be brought into a broader view of the nature of being human. Superiority for Al meant respect for one's fellow human beings. . . . The thing that I admired about Al Lee was that social science and social philosophy were never to be isolated from humanity and the quest for social justice and the total pattern of concern for the welfare of his fellow human beings.[19]

In some ways, like a celluloid super-hero, Al led a life-long "search for truth, justice, and the American way." Al quickly developed a self-concept that demanded of him an absolute duty to challenge what he saw as threats to academic freedom and equality for all people. It is safe to say that Al was driven by this self-concept. To fight continuously the forces of evil, one must of course locate this evil continuously. At this Al was a master. Some argue that he was indeed too proficient at it; he saw such evils even where they did not exist. Betty, on the other hand, often has been described as the one who smoothed things over and was the peacemaker in interpersonal relations. Al reflected on his life as follows: "I certainly did not want to be unlikable, but I do value being a nonconformist, and I feel that taking the initiative is a part of being alive."

THE IMPACT OF THE LEE'S IDEAS ON THE MAINSTREAM ACADEMIC CULTURE

The Lees worked at the margins of the sociological mainstream, their efforts animated not just by Chicago sociology but also by investigative journalism—Al's first career. Their style of muckraking, investigative journalism made them outsiders to the sociological establishment. The ideas and activities of these "outsider" sociologists represent at the least an implicit criticism of the mainstream of contemporary sociology. Histories of sociology often neglect all but the dominant themes in a given era. For example, the period after World War II has been characterized as an era of widespread "optimism and satisfaction" both in society and among sociologists, with other themes going unmentioned.[20] The lives of Betty and Al Lee demonstrate, however, that throughout this period there were other sociologies representing a deep-seated resistance to this self-satisfied perspective. Organizations founded by the Lees tapped intellectual dissatisfactions that were in turn tied to intellectual traditions. The Lees' organizational abilities, more than their research, tapped resistance to dominant trends in the discipline. The Lees fostered an intellectual pluralism that attempted to keep the social problems, fieldwork and symbolic-interactionist tradition of the Chicago school of sociology alive.

Few contemporary sociologists make a serious attempt to bring sociological analysis to the general public—a life-long emphasis of the Lees. Compared to Al Lee's readiness to speak out against leaders such as Fr. Coughlin and Rep. Martin Dies, sociologists then and now seem much more reluctant to engage in such criticism. Indeed, it is easy for contemporary American sociologists to ignore injustice, because much of modern sociology is largely irrelevant to problems of human misery and oppression. The situation seems similar to the late nineteenth century, when academic freedom was justified by claims of objectivity and value neutrality, as noted in Chapter One. On the other hand, the Lees' challenge to the Parsonian hegemony appears successful, since systems theory and functionalism are no longer so dominant as they were during the 1950s. Perhaps the war in Viet Nam as well as the civil rights' and women's movements have made it clear that conflict rather than consensus is the norm in social life. To be fair, it must be added that the Lees were not the only critics and not necessarily the most prominent critics of Parsonianism, for many realized that the reliance on systems theory and functionalism was unwarranted. Critical theory, Marxism, and symbolic interactionism were just a few of the attacks on this theoretical perspective. Symbolic interactionism and especially labeling theory were encouraged by the SSSP and by *Social Problems*.[21]

If the SSSP was successful in helping to dislodge functionalism, the Lees had less success elsewhere. More than ever the *ASR* is dominated by statistical studies, as are most professional journals. Along with the typical statistical analysis there is a good deal of "cow sociology," where people are used as a means to an end. As noted in Chapter 1, an apt illustration is research on crime deterrence, where there is no concern expressed for the people studied. The major premise or the underlying justification for the research is typically utilitarian and consideration of ethics is proudly eschewed. Much of this research has studied the empirical relationships between crime rates and criminal punishments, including the death penalty, which are glibly reported with no attention paid to the political consequences of these findings for the communities studied.

Qualitative research, and especially fieldwork, is much more the exception than when Al founded the SSSP. One reason fieldwork is so rare is that it is not attractive to funding agencies.[22] Attraction of research grant money has become equally or more important for sociologists' careers than research and publication itself. Major universities are increasingly recruiting faculty with this in mind and decisions regarding promotion and tenure are made on this basis. Moreover, fieldwork is too time-consuming to be attractive. There are, in addition, the usual problems of possible subpoenas of fieldworkers studying illegal behavior.[23] Scholars are also undoubtedly concerned about poor reception for this type of research in leading social science journals, except of course for *Social Problems*. During the past 20 years there have also developed problems involving federally mandated university Institutional Review Boards and the protection of human subjects. It is now illegal for university-based researchers to conduct covert observational research on any individuals or groups from the weakest to the most powerful.[24]

Studying powerful groups is nearly impossible. The question is, how can public figures in industry, in government, or in universities be made accountable? Indeed, the noted anthropologist Laura Nader has called for social scientists to study upward in the stratification system.[25] And Wax noted that federal regulations incorrectly assume that the researcher is always more powerful than the research subject.[26] Ultimately the question becomes, what kind of ethical code or ethical system defines it as wrong to embarrass, harass, and discredit those who contribute to racism and economic exploitation? The type of fieldwork that the Lees have championed is now largely if not totally impossible, given current restrictions. Current federal regulations explicitly protect the right of privacy and dignity of treatment, and require the researcher to avoid causing personal harm, as well as always to provide explicit informed consent. And there has been only slight opposition to such changes.[27]

In any case, one could not now conduct the Rosenhahn study of psychiatric hospitals,[28] the Schwartz and Skolnick study of employment discrimination,[29] the Duster study of discrimination practiced by realtors,[30] and the Reiss study of police discrimination,[31] all of which involved clandestine fieldwork. These studies demonstrated oppression on the part of police, the business community, and in the practice of medicine. None of these research projects caused documented harm to subjects of the investigations. Yet none of these studies actually provided for informed consent to research subjects. To do so would have made the studies impossible, for by putting the research subjects on their guard they could have altered their typical behavior. The Lees conclude that the ASA Code of Ethics is not an

instrument for protecting research subjects, or for internal professional social control, or a device to build higher ethical standards
among sociologists, but rather it is a public relations device to
make the profession less threatening to elites and more acceptable to
funding agencies.[32]

The debate between the Lees and James Coleman, representing
one aspect of a continuing controversy in the discipline involving
ethical standards, can never be resolved, because those on each side of
this issue obviously appealed to very different audiences. The Lees
have been in search of a sociology responsive to racial and religious
minorities rather than to funding agencies, and a sociology with a
methodological and theoretical base upon which to build humane
social change. According to this view, sociology should be readily
accessible to the average citizen, and not limited to the disciples of
higher mathematics and to government leaders. It would be a sociology that sees change as necessary and even healthy, as opposed to
what the Lees saw as the mutually exclusive type of discipline that
defines all change as somehow representing a breakdown in the
"social system." Many social scientists recognize that values influence
their research, especially in the initial selection of topics for research.
Yet many others in the profession undoubtedly agree with Tumin that
championing the rights of blacks, women, or the poor makes honest
reporting of facts impossible. Thus, as has often been noted, such
disputes are resolved by inaction or symbolic legislation.[33] This deep
and continuing division of opinion helps explain why the ASA Code
of Ethics has been merely a facade.[34] The question Al raised about
James Coleman's research involves whether a case involving the
relationship of data to interpretation can be seen as an ethical issue.
The answer is reflected in the fact that Coleman was not censured by
the ASA, and indeed was elected president in 1991.

Al Lee's opposition to the increasing professionalism of the
discipline, reflected in his continuing complaints about the autocracy
of ASA leaders and the movement of the association offices to
Washington, D.C., went unheeded. For its part, the ASA leadership
continues to be dominated by those from elite universities. Al Lee
was the last successful write-in candidate for ASA president. Correspondingly, this organization has typically refused to take positions
on significant world matters, including the war in Viet Nam. One
measure of the success of the Lees' efforts in the SSSP is that some of
its innovations, such as the involvement of women and minorities,
have been taken over by the ASA. The irony is that women have
become much more involved in the ASA, with little apparent impact
on the direction of the association. The ultimate outcome is that Al

and Betty Lee had little or no impact upon the overall direction of the ASA or for that matter on the *ASR*. As the former Executive Officer of the ASA observed in Chapter 5 Al made little or no impact on "the dominant professional ideology—intellectually or organizationally."

A Summing Up of the Lives of Betty and Al Lee

Chapters 1 and 2 demonstrate that as a young scholar Betty Lee had few female role models in the social sciences. The leaders of the discipline were all white males; Florence Teagarden at the University of Pittsburgh was an exception. Indeed, without her encouragement Betty might not have gone on to graduate school. And during her graduate school experience, Betty did not always receive encouragement or fair treatment. In her pursuit of professional training Betty had an uphill battle among women of her generation, even in her own family. In the decades after she received her Ph.D. women were in general relegated to marginal roles in universities and professional associations. And so it was with Betty. Through much of her life, women could only play a role behind the scenes in professional associations and in academic departments. As with many professionally trained women of her generation, she was not allowed to teach, due both to outright prejudice and to gender discrimination masquerading as nepotism rules. Even in the relatively egalitarian Society for the Study of Social Problems, Betty was never accorded the recognition one would have expected for a co-founder. She was never elected the association president. In addition to these obstacles she had the primary responsibility of rearing two children while at the same time attempting to begin her career. Her children consumed much of her time for several decades.

On the other hand, Betty had the advantage of total loyalty and intellectual support from Al. She did serve with Al on the ASS Public Relations Committee, and she co-authored books with him. For example, she and Al co-authored *Marriage and the Family*, which, as noted earlier, was a traditional textbook written by a man and woman with a relatively traditional relationship for the time. Because these two lives were so closely intertwined it is impossible to know precisely how the ideas the Lees produced were influenced by each partner. Without information to the contrary, we can only assume that nothing would have been the same in any of their ideas without the contributions of their partner. But Betty was also limited in employment because of Al. Thus she both benefitted and was hampered by her marriage to a fellow sociologist.

But through all the conflict Betty and Al retained their sense of humor. As one colleague observed: "Somehow the fact that they always contribute[d] a few six-packs of Guiness Stout to the anthropology department's ethnic dinners (as being the national food of Ireland) doesn't seem quite appropriate."[35] Another observer lauded Al's character and in addition emphasized his buoyant spirit: "Alfred McClung Lee remained all his life the conscience of sociology. The juicy rewards of joining the establishment were not for him. He preferred the maverick style of the early SSSP, with its democratic thrust. . . . Yet despite all his experiences with manipulation and repression, with evasion by the powerful, in and out of the field, he remained optimistic."[36] This optimism is reflected in a recent book in which the Lees conclude: "Parts of this chapter may look to some like a sad dirge, the sour grapes of an outsider, but it is really nothing of the kind. It should rather be interpreted as a song of joy that there are so many who know where sociological wisdom can be found and who are willing to dedicate themselves to that search. . . . That there are so many making such efforts turns one from discouragement with the darkening national and international scene to the encouraging possibilities that do exist."[37] What the Lees have not said here is that one of the reasons that there are those who continue this "search for sociological wisdom" is the lifelong effort of Betty and Al.

At the 1991 annual AHS meetings, a special plenary session was organized to pay tribute to the Lees. Six of their friends were asked to indicate briefly what a particular book of Lees had meant to them in their intellectual development. After these presentations, members of the panel and the audience one by one came forward to discuss the instances where Al was ready to speak up for friends in cases such as tenure battles. Next, since the Lee's health no longer allowed them to attend meetings, a taped message from the Lees was played, in which they urged all present to commit themselves to making the AHS a success. The entire proceeding, according to one observer, created a situation where among "those in attendance, everyone sat in their seats glowing, smiling."[38] Another observer summed the session up this way: "We organized the session on the basis of what it meant to the Lees, yet as it turned out its greatest significance was not what it meant for them, but rather what it meant for us."[39]

A question remains: Would it be possible for someone to begin careers like Al and Betty's today? The easiest answer is that no one has done so. We need look no further than government to understand why this is so. Since the Lees entered the profession during the 1930s, there has been massive growth in government and private foundation support for social science research. As the Lees recognized, this makes relatively small-scale research and writing projects such as theirs seem increasingly less legitimate to many sociologists, as well as to many universities. Were it not for the associations founded by the Lees and the publication outlets these associations have provided, the type of sociology that the Lees supported would be even rarer than it is today.

Parsons' view of propaganda as a vehicle for national mobilization, compared to the Lees' emphasis on the problem of individual dignity and liberty, reflects the consequences of the secularization and nationalization of much of contemporary sociology. The nature of the recurrent conflicts in the six decades of the Lees' careers show as much about the changing nature of sociology as about the Lees themselves. Much of this change in the profession is known to be a consequence of state-supported technological empiricism. While those sociologists adhering to the value-neutral position often portray these changes from nineteenth- to late twentieth-century sociology as a shift from ideology to technology, a better case can be made for this shift as being from one type of ideology to another.

In the *Humanist Sociologist* Betty quoted the late Russell Gordon Smith's essay, "The Philosophy of a Fool," in which he claimed that with imagination "we might remake an ugly universe in the likeness of our dreams." Smith argued that "nothing matters at all save laughter, beauty, and love—these three, Blessed Trinity, one and inseparable."[40] For his part, Al penned the following words many years ago in *The Humanist*: "But it does not take very great insight into the teachings of Jesus, into the spirit of the Prince of Peace, to recognize the authenticity of the Quaker way in this regard, the way of patient inquiry, and intelligent compromise as the way most likely to yield some relief from the world's international tensions and sacrifices of its young manhood."[41] Throughout their professional lives the Lees have attempted to use their craft in the service of humanity. This includes their research and writing, activities in professional associations, and classroom teaching. The Lees' contributions to sociology have been intellectual, ethical, and organizational.

NOTES

1. Howard S. Becker. "Notes on the Concept of Commitment." *American Journal of Sociology* 66 (July 1960): 32–40.

2. Robert N. Bellah, Richard Madsen, William M. Sullivan, Ann Swidler, and Steven M. Tipton. *Habits of the Heart* (New York: Harper and Row, Publishers, 1985).

3. Ibid.: 76.

4. Ibid.: 115.

5. Frederick Elwood. Letter to John F. Galliher (May 13, 1990).

6. Arthur J. Vidich and Stanford M. Lyman. *American Sociology: Worldly Rejections of Religion and Their Directions* (New Haven: Yale University Press, 1985): 3.

7. Martin Oppenheimer, Martin J. Murray, and Rhonda F. Levine, eds. "Introduction: The Movement and the Academy." *Radical Sociologists and the Movement: Experiences, Lessons, and Legacies* (Philadelphia: Temple University Press, 1991): 3–14.

8. Barry Skura. "Constraints on a Reform Movement: Relationships between SSSP and ASA, 1951–1970." *Social Problems* 24 (October 1976): 15–36.

9. Michael Patrick Allen. "The 'Quality' of Journals in Sociology Reconsidered: Objective Measures of Journal Influence." *ASA Footnotes* 18 (November 1990): 4–5.

10. *The Communist*. Review. Vol. 18 (December 1939): 1167.

11. Albert Szymanski. Review. *Social Forces* 52 (June 1974): 585.

12. Alvin W. Gouldner. *The Coming Crisis of Western Sociology* (New York: Basic Books, Inc., 1970).

13. Russell Jacoby. *The Last Intellectuals: American Culture in the Age of Academe* (New York: Basic Books, Inc., 1987).

14. John F. Galliher and Robert A. Hagan. "L.L. Bernard and the Original *American Sociologist*." *The American Sociologist* 20 (Summer 1989): 134–43.

15. Mark S. Gaylord and John F. Galliher. *The Criminology of Edwin Sutherland* (New Brunswick, NJ: Transaction Books, 1988).

16. Daniel Claster. Letter to John F. Galliher (December 8, 1990).

17. The Rev. M.C. Van de Workeen. Letter to John F. Galliher (December 17, 1990).

18. Stansfield Sargent. Letter to John F. Galliher (July 5, 1990).

19. Kenneth B. Clark. "Tribute Session: Remembering Alfred McClung Lee." Annual Meetings of the Society for the Study of Social Problems, Pittsburgh, PA (August 20, 1992); *SSSP Newsletter* 23 (Fall 1992): 10.

20. Ted R. Vaughan. "The Crisis in Contemporary American Sociology: A Critique of the Discipline's Dominant Paradigm." *A Critique of Contemporary American Sociology*. Ted R. Vaughan, Gideon Sjoberg and Larry T. Reynolds, eds. (Dix Hills, N.Y.: General Hall, Inc., 1993): 10–53.

21. Malcolm Spector. "Labeling Theory in *Social Problems*: A Young Journal Launches a New Theory." *Social Problems* 24 (October 1976): 69–75.

22. James L. McCartney. "On Being Scientific: Changing Styles of Presentation of Sociological Research." *The American Sociologist* 5 (February 1970): 30–35.

23. See, for example: "Sociology Grad Student Jailed; Scholars' Privilege Under Attack." *ASA Footnotes* 21 (August 1993): 2; "Scarce Released From Jail." *ASA Footnotes* 21 (November 1993): 1.

24. Richard M. Hessler and John F. Galliher. "Institutional Review Boards and Clandestine Research: An Experimental Test." *Human Organization* 42 (Spring 1983): 82–87.

25. Laura Nader. "Up the Anthropologist—Perspectives Gained from Studying Up." *Reinventing Anthropology.* Dell Hymes, ed. (New York: Random House, 1969).

26. Murray C. Wax. "Paradoxes of 'Consent' to the Practice of Fieldwork." *Social Problems* 27 (February 1980): 272–83.

27. John F. Galliher. "The Protection of Human Subjects: A Reexamination of the Professional Code of Ethics." *The American Sociologist* 8 (August 1973): 93–100; John F. Galliher, "Social Scientists' Ethical Responsibilities to Superordinates: Looking Upward Meekly." *Social Problems* 27 (February 1980): 298–308.

28. D.L. Rosenhahn. "On Being Sane in Insane Places." *Science* 179 (January 1973): 250–58.

29. Richard D. Schwartz and Jerome H. Skolnick. "Two Studies of Legal Stigma." *Social Problems* 10 (Fall 1962): 133–42.

30. Troy Duster, David Matza, and David Wellman. "Fieldwork and the Protection of Human Subjects." *The American Sociologist* 14 (August 1979): 136–42.

31. Albert J. Reiss, Jr. "Police Brutality—Answers to Key Questions." *Transaction* 5 (July/August 1968): 10–19.

32. Alfred McClung Lee. *Sociology for Whom?* 2nd ed. (Syracuse, NY: Syracuse University Press, 1986).

33. Joseph R. Gusfield. *Symbolic Crusade: Status Politics and the American Temperance Movement* (Chicago: University of Chicago Press, 1963).

34. Galliher. 1973 op. cit.; Galliher. 1980 op. cit.

35. Philip Peek. Letter to John F. Galliher (June 17, 1990).

36. Martin Oppenheimer. "Tribute Session: Remembering Alfred McClung Lee." Annual meetings of the Society for the Study of Social Problems, Pittsburgh, PA (August 20, 1992); *SSSP Newsletter* 23 (Fall 1992): 15–16.

37. Alfred McClung Lee. *Sociology for People: Toward a Caring Profession* (Syracuse, NY: Syracuse University Press, 1988): 31.

38. Henry H. Brownstein. Letter to John F. Galliher (November 4, 1991).

39. Jerold Starr. Interview (November 7, 1991).

40. Elizabeth Briant Lee. "Thoughts about Present-day American Middleclass Marriage and Family Living." *The Humanist Sociologist* 6 (September 1981): 13.

41. Alfred McClung Lee. "The Hoary Human Dilemma." *The Humanist,* (1954): 93–94.

Epilogue

Writing this biography of two dear friends was a tortured process, including as it does several episodes that are unflattering to the memory of Al Lee. In retrospect it seems predictable that a person with such strongly held positions and such personal commitment, energy, zeal, and passion would from time to time make mistakes. Al was known for his sense of mission, not for prudence or caution. Yet it was only after repeated proddings from friends, colleagues, reviewers and editors, over a period of three years, that the authors concluded that withholding information would do a disservice to the sociological community and ultimately to the memory of the Lees. It somehow seems appropriate that the struggle in producing this record illustrates in microcosm the conflict between fact and values in social science research, the conflict at the heart of the dispute between the Lees and much of the sociological establishment. The authors' experience in writing this biography suggests that the reason for this enduring tension is that there are no easy answers that can resolve this dispute. Clearly the bromides of simply reporting every detail in research, or the other extreme, of reporting only good news, are not helpful in resolving this issue. Yet the values which originally motivated the creation of this joint biography involve the undiminished belief of the authors in the essential goodness and wisdom of this sociological couple.

Bibliography

ELIZABETH BRIANT LEE BIBLIOGRAPHY (1931–1991)

"Personnel Aspects of Social Work in Pittsburgh." M.A. Thesis, University of Pittsburgh (1931).

"Eminent Women: A Cultural Study." Ph.D. Dissertation, Yale University (1937).

with A. Mc. Lee. *The Fine Art of Rabble-Rousing: A Popular Guide.* Illustrated with the Propaganda of the Rev. Charles E. Coughlin (New York: Institute for Propaganda Analysis, 1939). Confidential. Not for release. Mimeo and paper-bound.

———. *The Fine Art of Propaganda: A Study of Father Coughlin's Speeches* (New York: Institute for Propaganda Analysis and Harcourt, Brace and Co., 1939).

———. Three statistical tables on size and competitiveness of daily newspapers. Washington, D.C.: Federal Communications Commission No. 52296 (July 23, 1941). Mimeo.

———. "Activity 19." W. M. Tanner and W. E. Cheaver. *English for Every Use* (New York: Ginn and Co., 1947): 85.

———. "Propaganda." *English: Fourth Course.* by A. J. Stoddard and Matilda Bailey (New York: American Book Co., 1948): 188–89.

———. *Social Problems in America: A Source Book* (New York: Henry Holt and Co., 1949).

———. "The Devices of Propaganda." *Mass Communications.* Wilbur Schramm, ed. (Urbana: University of Illinois Press, 1949): 381.

———. *Social Problems in America: A Source Book.* Rev. ed. (New York: Henry Holt and Co., 1955).

———. "The Tricks of the Trade." Leonard Broom and Philip Selznick, *Sociology: A Text with Adapted Readings* (Evanston: Row, Peterson and Co., 1955): 290.

with Harold W. Pfautz, Ray H. Adams and S. M. Miller. "The Climate of Opinion and the State of Academic Freedom." *American Sociological Review* 21 (June 1956): 353–57.

"Editorial and Publications Committee." Report of the Chair, Society for the Study of Social Problems. *Social Problems* 4 (January 1957): 227.

with A. Mc. Lee. "Propaganda Techniques." Blaine E. Mercer. *The Study of Society* (New York: Harcourt, Brace and Co., 1958): 106–07.

————. "The Tricks of the Trade." Leonard Broom and P. Selznick. *Sociology* (Evanston: Row, Peterson and Col, 1958): 290.

"As the Twig is Bent." *Fellowship* 25 (March 1, 1959): 21–24.

————. "The Devices of Propaganda." *Mass Communications*. 2nd ed. Wilbur Schramm, ed. (Urbana: University of Illinois Press, 1960).

————. "Che Cosa Accade agli Schemi di Vita Familiare negli Stati Uniti." *Quaderni de Sociologia* 39 (Winter 1961): 3–20.

————. *Marriage and the Family* (New York: Barnes and Noble, 1961).

————. *Marriage and the Family*. 3rd printing (New York: Barnes and Noble, 1964).

————. parts of *The Fine Art of Propaganda*. T. L. Engle and Louis Snellgrave *Psychiatry: Its Principles and Applications*. 5th ed. (New York: Harcourt, Brace and World, 1969): 519–21.

————. "The Tricks of the Trade." R. C. Jeffrey and Owen Peterson. *Speech* (New York: Harper and Row, 1971): 321–22.

————. *The Fine Art of Propaganda*. rev. ed. (New York: Octagon Books, 1972).

————. "Propaganda: The Tricks of the Trade." R. W. Mack and John Pease, *Sociology and Social Life*. 5th ed. (New York: D. Van Nostrand Co., 1973): 505.

————. "The Society for the Study of Social Problems: Visions of Its Founders." *SSSP Newsletter*. Vol. 5: 1 (Fall 1973–74): 2–5.

————. "The Tricks of the Trade." R. C. Jeffrey and Owen Peterson. *Speech*. 2nd ed. (New York: Harper and Row, 1975).

————. "The Society for the Study of Social Problems: Parental

Recollections and Hopes." *Social Problems*. Vol. 24: 1 (October 1976): 4–14.

———. "Some Common Propaganda Devices and Their Symbols." *The I-Opener: An Introduction to Philosophy* (Englewood Cliffs, N.J.: Prentice-Hall, 1976). R.W. Platted: 63–64.

———. "Widely Used Propaganda Techniques." C. F. Fisher and C. A. Terry. *Children's Language and the Language Arts* (New York: McGraw-Hill Book Co., 1977): 135–36.

———. "From the Fine Art of Propaganda." Ruth L. Opner, *Writing from the Inside Out* (New York: Harper and Row, 1977): 369–75.

"Women in America: The Oppressed Majority." Book review. *Contemporary Sociology*. Vol. 6 (November 1977): 716.

with A. Mc. Lee, "Expanding Humanism." Free Mind: *Newsletter of the American Humanist Association*. Vol. 21: 4 (April 1978): 2.

———. "Varieties of Techniques." Maxine Hairston, *A Contemporary Rhetoric*. 2nd ed. (Boston: Houghton Mifflin Co., 1978): 314.

"Social Factors Making for Eminence among American Women Social Scientists." Association for Humanist Sociology. Presidential Address, 1978.

with A. Mc. Lee, "Checking It Out: Propaganda: The Tricks of the Trade," Jean Lloyd, R. W. Mack, and John Pease. *Sociology and Social Life*. 6th ed. (New York: D. Van Nostrand Co., 1979): 534.

———. "The Fine Art of Propaganda Analysis—Then and Now." *Et Cetera*. Vol. 36: 2 (Summer, 1979): 117–27.

———. *The Fine Art of Propaganda*. Clothbound: New York: Octagon Books, 1979. Paperback: San Francisco, California: International Society for General Semantics, 1979.

———. "The Tricks of the Trade." R. C. Jeffrey and Owen Peterson. *Speech*. 3rd ed. (New York: Harper and Row, 1980).

"A History of Women's Participation in the Eastern Sociological Society." *SWS Network* 10 (July): 5–6.

with A. Mc. Lee, "Titillating, But—" *In These Times* (October 21–27, 1981): 13.

———. "Two Clinicians Tandem in Social Action." *Clinical Sociology*. Vol. 4: 10 (Fall 1981): 3–4.

————. "Propaganda Techniques." Ian Robertson. *Sociology*. 2nd ed. (New York: Worth Publishers, 1981): 580.

"Thoughts about Present-day American Middleclass Marriage and Family Living." *The Humanist Sociologist* 6 (September 1981): 13.

with A. Mc. Lee, "Varieties of Techniques." Maxine Hairston, *A Contemporary Rhetoric*. 3rd ed. (Boston: Houghton Mifflin Co., 1982): 382.

————. "Clarence Marsh Case (1874–1946)." *The Humanist Sociologist*. Vol. 9: 1 (January 1984): 7–8.

————. "Propaganda: The Tricks of the Trade." G. J. DiRenzo, *Sociological Perspectives*. 2nd ed. (Lexington, Massachusetts, 1984): 376.

————. "A Home for the Ethical Humanist." *Friends Journal*. Vol. 31: 2 (February 1, 1985): 21.

————. "Two Sociologists in Search of Action." B. B. Hess, E. W. Markson, and P. J. Stein. *Sociology* 2nd ed. (New York: Macmillan Co., 1985).

————. "Melting Pot Discriminates." *Friends Journal*. Vol. 31: 10 (June 1/15, 1985): 19.

————. "Some Thoughts on SSSP's Mission." *SSSP Newsletter*. Vol. 17: 1 (Fall 1985): 9–12.

"Coughlin and Propaganda Analysis." *Humanity and Society*. Vol. 10 (February 1986): 25–35.

with A. Mc. Lee, "Propaganda Analysis in 1937–42—And Now?" *Quarterly Review of Doublespeak*. Vol. 12: 2 (January 1986): 2–4.

————. "Seven Kinds of Propaganda." Maxine Hairston, *Contemporary Composition: Short Edition* (Boston: Houghton Mifflin, 1986): 384.

————. "Propaganda Techniques." Ian Robertson. *Sociology*. 3rd ed. (New York: Worth Publishers, 1981): 551.

————. "Teaching Humanist Sociology: An Introduction." *The Humanist Sociology Resource Book*. Martin D. Schwartz, ed. (Washington: ASA Teaching Resources Center, 1987).

————. "Differing Views." *Madison (N.J.) Eagle* (April 29, 1987): 2.

————. "Propaganda: The Tricks of the Trade." G. J. DiRenzo,

Sociological Perspectives. 3rd ed. (Lexington, MA: Ginn Press, 1987): 388.

———. Letter. *Fellowship*. Vol. 53: 7–8 (July–August 1987): 29.

"Mary Ellen Richmond (1861–1928)." *Humanity and Society*. Vol. 12 (May 1988): 160–65.

with A. Mc. Lee, "The Continuing Values of SSSP." *SSSP Newsletter*. Vol. 19: 1 (Winter 1988): 4–5.

———. "Developing a Humanist Perspective." *Studi e Ricerche: Omaggio a Franco Ferrarotti*. Roberto Cipriani and M. I. Macioti, eds. (Roma, Italia: SIARES, 1988): 295–304.

———. "An Influential Ghost: The Institute for Propaganda Analysis 1936–1942," *Propaganda Review* 3 (Winter 1988): 10–14.

———. "Humanist Challenges to Sociologists." *SSSP Newsletter*. Vol. 20: 2 (Summer 1989): 2–5.

———. "Humanist Challenges to Sociologists." *The Humanist Sociologist* (Winter, 1989–90): 28–30. Reprinted from *SSSP Newsletter*, 1989.

"How Some Women Became Eminent Social Scientists." *Humanity and Society*. Vol. 13: 1 (February 1989): 16–28.

with A. Mc. Lee, "Struggles toward Equality and Justice." Presentation at the Annual Meetings of the Society for the Study of Social Problems (August 1991).

"Reflections on the Education of Women." *The Liberal Arts in a Time of Crisis*. Barbara Ann Scott, ed. (New York: Praeger 1991): 135–40

ALFRED MCCLUNG LEE, BIBLIOGRAPHY (1927–1991)

Editor-in-chief. *The Owl:* 1927. Student annual of the University of Pittsburgh.

Editor. *Selected Prize Winning Essays: Third Annual Traffic Essay contest*. Pittsburgh: Better Traffic Committee, 1930. Pamphlet.

"How Traffic Group Will Aid in Selling Safety," *Public Safety*. Vol. 4: 9 (September 1930): 20–21.

Trends in Commercial Entertainment in Pittsburgh as Reflected in the Advertising in Pittsburgh Newspapers (1790–1860). M.A. Thesis, University of Pittsburgh (1931).

Abstract, M.A. Thesis. University of Pittsburgh Bulletin. Vol. 28: 4 (December 20, 1931): 408–09.

Editor. *Selected Prize Winning Essays: Fourth Annual Traffic Essay Context*. Pittsburgh: Better Traffic Committee, 1931. Pamphlet.

with L. W. McIntyre. "Educating Careless Motorists by Outdoor Displays." *Public Safety*. Vol. 5: 3 (March 1931): 15–16.

Many unsigned editorials in the *New Haven Journal-Courier* (1932–34; 1937–38).

"Men and Machines." Book review. *New Haven Journal-Courier* (May 31, 1933).

Trends in the Newspaper Industry: A Sociological Study of the American Daily Newspaper. Ph.D. dissertation, Yale University (1933).

"First Sunday Newspaper in U.S. Published in New York in 1809." *Editor and Publisher*. Vol. 66: 29 (December 2, 1933): 12, 38.

"Sunday Newspapers' Life Difficult Until After Civil War." *Editor and Publisher*. Vol. 66: 31 (December 16, 1933): 12.

"New York *Observer*, First Sunday Newspaper in United States, Came Out 125 Years Ago." *The Publishers' Auxiliary*. Vol. 69: 6 (February 10, 1934): 1, 6.

"Pioneer American Daily in 1783." *Editor and Publisher*. Vol. 66: 43 (March 10, 1934): 11, 37.

"First U.S. Daily '50 Years Too Early.' " *Editor and Publisher*. Vol. 66: 44 (March 17, 1934): 12, 40.

"The A.N.P.A. and Its Predecessors." *Editor and Publisher*. Vol. 66: 48 (April 21, 1934): 17, 74, 76.

"Dunlap and Claypoole: Printers and News–Merchants of the Revolution." *Journalism Quarterly*. Vol. 2 (June 1934): 160–78.

"Rebel Destiny." Book review. *New Haven Journal-Courier* (June 16, 1934).

"Fifty Years of Daily Newspapers." *Editor and Publisher*: Golden Jubilee Number. Vol. 67: 20 (July 21, 1934): 50–51; 294–95.

"First Sunday Paper in Baltimore." *Editor and Publisher*. Vol. 67: 15 (August 25, 1934): 7.

"Early American Books and Printing." Book review. *Journalism Quarterly*. Vol. 12: 3 (September 1935): 310–11.

"Inexperience." Allegheny *Valley Advance* (June 26, 1936): 6.

"Propaganda and the News." Book review. *American Journal of Sociology*. Vol. 42: 1 (July 1936): 137.

"Benjamin Franklin." Book review. *Journalism Quarterly*. Vol. 13: 3 (September 1936): 311–12.

"A 100% Humorist." *Allegheny Valley Advance* (October 23, 1936): 6.

"Report of the Research Committee to the Twenty-First Convention of Sigma Delta Chi, Dallas, Texas, November 13–15, 1936." Mimeo.

"The Negro in the Philadelphia Press." Book review. *Journalism Quarterly*. Vol. 14: 1 (March 1937): 53.

The Daily Newspaper in America: The Evolution of a Social Instrument (New York: Macmillan Co., 1937).

"Freedom of the Press: The Services of a Catch Phrase." *Studies in the Science of Society*. G. P. Murdock, ed. (New Haven: Yale University Press, 1937): 355–75.

"Rise and Fall of That Phrase." *The Guild Reporter*. Vol. 4: 20 (September 6, 1937): 8.

"Report of the Research Committee to the Twenty-Second Convention of Sigma Delta Chi, Topeka, Kansas, November 18–20, 1937." Mimeo.

"Recent Developments in the Daily Newspaper Industry." *Public Opinion Quarterly*. Vol. 2: 1 (January 1938): 126–33.

"The Daily Newspaper Today." Yale University News Statement (January 10, 1938). Mimeo.

"The Trend Towards Newspaper Monopoly." *The Guild Reporter*. Vol. 5: 5 (January 10, 1938): 5.

"The Press and World Affairs." Book review. *American Sociological Review*. Vol. 3: 1 (February 1938): 122–23.

"Violations of Press Freedom in America." *Journalism Quarterly*. Vol. 15: 1 (March 1938): 19–27.

Communication. *The Quill*. Vol. 26: 4 (April 1938): 21.

"What Did Jefferson Mean by Free Press?" *The Guild Reporter*. Vol. 5: 17 (April 4, 1938): 4.

with R. T. Rich. *Survey of the Laboratory of Anthropology* (New York: Raymond Rich Associates, 1938). Mimeo.

"Le Conflit sur la liberte' de la presse aux Stats-Unis d'Amerique." *Cahiers de la Presse*. Vol. 1: 4 (October–December 1938): 551–79.

"The Long Hard Road That Led to the Guild." *The Guild Reporter*. Vol. 5: 48 (December 15, 1938): 9–10.

with Elizabeth Briant Lee. *The Fine Art of Rabble-Rousing: A Popular Guide*. Illustrated with the Propaganda of the Rev. Charles E. Coughlin (New York: Institute for Propaganda Analysis, 1939). Confidential. Not for release. Mimeo and paper-bound.

————. *The Fine Art of Propaganda: A Study of Father Coughlin's Speeches* (New York: Institute for Propaganda Analysis and Harcourt, Brace and Co., 1939).

"Dailies in Towns Under 10,000 Gaining, Says Lee." *Editor and Publisher*. Vol. 72: 1 (January 7, 1939): 14.

Chairman. "Report of the Press Relations Committee." *American Sociological Review*. Vol. 4: 2 (April 1939): 264–65.

"Supplementary Report of the Press Relations Committee." *American Sociological Review*. Vol. 4: 2 (April 1939): 266.

"Trends Affecting the Daily Newspapers." *Public Opinion Quarterly*. Vol. 3: 3 (July 1939): 457–502.

"Selling Men's Apparel Through Advertising." Book review. *The Journal of Marketing*. Vol. 4: 4, Part 1 (April 1940): 417.

"Seven Common Propaganda Devices." George V. Denny, Jr. *Town Meeting Discussion Leader's Handbook* (New York: The Town Hall, 1940): 22–23.

"The Devices of Propaganda." *The War for Men's Minds*. Herbert Klein, ed. (Los Angeles: Los Angeles City College Press, 1940): 89–94.

Chairman. "Report of the Public Relations Committee, American Sociological Society." *American Sociological Review*. Vol. 5: 1 (February 1940): 104–05.

"Supplementary Report of the Public Relations Committee." *American Sociological Review*. Vol. 5: 3 (June 1940): 413–14.

"News and the Human Interest Story." Book review. *Survey-Graphic*. Vol. 29: 9 (September 1940): 475.

"At the Bar of Public Opinion." Book review. *American Journal of Sociology*. Vol. 46: 2 (September 1940): 275.

Chairman. "Report of the Committee on Public Relations." *American Sociological Review*. Vol. 6: 1 (February 1941): 95–97.

"Add Textbooks." *Tide*. Vol. 15: 6 (March 15, 1941): 72–73.

Chairman. "Supplementary Report of the Committee on Public Relations." *American Sociological Review*. Vol. 6: 2 (April 1941): 260–61.

Chairman. Proceedings of the Public Relations Workshop (New York: Public Relations Workshop, 1941). Mimeo.

with Elizabeth Briant Lee. Three statistical tables on size and competitiveness of daily newspapers. Washington: Federal Communications Commission No. 52296 (July 23, 1941). Mimeo.

"Problems of War Planning in Great Britain." Book review. *American Sociological Review*. Vol. 6: 4 (August 1941): 591–92.

"American Journalism." Book review. *Journalism Quarterly*. Vol. 18: 3 (September 1941): 309–11.

"American Journalism." Book review. *Saturday Review of Literature*. Vol. 24: 22 (September 20, 1941): 19–20.

"Reason and International Politics." Book review. *Saturday Review of Literature*. Vol. 24: 25 (October 11, 1941): 19.

"The Long Week End." Book review. *American Sociological Review*. Vol. 6: 6 (December 1941): 923–24.

"Brandeis Persistency." Book review. *Saturday Review of Literature*. Vol. 24: 36 (December 27, 1941): 21–22.

"The Basic Newspaper Pattern." *The Annals of the American Academy of Political and Social Science*. Vol. 219 (January 1942): 44–52.

Executive Director. *Propaganda Analysis*. periodical of the Institute for Propaganda Analysis. Vol. 4: 8–13 (1941–42).

"The Stardust Industry." *Saturday Review of Literature*. Vol. 25: 1 (January 5, 1942): 6.

Editor. *A Keller Scrapbook* (South Norwalk: William Graham Sumner Club, 1942).

"Report on a Survey of Program Effectiveness: National Conference of Christians and Jews." January 23, 1942. Mimeo.

Chairman. "Report of the Committee on Public Relations." *American Sociological Review*. Vol. 7: 1 (February 1942): 90–92.

"Supplementary Report of the Public Relations Committee." *American Sociological Review*. Vol. 7: 2 (April 1942): 230.

with Willard Waller. "Opinion Analysis and National Morale" (New York: National Association of Publicity Directors, 1942). Mimeo.

"Subversive Individuals of Minority Status." *The Annals of the American Academy of Political and Social Science*. Vol. 223 (September 1942): 162–72.

"Marketing Life Insurance." Book review in *The Journal of Marketing*. Vol. 7: 2 (October 1942): 190–91.

"Yale Sociologists in Wartime." *Bulletin of the William Graham Sumner Club*. Vol. 12: 1 (November 1942): 1–7.

"Towards Clear Thinking." *NAPD Topics* (December 18, 1942): 2–3.

Editor. *Bulletin of the William Graham Sumner Club*. Vol. 11: 4 nos., 1941–42; Vol. 12: 5 nos., 1942–43; Vol. 13: 2 nos., 1943.

Chairman. "Report of the Committee on Public Relations." *American Sociological Review*. Vol. 8: 1 (February 1943): 80–81.

"Public Relations." *The Adcrafter*. Vol. 21: 8 (February 23, 1943): 1, 3.

Communications, War Problems Clinic. *Detroit Evening Times* (February 23, 1943–December 16, 1943).

"More Definitions." *NAPD Topics* (March 17, 1943): 6.

"The American Mind." *Detroit Collegian* (March 22, 1943): 2.

"Such Was the Dawn of the American Daily." *The Quill*. Vol. 31: 5 (May 1943): 6–8, 14.

"The American Mind: A Brief Essay." *Public Relations Topics*. (May 11, 1943): 3–5.

"Affidavits." May 10, 20, and 22, 1943 in Dept. of Justice. Affidavits Filed in Support of Plaintiff's Action for Summary Judgment (U.S.A. v. A.P., Civil Action No. 19–163, Dist. Court of the U.S. for the Southern Dist. of N.Y.) Filed and served May 23, 1943. 1, 309 pp: 76–170.

with John L. Fortson. *How to Make Friends for Your Church: A Manual on Public Relations* (New York: Association Press, 1943).

"Public Relations Counseling as Institutional Psychiatry." *Psychiatry.* Vol. 6: 3 (August 1943): 271–76; 340–41.

"Kendall of the Picayune." Book review. *The Annals of the American Academy of Political and Social Science.* Vol. 229 (September 1943): 214.

Dry Propaganda: An Analysis of the New Prohibition Drive (New York: Dryden Press, 1943). Mimeo.

"Attacks on Social Science." *Bulletin of the William Graham Sumner Club.* Vol. 13: 2 (November 1943): 1–4.

"Overcoming Anti-Semitism." Book review. *Annals of the American Academy of Political and Social Science.* Vol. 230 (November 1943): 242.

"The Editor's Epilogue." *Bulletin of the William Graham Sumner Club.* Vol. 13: 2 (November 1943): 10–11.

"Introduction." *Winning the Peace.* Alexander Brede, ed. (Detroit: Wayne University Press, 1943): 1–4.

with N. D. Humphrey. "Eight Lessons from Detroit." Excerpts from *Race Riot.* New York PM (November 7, 1943).

———. *Race Riot* (New York: Dryden Press, 1943).

"Interracial Democracy is Coming Year's Need." *The People's Voice* (December 25, 1943).

"Is Sociological Methodology Sterile?" *Papers of the Michigan Academy of Science, Arts, and Letters.* Vol. 29 (1943): 599–604.

"Consumer and Opinion Research." Book review. *Public Relations Topics.* Vol. 2: 1 (January 1944): 7.

"Government & Business Tomorrow." Book review. *Public Relations Topics.* Vol. 2: 1 (January 1944): 7–8.

"Techniques of Social Reform: An Analysis of the New Prohibition Drive." *American Sociological Review.* Vol. 9: 1 (February 1944): 65–77.

"Chairman, drafting committee. Interracial Code for Protestant Churches: Detroit council of Churches." Adopted February 17, 1944. Pamphlet.

"To Stem This Tide." Book review in *Social Forces.* Vol. 22: 3 (March 1944): 339–40.

"What's to Be Done with Germany and Japan?" *Detroit Collegian* (March 3, 1944).

Techniques of Agitation: An Analysis of the New Prohibition Drive (New York: Dryden Press, 1944). Limited edition.

"Training and Education for Public Relations." *Public Relations Topics.* Vol. 2: 4 (August 1944): 2–3.

"The Development of the Colonial Newspaper." Book review. *Journalism Quarterly.* Vol. 21: 3 (September 1944): 267–68.

"Building a Popular Movement." Book review. *The Annals of the American Academy of Political and Social Science.* Vol. 236 (November 1944): 220–21.

"The Social Dynamics of the Physician's Status." *Psychiatry.* Vol. 7: 4 (November 1944): 371–77.

Contributing editor. *Dictionary of Sociology* (New York: Library of Philosophy, 1944). Contributed 45 signed definitions.

"Public Opinion in Relation to Culture." *Psychiatry.* Vol. 8: 1 (February 1945): 49–61.

Participant, Conference on Research in the Field of Anti-Semitism, Summary of Proceedings and Suggestions for a Program (New York: American Jewish Committee, March 1945). Pamphlet.

"Interest Criteria in Propaganda Analysis." *American Sociological Review.* Vol. 10: 2 (April 1945): 282–88.

"Overhauling the Machinery of Democracy." *Saturday Review of Literature.* Vol. 28: 16 (April 21, 1945): 12.

"La Moral y las Custumbres en el Control Social." *Revista Mexicana de Sociologia.* Vol. 7: 2 (Mayo-Agosto 1945): 185–93.

"Foundations of a New Future." Book review. *Saturday Review of Literature.* Vol. 28: 19 (May 12, 1945): 13.

Chairman. "Report on Postwar Planning." Wayne University, May 24, 1945. Mimeo.

Co-author, "Public Relations," Proceedings of the Institute on Race Relations and Community Organization. June 18–29, 1945. Sponsored by the University of Chicago and American Council on Race Relations: 31–33. Mimeo.

"Detail and Utility of Government." Book review. *Saturday Review of Literature.* Vol. 28: 26 (June 30, 1945): 34–35.

"Levels of Culture as Levels of Social Generalization." *American Sociological Review*. Vol. 10: 4 (August 1945): 485–95.

"Members Define Public Relations." *Public Relations Topics*. Vol. 3: 7 (August 1945): 4: 8 (September 1945): 4.

"The Analysis of Propaganda: A Clinical Summary." *American Journal of Sociology*. Vol. 51: 2 (September 1945): 126–35.

"Industry and Power Politics." Book review. *Saturday Review of Literature*. Vol. 28: 38 (September 22, 1945): 36–37.

Race Riots Aren't Necessary. Public Affairs Pamphlet 107 (New York: Public Affairs Committee and American Council on Race Relations, 1945).

"Observations on Another Peace." *Saturday Review of Literature*. Vol. 28: 46 (November 17, 1945): 48.

"The German Record." Book review. *American Sociological Review*. Vol. 10: 6 (December 1945): 810–11.

"The Unbridled Industrial War." *Saturday Review of Literature*. Vol. 28: 48 (December 1, 1945): 23.

with N. D. Humphrey. "The City of Detroit Interracial Commission: A Case Study." *Journal of Educational Sociology*. Vol. 19: 5 (January 1946): 278–88.

"Human Leadership in Industry." *The Annals of the American Academy of Political and Social Science*. Vol. 243 (January 1946): 172–73.

"The Beginnings of Social Science." *Saturday Review of Literature*. Vol. 29: 1 (January 5, 1946): 12.

"A Definition of 'Public Relations' Is Emerging." *Library Journal*. Vol. 71: 5 (March 1, 1946): 330–32.

"The Press in the Control of Intergroup Tensions." *The Annals of the American Academy of Political and Social Science*. Vol. 244 (March 1946): 144–51.

"Unwritten Treaty." Book review. *The Annals of the American Academy of Political and Social Science*. Vol. 245 (May 1946): 192.

"The Age of Nationalism." Book review. *Saturday Review of Literature*. Vol. 29: 19 (May 11, 1946): 8.

"Reveille for Radicals." Book review. *American Sociological Review*. Vol. 11: 3 (June 1946): 370.

"The First Freedom." Book review. *Journalism Quarterly*. Vol. 23: 2 (June 1946): 231–32.

"Peoples Speaking to Peoples." Book review. *The Annals of the American Academy of Political and Social Science*. Vol. 247 (September 1946): 206–07.

"Concentration Camp, U.S. Model." Book review. *Saturday Review of Literature*. Vol. 29: 39 (September 28, 1946): 12.

Editor, co-author. *New Outline of the Principles of Sociology* (New York: Barnes & Noble, 1946). Author of "The Socialization of the Individual." Chapters 30–35: 283–341.

"Midwest Arena." Book review. *Saturday Review of Literature*. Vol. 29: 47 (November 23, 1946): 18.

Interview. Radio station WJBK Detroit (7–7:15 p.m., November 4, 1946).

with N. D. Humphrey. "To Prevent Race Riots." *College Readings for Inductive Study*. Rev. ed. Arward Starback and Notley S. Maddox, eds. (New York: Dryden Press, 1946): 371–86.

"The Human Frontier." Book review. *The Annals of the American Academy of Political and Social Science*. Vol. 349 (January 1947): 211.

Communication. *Commentary*. Vol. 3: 1 (January 1947): 90–91.

"Social Determinants of Public Opinions." *International Journal of Opinion and Attitude Research*. Vol. 1: 1 (March 1947): 12–29.

"Trends in Public Relations Training." *Public Opinion Quarterly*. Vol. 11: 1 (Spring 1947): 83–91.

"Propaganda, Communication, and Public Opinion." Book review. *American Sociological Review*. Vol. 12: 3 (April 1947): 243–44.

"Just a Few Words About the National Association of Public Relations Counsel." *The Adcrafter*. Vol. 25: 15 (April 15, 1947): 266.

"Are Only the Russians Guilty?" *Public Opinion Quarterly*. Vol. 11 (1947): 173.

"La Ensenanza Popular de la Sociologia y la Antropologia en la Universidad de Wayne." *Boletin del Instituto de Sociologia*. Vol. 5 (1947): 119–24.

"Action for Unity." Book review. *Commentary*. Vol. 3: 5 (May 1947): 497–98.

"Sociological Theory in Public Opinion and Attitude Studies." *American Sociological Review*. Vol. 12: 3 (June 1947): 312–23.

"Public Opinion." J.S. Roucek and Associates. *Social Control* (New York: D. Van Nostrand Co., 1947): 385–407.

"Advancin." Oakmont (Pa.) *Advance-Leader*. (July 17, 1947): 1.

"A Free and Responsible Press." Book review. *American Sociological Review*. Vol. 12 (August 1947): 486–87.

"The American Radio." Book review. *American Sociological Review*. Vol. 12 (August 1947): 487.

"Propaganda Techniques of Religious Groups." *American Psychologist*. Vol. 2: 8 (August 1947): 280.

"Attitudes to Minority Groups." Book review. *International Journal of Opinion and Attitude Research*. Vol. 1: 3 (September 1947): 114–16.

"When Peoples Meet." Book review. *International Journal of Opinion and Attitude Research*. Vol. 1: 3 (September 1947): 116–17.

"So You Hate—!" *Unity*. Vol. 133: 4 (September–October 1947): 66–67.

"Our Fair City." Book review. *The Annals of the American Academy of Political and Social Science*. Vol. 254 (November 1947): 222–23.

"You and Your Public." Book review. *Public Opinion Quarterly*. Vol. 11 (1947): 458–460.

"A Definition of Public Opinion." *International Journal of Opinion and Attitude Research*. Vol. 1: 4 (December 1947): 103–06.

with E. B. Lee. "Activity 19." W. M. Tanner and W. E. Cheaver. *English for Every Use* (New York: Ginn and Co., 1947): 85.

with N. D. Humphrey. "The Riot Pattern." *Readings in General Sociology* R. W. O'Brian, ed. (Palo Alto, California: Pacific Books, 1947): 399–401.

"A Personal Public Relations Program." For Marshall Field, III. Project of the Fred Eldean Organization, 1947. Mimeo.

"El Poder Personal y la Accion Social." *Revista Mexicana de Sociologia*. Vol. 6: 3 (September–December 1947): 341–51.

"The Civic Services of a Local Opinion Survey." *Proceedings, Second International Conference on Public Opinion Research* (Williamstown,

Mass., September 2–5, 1947). Henry David, ed. (Chicago: National Opinion Research Center, 1948): 32–37.

"Propaganda." *Americana Annual 1948.* A. H. McDaniels, ed. (New York: Americana Corp., 1948): 551–52.

"The Press and Public Relations of Religious Bodies." *The Annals of the American Academy of Political and Social Science.* Vol. 256 (March 1948): 120–31.

And Then Came the Guild. Pamphlet (New York: American Newspaper Guild, 1948.

"Some Prerequisites of International Opinion Surveying." *International Journal of Opinion and Attitude Research.* Vol. 2: 1 (Spring 1948): 54–62.

Communication. *American Sociological Review.* Vol. 13 (1948): 341–42.

"Facing Facts." Book review. *Christian Register.* Vol. 187: 6 (June 1948): 14.

"The Psychology of Humor." Book review. *American Sociological Review.* Vol. 13: 3 (June 1948): 361.

"The Comics." Book review. *American Sociological Review.* Vol. 13 (August 1948): 500–501.

Chairman, National Awards Committee, Public Relations Society of America. "Annual Awards and Citations." *Public Relations Journal.* Vol. 4: 8 (August 1948): 30–40.

"Theorie des Opinions." Book review. *International Journal of Opinion and Attitude Research.* Vol. 2: 2 (Summer 1948): 245–47.

"Two-Way Street." Book review. *International Journal of Opinion and Attitude Research.* Vol. 2: 3 (Fall 1948): 413–15.

with E. B. Lee. "Propaganda." A. J. Stoddard and Matilda Bailey. *English: Fourth Course* (New York: American Book Co., 1948), pp. 188–89.

"How to Reduce Distribution Costs." Book review. *Journal of Marketing.* Vol. 13: 3 (January 1949): 418–19.

"The People's Choice." Book review. *The Annals of the American Academy of Political and Social Science.* Vol. 261 (January 1949): 194.

"The Communication of Ideas." *The Annals of the American Academy of Political and Social Science.* Vol. 261 (January 1949): 215.

"Working With Colleges and Universities." *Public Relations Journal.* Vol. 5: 1 (January 1949): 11–14.

"Civil Rights? 'Ha!' Practical Joke." *Christian Register.* Vol. 128: 2 (February 1949): 15–17.

"Public Opinion in Relation to Culture" and "Techniques of Social Reform: An Analysis of the New Prohibition Drive." *Sociological Analysis: An Introductory Text and Case Book* Logan Wilson and W. L. Kolb, eds., (New York: Harcourt, Brace and Co., 1949).

"Lee States His Views on Monopoly." *Journalism Quarterly.* Vol. 26: 1 (March 1949): 125–26.

with E. B. Lee. *Social Problems in America: A Source Book* (New York: Henry Holt and Co., 1949).

"Freedom and Civilisation." Book review. *International Journal of Opinion and Attitude Research.* Vol. 3: 1 (Spring 1949): 148–49.

"Science and Society in India." Book review. *International Journal of Opinion and Attitude Research.* Vol. 3: 2 (Summer 1949): 281–82.

"Experiences and Tasks of International Opinion Surveying." *International Journal of Opinion and Attitude Research.* Vol. 3: 2 (Summer 1949): 323–28; 334–35.

"Between the Scylla and Charybdis of Big Government and Big Business." *Christian Register.* Vol. 128: 7 (August 1949): 5–6.

"The American Soldier." *The Annals of the American Academy of Political and Social Science.* Vol. 265 (September 1949): 173–75 and vol. 267 (January 1950): 252.

"Communications Research: 1948–1949." *The Annals of the American Academy of Political and Social Science.* Vol. 265 (September 1949): 216–17.

"Introduction a la Sociologie." *International Journal of Opinion and Attitude Research.* Vol. 3: 3 (Fall 1949): 462.

"Psychology of Social Classes." Book review. *Social Science.* Vol. 24: 4 (October 1949): 248.

"The Nature-Nurture Controversy." *Scientific Monthly.* Vol. 4 (October 1949): 275–76.

"Sociology for Public Relations Practice." *Public Relations Journal.* Vol. 5: 10 (October 1949): 22–25.

"Experiments in Mass Communication." Book review. *The Annals of the American Academy of Political and Social Science.* Vol. 266 (November 1949): 236–37.

"A Sociological Discussion of Consistency and Inconsistency in Intergroup Relations." *Journal of Social Issues.* Vol. 5: 3 (1949): 12–18.

Co-author. *Diccionario de Sociologia.* H. P. Fairchild, ed. (Mexico-Buenos Aires: Fondo de Cultura Economica, 1949).

with E. B. Lee, "The Devices of Propaganda." *Mass Communications.* Wilbur Schramm, ed. (Urbana: University of Illinois Press, 1949): 381.

"Understanding Society." Book review. *International Journal of Opinion and Attitude Research.* Vol. 2: 4 (Winter 1948–49): 606.

"The Proper Study of Mankind." Book review. *Public Opinion Quarterly.* Vol. 12: 4 (Winter 1948–49): 742–744.

"Implementation of Opinion Survey Standards." *Public Opinion Quarterly.* Vol. 13: 4 (January 1950): 645–52.

"Can the Individual Protect Himself Against Propaganda Not in His Interest?" *Social Forces.* Vol. 20: 1 (October 1950): 56–61.

"Power-Seekers." *Studies in Leadership* A. W. Gouldner, ed. (New York: Harper & Brothers, 1950).

"Strategic Intelligence for American World Policy." Book review. *Christian Register.* Vol. 129: 4 (April 1950): 3–4.

"Social Structure." Book review. *International Journal of Opinion and Attitude Research.* Vol. 4: 1 (Spring 1950): 116–18.

"Prophets of Deceit." Book review. *Public Opinion Quarterly.* Vol. 14: 2 (Summer 1950): 347–48.

"Character Assassination." Book review. *Journalism Quarterly.* Vol. 27: 2 (Summer 1950): 335–37.

"Measurement and Prediction." Book review. *The Annals of the American Academy of Political and Social Science.* Vol. 272 (November 1950): 261–62.

"Public Opinion and Propaganda." Book review. *Social Forces.* Vol. 29: 2 (December 1950): 211–12.

"Reader in Public Opinion and Communication." Book review. *American Sociological Review.* Vol. 15: 6 (December 1950): 815–16.

Editor, co-author. *New Outline of the Principles of Sociology.* Rev. ed. (New York: Barnes & Noble, 1951).

"The Pall of Orthodoxy." *The Nation.* Vol. 173: 6 (August 11, 1951): 110–11.

"Individual and Organization Research in Sociology." *American Sociological Review.* Vol. 16: 5 (October 1951): 701–07.

Editor. *Readings in Sociology.* (New York: Barnes & Noble, 1951). Author of 1–7; 297–312; 407–11.

Participant in Public Affairs Committee Round Table: *Loyalty in a Democracy* (Allerton House, New York, N.Y., May 26, 1951). Mimeo.

with N. D. Humphrey. "The Riot Pattern." R. W. O'Brien, C. C. Schrag, and W. T. Martin. *Readings in General Sociology* (New York: Houghton Mifflin Co., 1951): 273–74.

"On Resolutions by the Society." *American Sociological Review.* Vol. 16: 1 (February 1951): 102–03.

"Civil Liberties on Our Campuses." As given at the University of Minnesota, February 23, 1951. Mimeo.

"Introduction." M. S. Stewart. *The Negro in America.* Public Affairs Pamphlet 95. March 1951: 2.

"Communications" to World Association for Public Opinion Research. *International Journal of Opinion and Attitude Research.* Vol. 5: 2 (Summer 1951): 290–92.

Chairman. "Report of the Committee on the Problems of the Individual Researcher." *American Sociological Review.* Vol. 16: 6 (December 1951): 263–64.

"The Recruitment, Selection, and Training of Social Scientists." Book review. *International Journal of Opinion and Attitude Research.* Vol. 4: 4 (Winter 1950–51): 594–97.

"Language of Politics." Book review. *International Journal of Opinion and Attitude Research.* Vol. 5: 1 (Spring 1951): 125–26.

"Current Trends in Social Psychology." Book review. *International Journal of Opinion and Attitude Research.* Vol. 5: 1 (Spring 1951): 126–27.

"Sales Engineering." Book review. *Journal of Marketing.* Vol. 15: 4 (April 1951): 509–10.

"Continuities in Social Research." Book review. *International Journal of Opinion and Attitude Research*. Vol. 5: 3 (Fall 1951): 422–24.

"Influences of Organizational Research Upon the Development of Sociology." *Sociologische Forschung in Underer Zeit*. K. G. Specht, ed. (Koln und Opladen: Westdeutschen Verlag, 1951).

"Sociological Insights Into American Culture and Personality." *Journal of Social Issues*. Vol. 7: 4 (1951): 7–14.

Chairman, Drafting Committee, ACLU, Academic Freedom and Academic Responsibility (New York: American Civil Liberties Association, April 1942). Pamphlet.

How to Understand Propaganda (New York: Rinehart & Co., 1952).

"Participant in Loyalty in a Democracy: A Roundtable Report." (New York: Public Affairs Committee, February 1952). Public Affairs Pamphlet 179.

"How to Understand Propaganda." *Psychological Book Previews*. Vol. 2: 2 (April 1952): 78–83.

"Four Who Defied Compromise." *Christian Register*. Vol. 131: 7 (September 1952): 17–19; 40.

"Seeing Through World Tensions." *The Intercollegian*. Vol. 70: 2 (October 1952): 16–17.

"Amen to Wide Range." Communication. *Christian Register*. Vol. 131: 7 (September 1952): 8.

"Communication." *Journalism Quarterly*. Vol. 29: 3 (Summer 1952): 381.

"Advertising Idea Book." *Journal of Marketing*. Vol. 16: 3 (January 1952): 379–80.

"The Comparative Study of Symbols." *The Annals of the American Academy of Political and Social Science*. Vol. 283 (September 1952): 196–97.

"Race and Culture." Book review. *The Humanist*. Vol. 12: 4 (July–August 1952): 191.

"Business Be Damned." Book review. *Scientific Monthly*. Vol. 75: 3 (September 1952): 194.

"The Community Press in an Urban Setting." Book review. *American Sociological Review*. Vol. 17: 5 (October 1952): 641–42.

"Listening Salesmanship." Book review. *Journal of Marketing*. Vol. 17: 2 (October 1952): 202–03.

"Cultural Sciences: Their Origin and Development." Book review. *The Humanist*. Vol. 12: 5 (September–October 1952): 241.

"Propaganda in War and Crisis." Book review. *Social Forces*. Vol. 31: 2 (December 1952): 174–75.

President, Unitarian Fellowship for Social Justice. "In Defense of Anti-Totalitarian Resolution—Our Liberties Endangered." *Christian Register*. Vol. 132: 6 (July 1953): 5.

"Let's Continue to Lead Toward a Church for Men of All Colors." *Christian Register*. Vol. 132: 5 (May 1953): 21.

"Seeing Through World Tensions." *Humanism World Digest*. Vol. 25: 2 (May 1953): 3–6. Also in *The Intercollegian*. Vol. 70: 2 (October 1952): 16–17.

"Comment on Humanist Manifesto." *The Humanist*. Vol. 13: 3 (May–June 1953): 138.

Editor. *Principles of Sociology*. Rev. ed. (New York: Barnes & Noble, 1953).

"Standards and Ethics in Sociological Research," Congres de Liege, Association Internationale de Sociologie. September 1953. Mimeo.

"Responsibilities and Privileges in Sociological Research." *Sociology and Social Research*. Vol. 37: 6 (July–August 1953): 367–74.

"Richtmasse und Ethische Grundsatze in der Soziologischen Forschung." *Kolner Zeitsrift fur Soziologie*. Vol. 5 (1952–53): 401–11.

"The Study of Public Opinion." *Sociology: A Book of Readings*. Samuel Koenig, R. D. Hopper, and Feliks Gross, eds. (New York: Prentice-Hall, 1953): 445–53.

Chairman. "Report of the Committee on Standards and Ethics in Research Practice." *American Sociological Review*. Vol. 18: 6 (December 1953): 683–84.

"Is Anybody Listening?" Book review. *American Journal of Sociology*. Vol. 58: 4 (January 1953): 437–38.

"Democracy and the Economic Challenge." Book review. *The Humanist*. Vol. 13: 1 (January–February 1953): 44.

With others. "Comments on the Humanist Manifesto: A Symposium." *The Humanist*. Vol. 13: 3 (May–June 1953): 136–41; Lee statement on 138.

"Moral Principles of Action." Book review. *The Humanist*. Vol. 13: 3 (May–June 1953): 143–44.

"Science as Morality." Book review. *Christian Register*. Vol. 132: 9 (November 1953): 4.

"The Tools of Social Science." Book review. *Social Forces*. Vol. 32: 2 (December 1953): 205.

"The Hoary Human Dilemma." *The Humanist*. Vol. 14: 2 (March–April 1954): 90–94.

"Public Relations or Propaganda?" *Adult Leadership*. Vol. 2: 10 (March 1954): 20–22.

"Statement." U.S. Senate, Committee on Labor and Public Welfare, Subcommittee on Civil Rights, Antidiscrimination in Employment . . . on S. 692. (Washington: Government Printing Office, 1954): 301–06. Testimony given March 3, 1954.

Chairman, Commission on Unitarian Intergroup Relations, American Unitarian Association. "How 'Open' Is the Unitarian Door?" *Christian Register*. Vol. 133: 4 (April 1954): 10–16.

Co-editor, co-author. *Public Opinion and Propaganda: A Book of Readings* (New York: Dryden Press, 1954).

"Discrimination in College Fraternities and Sororities." *School and Society*. Vol. 79 (June 26, 1954): 198–99.

"Your—and Their—Stratagems." *The Humanist*. Vol. 14: 5 (September–October 1954): 201–08.

"Die Weiterentwicklung von Parks Theorie der Grenzeituation." *Kolner Zeitschift fur Soziologie*. Vol. 6: 6 (1953–54): 234–43.

"Social Pressures and the Values of Psychologists." *The American Psychologist*. Vol. 9: 9 (September 1954): 516–22.

"Fraternities: Schools for Prejudice?" *The Committee Reporter* (American Jewish Committee). vol. 2: 5 (September–October 1954): 2–3.

"Attitudinal Multivalence in Relation to Culture and Personality." *American Journal of Sociology*. Vol. 60: 3 (November 1954): 294–99.

"Milford, Delaware, Round by Round." *The Crisis*. Vol. 61: 9 (November 1954): 521–32.

"Sociologists in an Integrating Society: Significance and Satisfaction in Sociological Work." *Social Problems.* Vol. 2: 2 (October 1954): 57–66.

"Standards and Ethics in Sociological Research." *Transactions of the Second World Congress of Sociology* (London: International Sociological Association, 1954): 156–61.

"Aryan Blood Nonsense on U.S. Campuses." *Christian Register.* Vol. 133: 10 (December 1954): 11, 18.

"Anthropology Today." Book review. *The Humanist.* Vol. 14: 1 (January–February 1954): 45–46.

"How to Lie With Statistics." Book review. *Christian Register.* Vol. 133: 4 (April 1954): 2.

"A General View of Positivism." Book review. *The Humanist.* Vol. 14: 6 (November–December 1954): 298–99.

"Reconsideracion de la Teoria de Park Sobre la Marginalidad." *Revista Mexicana de Sociologia.* Vol. 16: 3 (September–December 1954): 375–86.

"The Program of the National Committee on Fraternities in Education." *Social Problems.* Vol. 2: 3 (January 1955): 172–75.

"Education of an American Liberal." Book review. *Christian Register.* Vol. 134: 1 (January 1955): 2.

"Tendencias de las Fraternidades Socio-universitarias en los Estados Unidos." *Revista Mexicana de Sociologia.* Vol. 17: 1 (Enero–Abril 1955): 139–49.

"Delaware's Ku Klux Test Tube." *Christian Register.* Vol. 134: 2 (February 1955): 14–18.

"Social Science Role Cited." *Civil Liberties in New York.* Vol. 3: 4 (March 1955): 2.

"Specific Areas of Selectivity in Colleges." M.I.T. National Intercollegiate Conference on Selectivity and Discrimination in American Universities, Complete Agenda: Discussion Questions and Documentation, March 25–27, 1955: 18–19.

"Aryanism Goes Underground on American Campuses: *Journal of Human Relations.* Vol. 3: 3 (Spring 1955): 36–41.

With others. "Appendix to Appellants' Briefs: Statements by Social

Scientists in the Supreme Court of the United States, October Term 1952." *Social Problems.* Vol. 2: 4 (April 1955): 227–35.

"Can Social Fraternities Be Democratic?" *Journal of Higher Education.* Vol. 26: 4 (April 1955): 173–80.

"Toward Fraternity in Fraternities." *The Intercollegian.* Vol. 72: 8 (April 1955): 18.

Editor, co-author. *Principles of Sociology.* 2nd ed. (New York: Barnes & Noble, 1955).

with Elizabeth Briant Lee. *Social Problems in America: A Source Book.* Rev. ed. (New York: Henry Holt and Co., 1955).

"Groups at Work." Book review. *Psychological Bulletin.* Vol. 52: 3 (May 1955): 278–79.

"The Clinical Study of Society." *American Sociological Review.* Vol. 20: 6 (December 1955): 648–53.

Fraternities Without Brotherhood: A Study of Prejudice on the American Campus (Boston: Beacon Press, 1955).

"Foreword." *Mental Health and Mental Disorder: A Sociological Approach.* Arnold M. Rose, ed. (New York: W. W. Norton & Co., 1955): xi–xii.

"Contributing editor. *Dictionary of Sociology.* H. P. Fairchild, ed. Reissue (Ames, Iowa: Littlefield, Adams & Co., 1955).

"Foreword." *Sexual Behavior in American Society.* Jerome Himelhoch and Sylvia Fleis Fava, eds. (New York: W. W. Norton & Co., 1955): xiii–xiv.

with Elizabeth Briant Lee. "The Tricks of the Trade." Leonard Broom and Philip Selzniok. *Sociology: A Text with Adapted Readings* (Evanston: Row, Peterson and Co., 1955): 290.

"Who Forms *Your* Opinions and How? Where Do You Get Your Facts?" National Council of Churches, United Church Women, The Pursuit of Truth (1956): 3–6. Printed pamphlet.

"National Policies for Education, Health and Social Services." Book review. *American Sociological Review.* Vol. 21: 2 (April 1956): 254.

"The Process and Effects of Mass Communication." Book review. *American Sociological Review.* Vol. 21: 3 (June 1956): 408–09.

"Communication." *The Quill.* Vol. 44: 6 (June 1956): 5.

"Freedom Today." Book review. *The Humanist.* Vol. 16: 4 (July–August 1956): 195–96.

Advisory board member, with Lewis Leary, chairman, and others. "Articles in American Studies, 1955." *American Quarterly.* Vol. 8: 2 (Summer 1956): 171–82.

"Lo studio clinico della Societa." *Quaderni di Sociologia* (Torino) 19 (Inverno 1956): 3–23.

"Sociology and Liberal Religion." *The Ethical Outlook.* Vol. 42: 6 (November–December 1956): 186–90.

"The Direction of Human Development: Biological and Social Bases." Book review. *Christian Register.* Vol. 135: 10 (December 1956): 2.

"The Torment of Secrecy." Book review. *Social Problems.* Vol. 4: 3 (January 1957): 263–64.

"Communication." *Council on Public Relations Education Letter* (Association for Education in Journalism) 2 (January 1957): 3.

"Report of the Coordinator of Special Problems Committees." *Social Problems.* Vol. 4: 3 (January 1957): 276–77.

"Psychic Violence." *Fellowship.* Vol. 23: 4 (April 1957): 23–24. Book review of "The Rape of the Mind."

Editor. "Some Suggested Readings." College of the City of New York, Four College Teacher Education Conference, Communication Techniques in the Mass Media, April 5, 1957: 5–9.

"In the College Boom, What Is Going to 'Give'?" *The Humanist.* Vol. 17: 5 (September–October 1957): 269–75.

"Techniques of Identification." Pamphlet reprint of portion of Chapter 3, *How to Understand Propaganda* (Washington: National War College, Visual Aids, 1957): 68–77.

"Fattori Sociali dell 'Integrazione Europea." *Quaderni di Sociologia* 28 (Primavera 1958): 116–24.

"The Place of Introductory Sociology in General Education." *Journal of Higher Education.* Vol. 29: 5 (May 1958): 251–56.

"Centro di Ricerche Sociologiche sui Mezzi Audiovisivi." *Bollettino di Informazione* (Commissione Nazionale Italiana per 1 UNESCO). Anno 5: opuscoli 3–4. 15 luglio 1958: 8–11.

"The Sociological Research Centre on Audiovisual Means of the

Catholic University, Milan." *UNESCO International Social Science Bulletin.* Vol. 10: 4 (1958): 631–33.

"La Sociologia Industriale Americana e forse un'arte magica?" *Notiziario de Sociologia* 3 (July–August 1958): 1–4.

Vocabolario Audiovisivo Pamphlet (Milano: Italia: Universita Cattolica del Sacro Cuore, Centro di Ricerche Sociologiche sul Mezzi Audiovisivi, 1958).

How Customs and Mentality Can Be Changed (The Hague: Institute of Social Studies. Publications on Social Change 8, 1958). Pamphlet. 12 pp. digest of pamphlet in *Sociological Abstracts.* Vol. 7: 2 (April 1959): 145.

"On the Social Scene." Proceedings of the Fiftieth Anniversary Observance of the American Jewish Committee, April 10–14, 1957 (New York: American Jewish Committee, 1958): 49–54.

with Elizabeth Briant Lee. "Propaganda Techniques." Blaine E. Mercer. *The Study of Society.* (New York: Harcourt, Brace and Co., 1958): 106–07.

with Elizabeth Briant Lee. "The Tricks of the Trade." Leonard Broom and Philip Selzniok. *Sociology: A Text with Adapted Readings* (Evanston: Row, Peterson and Co., 1955): 290.

"Propaganda." Book review. *American Sociological Review.* Vol. 23: 3 (June 1958): 354.

Editor. *Readings in Sociology* (New York: Barnes & Noble, 4th printing, 1959).

Editor, co-author. *Principles of Sociology.* 2nd ed. (New York: Barnes & Noble, 1959).

"Sociologia e Studio delle Comunicazione di Massa." *Lo Spettacolo.* Vol. 9: 4 (October–December 1959): 209–17.

"Sociologie et etude des communications de masse." *Lo Spettacolo.* Vol. 9: 4 (October–December 1959): xii–xxi.

"Sociologia e Studio delle Comunicazione di Massa" (Roma: Societa Italiana degli Autori ed Editori, 1959).

"The New Prohibition Drive." chapter 30 in *Drinking and Intoxication: Selected Readings.* R. G. McCarthy, ed. (New Haven: Publications Division, Yale Center of Alcohol Studies; Glencoe, Il.: The Free Press, 1959): 412–28.

"The Great Famine." Book review. *Social Problems*. Vol. 6: 3 (Winter 1959): 280–81.

"Una Comunita Meridionale." Book review. *Social Problems*. Vol. 6: 4 (Spring 1959): 374–75.

"They Failed as Killers." Book review of "The Ineffective Soldier." *Fellowship*. Vol. 25: 17 (September 1, 1959): 12–13.

"Aspects of Islam in Post-Colonial Indonesia." Book review. *Social Problems*. Vol. 7: 2 (Fall 1959): 173.

"La Cosiddetta Analisi del Contenuto." *Centro Nazionale per Gli Studi su l Informazione*. Vol. 4: 3 (March 1960): 2–4.

"The Impact of Segregated Housing on Public Schools." *School and Society*. Vol. 88: 2174 (May 7, 1960): 241–43.

"El Impact de la Alojamientos Desegregado sobre los Escuelas Publicas." *Revista Mexicana de Sociologia*. Vol. 22: 3 (September–December 1960): 989–93.

Editor. *Readings in Sociology. 5th printing. rev.* (New York: Barnes & Noble, 1960).

"Gli Irlandesi d'America." *Communita*. Vol. 14: 81 (July–August 1960): 24–28.

La Sociologia delle Comunicazioni (Torino: Taylor Editore, 1960).

with L. G. A. Schlichting and F. Fettorella. "Concetto e Formazione dell 'Opinione Pubblica." *Notizie e Commenti*. Vol. 4: 12 (December 1960): 1–4.

"Ricerca sulla Formazione della 'Opinione Pubblica." *Annali della Universita di Macerata*. Vol. 24 (1960): 37–45.

"Editor's Foreword." To George Simpson. *People in Families* (New York: Thomas Y. Crowell Co., 1960): vii–ix.

"The Impact of Segregated Housing on Public Schools." *The Countdown on Segregated Education*. W. W. Brickman and S. Lehrer, eds. (New York: Society for the Advancement of Education, 1960).

"A Sociologist Looks at Liberal Religion." *Contemporary Accents in Liberal Religion:* 1960. Bradford Gale ed. (Boston: Beacon Press, 1960): 210–18.

with Elizabeth Briant Lee. "The Devices of Propaganda." pp. 417–18 in *Mass Communications*. 2nd ed. Wilbur Schramm, ed. (Urbana: University of Illinois Press, 1960).

"Book Selection and Censorship." Book review. *American Sociological Review*. Vol. 25: 2 (April 1960): 303.

"Road to Propaganda." Book review. *American Sociological Review*. Vol. 25: 2 (April 1960): 317.

"The Muqaddimah." Book review. *Unitarian Register*. Vol. 139: 4 (April 1960): 15–16.

"Value in Social Theory." Book review. *The Annals of the American Academy of Political and Social Science*. Vol. 329 (May 1960): 191.

"Propaganda Analysis." Book review. *American Sociological Review*. Vol. 25: 3 (June 1960): 432–33.

"Crime and Conformity." Book review. *Fellowship*. Vol. 26: 13 (July 1, 1960): 26–27.

"Class in American Society." Book review. *American Quarterly*. Vol. 12 (1960): 422.

"Mobilita e Stratificazione Sociale." Book review. *Social Problems*. Vol. Social Problems. Vol. 8: 2 (Fall 1960): 275–76.

with Elizabeth Briant Lee. "Che Cosa Accade agli Schemi di Vita Familiare negli Stati Uniti." *Quaderni di Sociologia* 39 (Winter 1961): 3–20.

"Come Intendere la Propaganda." *Lo Spellacolo*. Vol. 11: 1 (January–March 1961): 8–15.

"Partecipazione ed Analisi nella Ricerca Sociologica." *Rassegna Italiana di Sociologia*. vol. 2 (1961): 43–59.

"Ricerche sulla Formazione della Opinione Pubblica." *L'Ufficio Moderno—la Pubblicita* 8 (August 1961): 1–5.

Come Intendere la Propaganda (Roma: Societa Italiana degli Autori ed Editori, 1961).

"Editor's Foreword." Milton L. Barron. *The Aging American* (New York: Thomas Y. Crowell Company, 1961): vii–ix.

"Individual and Organizational Research in Sociology." *Sociology: The Progress of a Decade*. S. M. Lipset and N. J. Smelser, eds. (Englewood Cliffs, N.J.: Prentice-Hall, 1961).

"Autocracy and Democracy." Book review. *The Annals of the American Academy of Political and Social Science*. Vol. 335 (May 1961): 230–31.

"The Calas Affair." Book review. *American Sociological Review*. Vol. 26: 3 (June 1961): 489–90.

"Genesis and Structure of Society." Book review. *American Sociological Review*. Vol. 26: 4 (August 1961): 640–41.

Che Cos 'e la Propaganda (Torino: Casa Editrice Taylor, 1961).

with Elizabeth Briant Lee. *Marriage and the Family* (New York: Barnes & Noble, 1961).

"Alcuni problemi di orientamento nelle Scienze Sociali." *Rassegna Italiana di Sociologia*. Vol. 2: 4 (October–December 1961): 435–44.

"La Sociologia delle Comunicazioni." Book review. *Estudios de Sociologia*. Vol. 1 (Buenos Aires, 1961): 225–26.

"An Interim Report to the Membership of the Society for the Study of Social Problems." *Social Problems*. Vol. 9: 3 (Winter 1962): 289–92.

Editor. *Principios de Sociologia* (Sao Paulo, E. U. do Brasil, 1962).

"Preface." J. A. Ponsioen. *The Analysis of Social Change Reconsidered*. Vol. 4 (Institute of Social Studies, 1962): 7–10.

"Impacto de los Medios de Masas Sobre la Politica Estadounidense." *Revista Mexicana de Sociologia*. Vol. 24: 1 (January–April 1962): 127–37.

"To the Editor." *Social Problems*. Vol. 9: 4 (Spring 1962): 386–89.

"S. S. S. P. Delegate to I. S. A. Chosen by A. S. A. Without Consultation: A Report." *Social Problems*. Vol. 9: 4 (Spring 1962): 400–01.

"Influenza dei Mezzi di Comunicazione di Massa sulla Politica Americana." *Quaderni di Sociologia*. Vol. 11: 2 (April–June, 1962): 154–64.

"S. S. S. P. Delegate to I.S. A. Chosen by A. S. A. Without Consultation: A Second Report." *Social Problems*. Vol. 10: (Summer 1962): 97–100.

"Problemi di Sociologia." Book review. *Social Problems*. Vol. 9: 3 (Winter 1962): 296–97.

"Ricera sulla formazione della 'opinione pubblica." *Problemi della Pubblica Amministrazione* (Universita di Bologna). Vol. 5 (1963): 155–63.

"Roles of Marginality in Mobility and in Social Change." Institut International de Sociologie, La Sociologia y las sociedades en Desarrollo Industrial Vol. III. (Universidad Nacional de Cordoba, Argentina, 1963): 223–37.

"Sobre la confusion de los Tejidos de la Ortodoxia y la Legitimidad de la Sociedad con el 'sistema' y el 'orden.' " *Revista Mexicana de Sociologia*. Vol. 25: 2 (May–August 1963): 647–56.

"Editor's Foreword." M. R. Davie. *William Graham Sumner* (New York: Thomas Y. Crowell Co., 1963): v–vi.

"Editor's Foreword." Israel Gerver. *Lester Frank Ward* (New York: Thomas Y. Crowell Co., 1963): v–vi.

"Editor's Foreword." S. M. Miller. *Max Weber* (New York: Thomas Y. Crowell Co., 1963). iii–iv.

"Editor's Foreword." Bernard Rosenberg. *Thorstein Veblen* (New York: Thomas Y. Crowell Co., 1963): v–vi.

"Editor's Foreword." George Simpson. *Emile Durkheim* (New York: Thomas Y. Crowell Co., 1963): vii–viii.

"The 1962 Meetings of the ASA Council: A Report from the SSSP Delegate." *Social Problems*. Vol. 10: 3 (Winter 1963): 293–97.

"The Special January 12, 1963 Meeting of the ASA Council: Comments by the SSSP Representative." *Social Problems*. Vol. 10: 4 (Spring 1963): 409–11.

"The Muqaddimah." Book review. *Social Problems*. Vol. 10: 3 (Winter 1963): 199–201.

"The Scotch-Irish: A Social History." Book review. *The Annals of the American Academy of Political and Social Science*. Vol. 346 (March 1963): 202–03.

"The Irish Border as a Cultural Divide." Book review. *American Anthropologist*. Vol. 65 (1963): 1173–74.

with Elizabeth Briant Lee. *Marriage and the Family*. 3rd printing (New York: Barnes & Noble, 1964).

"L'uomo multivalente in una societa multivalente: basi per una sociologia piu dinamica." *Studi di Sociologia*. Vol. 2: 2 (April–June 1964): 115–24.

Windows on the World: A Career Field-Study Project (Boston: Program Survey Committee of the [Unitarian] Laymen's League, 1964).

"Levels of Culture as Levels of Social Generalizations." "Individual and Organizational Research in Sociology." *Contemporary Sociology*. M. L. Barron, ed. (New York: Dodd, Mead & Co., 1964): 109–19; 524–32.

"Annual Report for 1962–63 of the SSSP Representative to the ASA Council." *Social Problems*. Vol. 11: 3 (Winter 1964): 319–21.

Part of: "PRSA Conference Sees Accreditation Program Established." *Public Relations Journal*. Vol. 20: 1 (January 1964): 6–13, esp. 9.

"The Program Survey Report." *The Lamplighter* (Unitarian Laymen's League, Boston, June 1964): 2–4.

"The American Federal Executive." Book review. *The Annals of the American Academy of Political and Social Science*. Vol. 353 (May 1964): 187–88.

"The Concept of System." *Social Research*. Vol. 32: 3 (Autumn 1965): 229–38.

Windows on the World: First Hand Explorations in Careers: A Project for Youth and Adults. Reviews ed. (Boston: Laymen's League, 1965).

"Items for the Agenda of Social Science." *Applied Sociology: Opportunities and Problems* A. W. Gouldner and S. M. Miller, eds. (New York: Free Press, 1965): 421–28.

Editor's foreword. Joseph Lopreato, *Vilfredo Pareto* (New York: Thomas Y. Crowell Co., 1965): v–vi.

"Annual Report for 1963–64 of SSSP Representative to the ASA Council." *Social Problems*. Vol. 12: 3 (Winter 1965): 356–360.

"The Voice of the I. F. J." *The Journalist's World*. Vol. 2: 4 (1965): 25.

"Reply to Bierstedt." *American Sociological Review*. Vol. 30 (1965): 131.

"Church/State/Education." *The Lamplighter* (April 1965): 7.

"Report of the Program Survey Committee." *The Lamplighter* (June 1965): 5–6.

Chairman, Committee on Public Opinion. "Report to the Commission to Study the Arts in New Jersey." September 1965 (Trenton: State of New Jersey).

Statement at Public Hearing before Commission to Study the Arts in New Jersey (September 14, 1965): 68–75.

"Race Riot in East St. Louis: July 2, 1917." Book review. *The Annals of the American Academy of Political and Social Science.* Vol. 358 (March 1965): 231–32.

"The Irish in Britain." Book review. *The Annals of the American Academy of Political and Social Science.* Vol. 362 (November 1965): 204.

"The Opinion Makers." Book review. *Register-Leader.* Vol. 148: 1 (January 1966): 16.

"Dissenting Appraisal." *Register-Leader.* Vol. 148: 4 (April 1966): 20.

Chairman, Committee on Public Opinion. "Summary of the Committee's Recommendations to the Commission." *The Arts in New Jersey* (Trenton, 1966): 150–55.

Multivalent Man (New York: George Braziller, 1966).

Editor's foreword. George Simpson. *People in Families* (Cleveland and New York: Meridian Books, 1966): vii–ix.

"Il persistere delle ideologie." *La Critica Sociologica* (Rome). Vol. 1 (Spring, 1967): 5–15.

"Institutional Structures and Individual Autonomy." *Human Organization.* Vol. 26: 1–2 (Spring–Summer 1967): 1–5.

"Organizational Leadership in Liberal Religion." *Journal of the Liberal Ministry.* Vol. 7: 2 (Spring 1967): 54–60, 65.

"Communication," *American Sociologist.* Vol. 2: 2 (May 1967): 100.

"Report of the Delegate-Elect to the Council of ISA." *Social Problems.* Vol. 14: 3 (Winter 1967): 351.

"A Starting Point for Symposium." *The Quill.* Vol. 55: 9 (September 1967): 7.

Report as Delegate to the International Sociological Association. *American Sociologist.* Vol. 2: 4 (November 1967): 240–50.

"Rebellion in Newark." Book review. *Civil Liberties Reporter* (ACLU of New Jersey). Vol. 3: 4 (November 1967): 2, 4.

"Improvised News." Book review. *The Annals of the American Academy of Political and Social Science.* Vol. 374 (November 1967): 213–14.

"Report to Bureau of Education and Cultural Affairs, U.S. Department of State." Activities under U.S. Specialist Grant No. 740181 (December 28, 1966 to May 26, 1967 inclusive).

"Race Riots Are Symptoms." New introductory essay. Lee and N. D. Humphrey. *Race Riot* (New York: Octagon Books, 1968): vii–xxviii.

"On Formula Liberalism." *Journal of the Liberal Ministry.* Vol. 8: 3 (Fall 1968): 47–50.

"I Moti Raziali Sono Sintomi." *La Critica Sociologica* 5 (Spring 1968): 36–52.

"Report of SSSP Representative to the International Sociological Association." *SSSP Newsletter.* Vol. 1: 1 (Winter 1968): 9–11.

"Report of the Representative on the Intersociety Committee." *SSSP Newsletter.* Vol. 1: 1 (Winter 1968): 14.

Communication. *SSSP Newsletter.* Vol. 1: 3 (Summer 1968): 4–5.

"Red Lessons for Blacks." Book review. *Saturday Review* Vol. 51: 31 (August 1, 1968): 20–21.

"Beyond Alienation." Book review. *American Sociological Review.* Vol. 33: 1 (November 1968): 163–64.

Editor, co-author. *Principles of Sociology.* 3rd ed. (New York: Barnes & Noble, 1969). Lee author of 1–64, 287–362.

Associate Editor and co-author. Worterbuch der Soziologie. 2nd ed. Wilhelm Bernsdorf, ed. (Stuttgart: Ferdinand Enke, 1969). Lee articles: 565–68, 724–25, 851–53, 856–57, and 986–89.

with N. D. Humphrey. "Race Riot." *Racial Violence in the United States.* A. D. Grimshaw, ed. (Chicago: Aldine Publishing Co., 1969).

with Elizabeth Briant Lee. *The Fine Art of Propaganda,* T. L. Engle and Louis Snellgrove. *Psychology: Its Principles and Applications.* 5th ed. (New York: Harcourt, Brace and World, 1969): 519–21.

"Report of SSSP Representative to the International Sociological Association." *SSSP Newsletter.* Vol. 1: 4 (Winter 1969): 17–19.

"Report of Delegate to the International Sociological Association." *American Sociologist.* Vol. 4: 4 (1969): 362–63.

"Tapes as Strikebreakers." *American Teacher* (December 1969): 14.

"The Anthropology of Armed Conflict and Aggression." Book review. *Fellowship.* Vol. 35: 1 (January 1969): 27–28.

"Anglo-Saxons and Celts." Book review. *The Annals of the American Academy of Political and Social Science.* Vol. 382 (March 1969): 169.

"Celtic Nationalism." Book review. *The Annals of the American Academy of Political and Social Science.* Vol. 384 (July 1969): 154–55.

"The Behavior Sciences." Book review. *Religious Humanism.* Vol. 3: 3 (Summer 1969): 143–44.

"Censorship: The Irish Experience." Book review. *The Annals of the American Academy of Political and Social Science.* Vol. 386 (November 1969): 188–89.

Multivalent Man. paperback ed. (New York: George Braziller, 1970).

"Ph.D.s for Whom at 42nd Street?" *United Federation of College Teachers Action.* Vol. 7: 4–5 (January–February 1970): 4.

L'Uomo Polivalente (Unione Tipografico-Editrice Torinese, 1970).

"On Context and Relevance." *The Participant Observer.* Glenn Jacobs, ed. (New York: George Braziller, 1970).

with N. D. Humphrey. "June 1943." Jeffrey Schrank. *Violence: A Discussion Series* (Morristown, N.J.: Silver Burdett Company, 1970): 43.

with Elizabeth Brown Little and others. *Study Guide: Introductory Sociology* (Southport, Connecticut: Future Resources and Development Corporation, 1970).

with Elizabeth Brown Little, eds. *Reader in Sociology* (Southport, Connecticut: Future Resources and Development Corporation, 1970). Looseleaf.

with E. T. Campbell. *Does Religion Bring Happiness?* (Public Affairs International, 1970).

"Unfortunate Propaganda." *Friends Journal.* Vol. 16: 7 (April 1, 1970): 204.

"AAUP's Salary Reports." *American Teacher.* Vol. 54: 9 (April 1970): 23.

"Use of Register Questioned." *Newsletter of the American Anthropological Association.* Vol. 11: no. 6 (June 1970): 15.

"Report of SSSP Representative to the International Sociological Association." *SSSP Newsletter.* Vol. 2: 1 (Spring 1970): 11–12.

Communication, *AHP Newsletter* (Association for Humanistic Psychology). Vol. 7: 1 (October 1970): 10.

"The End of Liberalism." Book review. *The Annals of the American Academy of Political and Social Science.* Vol. 387 (January 1970): 187.

"The Irish Countryman." Book review. *American Anthropologist.* Vol. 72: 1 (February 1970): 130–32.

Taped lecture. "What Sociology Offers." Cassette 1, Side A (No. 170–1). Future Resources and Development, 1970.

Taped lecture. "Sociological Views of Growing Up in Society." Cassette 2, Side A (No. 170–2). Future Resources and Development, 1970.

Taped lecture. "The Struggle for Your Mind." Cassette 7, Side A (No. 170–7). Future Resources and Development, 1970.

Taped lecture. "Current Challenges in Research on Social Problems." Cassette 7, Side B. (No. 170–7). Future Resources and Development, 1971.

with Elizabeth Brown Little, *Introductory Sociology: Master Teacher Guide* (Westport, Connecticut: Future Resources and Development, 1971): pp. 24–37.

with N. D. Humphrey. "Race Riot (Detroit, 1943)." *The Politics of Riot Commissions,* 1917–1970. A. M. Platt, ed. (New York: Collier Books, 1971): 229–58.

with Elizabeth Briant Lee. "The Tricks of the Trade." C. Jeffrey and Owen Peterson. *Speech* (New York: Harper and Row, 1971): 321–22.

with N. D. Humphrey. 1968 ed. Tape recording for the blind and physically handicapped. (Franklin, Michigan: Readings for the Blind, 1971).

"1969–1970 Report SSSP Representative to the International Sociological Association." *SSSP Newsletter.* Vol. 2: 3 (Winter 1971): 9–11.

"Re: Action." *AHP Newsletter.* Vol. 7: 6 (April 1971): 11.

Communication. *SPSSI Newsletter* 128 (July 1971): 2.

"College Unionism." *American Teacher.* Vol. 56: 1 (September 1971): 30.

"Report of Representative to the International Sociological Association." *American Sociologist.* Vol. 6: 4 (November 1971): 361–63.

"Maria Comberti and Friends in Italy." *Friends Journal.* Vol. 17: 20 (December 1, 1971): 642.

"Our Long Violent History." Book review. *Fellowship.* Vol. 17: 3 (March 1971): 21–22.

"The Chief Secretary." Book review. *The Annals of the American Academy of Political and Social Science.* Vol. 396 (July 1971): 153–54.

"Mechanical Man." Book review. *Philosophy Forum.* Vol. 9 (1971): 336–41.

"On Context and Relevance." J. F. Glass and J. R. Staude. *Humanistic Society* (Pacific Palisades, CA: Goodyear Publishing Co., 1972): 247–56.

"Let's Describe Interreligious Conflicts Like They Are." *Journal of the Liberal Ministry.* Vol. 12: 2 (Spring 1972): 43–46.

"An Obituary for 'Alienation.'" *Social Problems.* Vol. 20: 1 (Summer 1972): 121–27.

"Northern Ireland." Book review. *The Annals of the American Academy of Political and Social Science.* Vol. 400 (March 1972): 195–96.

"Church and State in Modern Ireland, 1923–1970." Book review. *The Annals of the American Academy of Political and Social Science.* Vol. 401 (May 1972): 181–82.

Communication. *Insurgent Sociologist.* Vol. 2: 2 (Spring 1972): 42.

Communication. *Insurgent Sociologist.* Vol. 2: 4 (Summer 1972): 50–51.

with Elizabeth Briant Lee. *The Fine Art of Propaganda.* Rev. ed. with new introduction (New York: Octagon Books, 1972).

"Foreword," Jerre Mangione, *The World Around Danilo Dolci: A Passion for Silicians* (New York: Harper & Row, 1972): xiii–xix.

"The Myth and the Truth of Irish Violence." *Fellowship.* Vol. 38: 9 (September 1972): 12–16.

"The Northern Ireland Problem." Book review. *Unitarian Universalist World.* Vol. 3: 18 (December 15, 1972): 8.

"Sociological Paradigms in Social Struggles." Document No. 40, XXIII Congreso International de Sociologia, Institut International de Sociologie (Caracas, Venezuela, 20–25 November 1972).

"Modern Civilization and Human Survival: A Social-Scientific View." *Philosophy Forum*. Vol. 12 (1972–73): 29–66.

Toward Humanist Sociology (Englewood Cliffs, N.J.: Prentice-Hall, 1973).

"Random Notes on Radicalism in Sociology." *Insurgent Sociologist*. Vol. 3: 2 (Winter 1973): 20–24.

"The Northern Ireland Problem." Book review. *Friends Journal* (January 1, 1973): 14–15.

"More About Ulster." Book review. *Church and State*. Vol. 26: 1 (January 1973): 17.

"More on B. F. Skinner." *The Humanist*. Vol. 33: 1 (January–February 1973): 46.

Communication. *The Humanist*. Vol. 33: 3 (May–June 1973): 44.

"The Northern Ireland Problem." Book review. *The Annals of the American Academy of Political and Social Science*. Vol. 406 (March 1973): 209–10.

The Daily Newspaper in America. Re-issue (New York: Octagon Books, 1973).

Letter. *Insurgent Sociologist*. Vol. 3: 4 (Summer 1973): 98–99.

with Elizabeth Briant Lee. "Propaganda: The Tricks of the Trade." R. W. Mack and John Pease, *Sociology and Social Life*. 5th ed. (New York: D. Van Nostrand Co., 1973): 505.

"That Most Distressful Nation: The Taming of the American Irish." Book review. *The Annals of the American Academy of Political and Social Science*. Vol. 407 (May 1973): 221–22.

"Insurgent and 'Peacekeeping' Violence in Northern Ireland." *Social Problems*. Vol. . Vol. 20: 4 (Spring 1973): 532–46.

"Sexist Language." *Newsweek* (October 8, 1973): 18.

"Inventiveness Urged." *UU World* (October 15, 1973): 5.

"Our 'Motherland' Is the Entire World." *New York Teacher* (November 4, 1973): 10.

"Race and Law in Great Britain." Book review. *The Annals of the American Academy of Political and Social Science*. Vol. 410 (November 1973): 200–201.

"Radical Sociology"; "Humanist Sociology"; "Propaganda." *Encyclo-*

pedia of Sociology (Guilford, Connecticut: Dushkin Publishing Co., 1974): 236–37; 129–30; 226.

"The Fourth World." Book review. *The Annals of the American Academy of Political and Social Science.* Vol. 411 (January 1974): 229–30.

"UU Principles." *UU World* (May 1, 1974): 5.

"The Irish." Book review. *The Annals of the American Academy of Political and Social Science.* Vol. 412 (March 1974): 213–14.

"To What Is Northern Ireland's Civil War Relevant?" *Holy Cross Quarterly.* Vol. 6 (1974): 1–4: 94–100.

with Elizabeth Briant Lee. "The Society for the Study of Social Problems: Visions of Its Founders." *SSSP Newsletter.* Vol. 5: 1 (Fall 1973–74): 2–5.

"Man's Quest for Autonomy." Book review. *UU World* (September 1915, 1974): 8.

"Man's Quest for Autonomy." Book review. *The Annals of the American Academy of Political and Social Science.* Vol. 415 (September 1974): 279–80.

"Church, State and Nation in Ireland." Book review. *The Annals of the American Academy of Political and Social Science.* Vol. 415 (September 1974): 241–42.

"Efforts to Control Insurgency in Northern Ireland." *International Journal of Group Tensions.* Vol. 4: 3 (September 1974): 346–58.

with Elizabeth Briant Lee. "The Tricks of the Trade." R. C. Jeffrey and Owen Peterson. *Speech. 2nd ed.* (New York: Harper & Row, 1975): 309–10.

with others. "Cussler Legal Defense Fund." *ASA Footnotes.* Vol. 3: 4 (April 1975): 6.

Participant: "Open Social Science Colloquim on Neo-Coleman Rejection of Social Desegregation." Metropolitan Applied Research Council, New York, N.Y. (June 24, 1975).

"Sociology for Whom?" *ASA Footnotes.* Vol. 3: 6 (August 1975): 1, 3.

Chairperson. "Deadlines & Procedures Posted for 1976 Program in New York." *ASA Footnotes.* Vol. 3: 6 (August 1975): 3–5.

"The Peace-Loving Irish?" *Human Behavior.* Vol. 4: 9 (September 1975): 43.

"Humanist Challenges to Positivists." *Insurgent Sociologist.* Vol. 6: 1 (Fall 1975): 41–50.

"Pegler's Not So Grand." *The Quill* (September 1975): 5.

"Organizing within the ASA." *Invisible Socialist University Newsletter of East Coast Conference of Socialist Sociologists.* Vol. 2: 2 (August 1, 1975): 1, 20–23.

"The Irish." Book review. *The Annals of the American Academy of Political and Social Science.* Vol. 421 (September 1975): 173–74.

"Humanistic Society." Book review, *Contemporary Sociology.* Vol. 4: 5 (September 1975): 557.

"Humanism as Demystification." *Sociological Analysis and Theory.* Vol. 5: 3 (October 1975): 267–88.

"Human Values in a Changing Society." Proceedings of the Conference on Planning and Public Policy in the Regional Setting. F. J. Costa, ed. (Akron: University of Akron, 1975): 54–70.

"Report of the President." *ASA Footnotes.* Vol. 3: 9 (December 1975): 8.

"Northern Irish Socialization in Conflict Patterns." *International Review of Modern Sociology.* Vol. 5: 2 (Autumn 1975): 127–34.

"The First Amendment as a Charter for Nonviolent Action." *To Secure Peace and Liberty.* Larry Gara, ed. (New York: War Resisters League, 1976). Vol. 21.

"Humanism as Demystification." *Journal of Sociology and Social Welfare.* Vol. 3: 3 (January 1976): 347–68.

"Humanism as Demystification." Proceedings of the Second Annual Conference, Sociological Association of Ireland (Belfast: Queen's University of Belfast, 1976): 10–33.

"Inaugural Remarks by ASA President." *ASA Footnotes.* Vol. 4: 1 (January 1976): 1, 3.

"ASA Referendum." *Sociologists for Women in Society Newsletter.* Vol. 6: 1 (March 1976): 13.

"On the Fate of Humanism in Social Science." *SSSP Social Problems Theory Division Newsletter* 5 (Winter 1976): 18–19.

"Report of the President." *ASA Footnotes.* Vol. 4: 3 (March 1976): 6.

"Petition from the Membership." *ASA Footnotes.* Vol. 4: 3 (March 1976): 7.

with others. "In Favor of Referendum Proposals." *ASA Footnotes.* Vol. 4: 4 (April 1976): 1, 9.

"Is Ulster's Conflict Religious?" *Church and State.* Vol. 29: 5 (May 1976): 9–11.

"The Mafia of a Sicilian Village, 1860–1960." Book review. *The Annals of the American Academy of Political and Social Science.* Vol. 425 (May 1976): 182.

"Report of the President." *ASA Footnotes.* Vol. 4: 5 (May 1976): 8.

with others. Letter concerning Referendum. *ASA Footnotes.* Vol. 4: 3 (May 1976): 2.

"Theme: Sociology for Whom?" American Sociological Association: 71st Annual Meeting: Preliminary Program 1976 (New York Hilton, August 30–September 3, 1976): 2–3.

"Ernest Becker's Lost Science of Man." *La Critica Sociologica* 37 (Primavera 1976): 89–93.

"Letter to the Editors." *Sociological Practice.* Vol. 1: 1 (Spring 1976): 7–9.

"Valedictory: A Report on the Year 1975–1976." *ASA Footnotes.* Vol. 4: 6 (August 1976): 1, 9, 10.

"What Kind of Sociology is Useful to Social Workers?" *Journal of Sociology and Social Welfare.* Vol. 4: 1 (September 1976): 4–13.

"Sociology for Whom?" *Anthropology and Humanism Quarterly.* Vol. 1: 2 (September 1976): 8–9.

"Report of the President." *ASA Footnotes.* Vol. 4: 9 (December 1976): 4.

with Elizabeth Briant Lee. "The Society for the Study of Social Problems: Parental Recollections and Hopes." *Social Problems.* Vol. 24: 1 (October 1976): 4–14.

"Sociology for Whom?" *American Sociological Review.* Vol. 41: 6 (December 1976): 925–36.

with Elizabeth Briant Lee. "Some Common Propaganda Devices and Their Symbols." *The Eye Opener: An Introduction to Philosophy.* R. W. Platt, ed. (Englewood Cliffs, N.J.: Prentice-Hall, 1976): 63–64.

Testimony before University of Pittsburgh Hearing Board in Paul Nyden versus University of Pittsburgh. Excerpt of Proceedings. Vol. 2, 175–259. 1976.

"The Nyden Case: An Alumnus Revisits Pitt." *Insurgent Sociologist.* Vol. 7: 1 (Winter 1977): 70–73.

"Intercolonialism." Book review. *The Annals of the American Academy of Political and Social Science.* Vol. 429 (January 1977): 162–63.

with Elizabeth Briant Lee. "Widely Used Propaganda Techniques." C. F. Fisher and C. A. Terry. *Children's Language and the Language Arts* (New York: McGraw-Hill Book Co., 1977): 135–36.

with Elizabeth Briant Lee. "From the Fine Art of Propaganda." Ruth L. Opner. *Writing from the Inside Out* (New York: Harper & Row, 1977): 369–75.

"Sane Asylum." Book review. *Fellowship* (January–February 1977): 27–28.

"Corrymeela." Book review. *Fellowship* (March–April 1977): 27.

"The Quality of Interpersonal Experience." *Anthropology and Humanism Quarterly.* Vol. 2: 1 (March 1977): 2–3.

"Humanism as Demystification." *Anthropology and Humanism Quarterly.* Vol. 2: 1 (March 1977): 5–13.

"A Conversation with Alfred McClung Lee." ed. Tom Reilly. *Journalism History.* Vol. 4: 1 (Spring, 1977): 2–7.

"Letter to the American Sociological Association." *Insurgent Sociologist.* Vol. 7: 3 (Summer 1977): 85.

"A Different Kind of Sociological Society." *Humanity and Society.* Vol. 1: 1 (Summer 1977): 1–11.

"The Challenge of Social Inequality." Book review. *Humanity and Society.* Vol. 1: 1 (Summer 1977): 176–77.

"Conflict in Northern Ireland." Book review. *The Annals of the American Academy of Political and Social Science.* Vol. 433 (September 1977): 188–89.

"Insult and Society." Book review. *Contemporary Sociology.* Vol. 6: 5 (September 1977): 615–16.

"What Americans Should Do About Crime." Book review. *Fellowship.* Vol. 43: 12 (December 1977): 23.

"Evaluation and/or Policy Research in the Development of Social Problems Theory." *Social Problems Theory Division Newsletter* (Fall 1977): 8–9.

"Responsibility and Accountability in Sociology." K. H. Ferguson, and others, eds. *Sociological Research Symposium,* VII (Richmond: Delta Chapter, Alpha Kappa Delta, Virginia Commonwealth University, 1977): 2–13.

"Imperialism, Class and Northern Ireland's Civil War." *Crime and Social Justice* 8 (Fall–Winter 1977): 46–52.

"Fellow Members of the 1977 A.S.A. Council." *Insurgent Sociologist.* Vol. 8: 1 (Winter 1978): 102.

"To the Council." *Insurgent Sociologist.* Vol. 8: 1 (Winter 1978): 101–02.

"The Cult of the Wild." Book review. *Fellowship.* Vol. 44: 1–2 (January–February 1978): 20.

"How We Humanists Can Cooperate." *Religious Humanism.* Vol. 12: 1 (Winter 1978): 41–45.

"Letter from an Honorary Member." *Bulletin, Sociological Association of Ireland,* 11 (March 1978): 1.

"Church-State Separation: A Sociologist's View." *Church and State.* Vol. 31: 3–4 (March–April 1978): 17–18.

with Elizabeth Briant Lee. "Expanding Humanism." *Newsletter of the American Humanist Association.* Vol. 21: 4 (April 1978): 2.

Sociology for Whom? (New York: Oxford University Press, 1978).

"The Struggle for Humanity." Book review. *The Annals of the American Academy of Political and Social Science.* Vol. 437 (May 1978): 183–84.

with Elizabeth Briant Lee. "Varieties of Techniques." Maxine Hairston, *A Contemporary Rhetoric, 2nd ed.* (Boston: Houghton Mifflin Co., 1978): 314.

"The Psychology of Rigorous Humanism." Book review. *Religious Humanism.* Vol. 12: 3 (Summer 1978): 144–14.

"Irish Muppets Show." *In These Times.* Vol. 2: 36 (August 2–8, 1978): 18.

Una Sociologia per l 'Uomo. Traduzione di Sergio Miletti (Napoli: Liguori Editore, 1978).

"Human Values in a Changing Society." *Public Rule or Ruling Classes?* R. S. Sterne and F. J. Costa, eds. (Cambridge, Massachusetts: Schenkman Publishing Co., 1978).

"Church and State." *Unitarian Universalist World* (December 1978): 5.

"The Guyana Tragedy." *Church and State*. Vol. 32: 1 (January 1979): 26.

"Sociology: Humanist Emphasis is Increasing in Studies." Book review. *The Churchman*. Vol. 193: 9 (December 1979): 19.

"Explorers of Humankind." Book review. *The Churchman*. Vol. 193: 8 (November 1979): 17.

"Human Rights and American Foreign Policy." Book review. *Humanity and Society*. Vol. 3: 4 (November 1979): 325–27.

"The Irish Triangle." Book review. *American Committee for Irish Studies Newsletter*. Vol. 9: 1 (October 1979): 4.

"Ireland's Representatives." *The Churchman*. Vol. 193: 7 (October 1979): 2.

with Elizabeth Briant Lee. "Checking It Out: Propaganda: The Tricks of the Trade." Jean Lloyd, R. W. Mack, and John Pease. *Sociology and Social Life. 6th ed.* (New York: D. Van Nostrand Co., 1979): 534.

"How Humanists Can Cooperate." *Humanist in Canada 50*. Vol. 12: 3, 1979: 34–36.

"Beyond the Jungle." Book review. *The Humanist*. Vol. 39: 5 (September–October 1979): 65–66.

"The Art of Social Conscience." Book review. *The Humanist*. Vol. 39: 5 (September–October 1979): 64.

Chair, Editorial and Publications Committee. "Working Draft of Proposals." *Newsletter of Association for Humanist Sociology*. Vol. 4: 3 (September 7, 1979): 2–4.

"A Michigan Predecessor of Americans United." *Church and State*. Vol. 32: 7 (July–August 1979): 19–20.

"Toward the Social Production of the Sacred." Book review. *The Humanist*. Vol. 32: 4 (July–August 1979): 65.

"An Ethnic at Large." Book review. *The Humanist.* Vol. 39: 4 (July–August 1979): 65–66.

with Elizabeth Briant Lee. "The Fine Art of Propaganda Analysis— Then and Now," *Et Cetera.* Vol. 36: 2 (Summer 1979): 117–27.

"Humanism in Sociology." Book review. *Contemporary Sociology.* Vol. 8: 4 (July 1979): 590–91.

"Social Stratification in Australia." Book review. *The Annals of the American Academy of Political and Social Science.* Vol. 444 (July 1979): 183–84.

with Elizabeth Briant Lee. *The Fine Art of Propaganda.* Clothbound: New York: Octagon Books, 1979. Paperback: San Francisco, California: International Society for General Semantics, 1979. Re-issues.

"Interethnic Conflict in the British Isles." *Anthropology and Humanism Quarterly.* Vol. 4: 2 & 3 (June–September, 1979): 6–16.

"Mark Twain: One of the Enduring Voices." *The Humanist.* Vol. 39: 3 (May–June 1979): 52–53.

"Sociology for People." *Humanity and Society.* Vol. 3: 2 (May 1979): 81–91.

"Query on AI's N. Ireland Work." *Matchbox* (of Amnesty International). Spring 1979: 11.

"How We Humanists Can Cooperate." *AHP Newsletter* (April 1979): 26–28.

"Section on Irish an 'Understatement.' " *New York Teacher* (April 1, 1979): 8.

"The Services of Clinical Sociology." *American Behavioral Scientist.* Vol. 23: 3 (March–April 1979): 487–512.

"On the Dread of Innovation in Universities." *Practicing Anthropology.* Vol. 2: 1 (October 1979): 3, 18–20.

"Workaholics." Book review. *The Churchman.* Vol. 194: 1 (January 1980): 17.

"The Genesis Factor." Book review. *The Churchman.* Vol. 194: 1 (January 1980): 17.

"Humanist Strength: Reality." *The Humanist.* Vol. 80: 1 (January– February 1980): 5–13, 48.

"Peace People of Northern Ireland." Book review. *The Churchman.* Vol. 194: 2 (February 1980): 15.

"Introduction." *W. G. Sumner, Earth-Hunger and Other Essays.* A. G. Keller, ed. New ed. (New Brunswick, N.J.: Transaction Books, 1980): v–xxvii.

"The Evolution of Sexuality." Book review. *The Humanist.* Vol. 40: 3 (May–June 1980): 38–39.

"Terrorism: Theory and Practice." Book review. *The Humanist.* Vol. 40: 3 (May–June 1980): 39–40.

Chairperson, Press Relations Committee, 1938–39, American Sociological Society, report reprinted in L. J. Rhoades. "75th Anniversary." *ASA Footnotes.* Vol. 8: 4 (April 1980): 4.

"Humanists Can Be Conscientious Objectors to War." *The Humanist.* Vol. 40: 3 (May–June 1980): 61.

"The MXs in Our Midst." *In These Times* (May 7–13, 1980): 15.

"Trimming the VAT." *Commonweal.* Vol. 107: 10 (May 23, 1980): 290.

"N Block Prisoners." *In These Times.* Vol. 4: 25 (May 21–27, 1980): 16.

with Elizabeth Briant Lee. "The Tricks of the Trade." R. C. Jeffrey and Owen Peterson. *Speech. 3rd ed.* (New York: Harper & Row, 1980): 287–88.

"Violence in America." Book review. *The Humanist.* Vol. 40: 4 (July–August 1980): 44.

"Experiences in Graduate Training." *The Wisconsin Sociologist.* Vol. 17: 2 & 3 (Spring, Summer 1980): 62–63.

Editor, co-author. "Human Rights in the Northern Ireland Conflict: 1968–1980." *International Journal of Politics.* Vol. 10: 1 (Spring 1980): 1–146.

"Who Helps Whom Among Scholarly Communicators? Who Profits?" *Practicing Anthropology.* Vol. 2: 4 (April–May 1980): 12, 28.

"Nonviolent Agencies in the Northern Ireland Struggle." *Journal of Sociology and Social Welfare.* Vol. 7: 4 (July 1980): 601–23.

"Attitudes in the Republic of Ireland Relevant to the Northern Ireland Problems." Book review. *The Humanist.* Vol. 40: 5 (September–October 1980): 47–48.

"The Intercollegiate Socialist Society, 1905–1921." Book review. *The Annals of the American Academy of Political and Social Science*. Vol. 451 (September 1980): 186–87.

"An Alternative Sociology." Book review. *Contemporary Sociology*. Vol. 9: 6 (November 1980): 844.

"Foreword." Rona M. Fields. *Northern Ireland: Society Under Siege* (New Brunswick and London: Transaction Books, 1980): vii–ix.

"Journalists Take the Wraps Off the IRA's Secret Army." Book review. *In These Times*. Vol. 5: 11 (February 4–10, 1981): 21.

"American Opinion and the Irish Question." Book review. *American Committee on Irish Studies Newsletter*. Vol. 11 (February 1981): 4.

"American Taxes." *New Society*. Vol. 55: 951 (February 5, 1981): 256.

Communication. *Fellowship*. Vol. 47: 1–2 (January–February 1981): 2.

"Attitudes in the Republic of Ireland Relevant to the Northern Ireland Problem." Book review. *Contemporary Sociology*. Vol. 10: 2 (March 1981): 307–08.

"Mass Media Mythmaking in the United Kingdom's Interethnic Struggles." *Ethnicity*. Vol. 8 (1981): 18–30.

"Social Origins of the Irish Land War." Book review. *The Annals of the American Academy of Political and Social Science*. Vol. 454 (March 1981): 218–19.

"The Forgotten Sumner." *Journal of the History of Sociology*. Vol. 3: 1 (Fall–Winter, 1980–81): 87–105. Reprint of introduction to Transaction edition of Sumner's *Earth Hunger*.

"Apocalypse." Book review. *Fellowship*. Vol. 47: 4–5 (April–May 1981): 26–27.

"The Dynamics of Terrorism in Northern Ireland, 1968–1980." *Social Research*. Vol. 48: 1 (Spring 1981): 100–34.

"How Can the American Sociological Association Become More Useful?" *American Sociologist*. Vol. 16: 2 (May 1981): 93–97.

"Knows It Well." *In These Times*. Vol. 5: 28 (June 17–30, 1981): 15.

"The Real Adam Smith." *The Nation*. Vol. 232: 25 (June 27, 1981): 778.

"KKK Resurgence." *The Crisis*. Vol. 88: 5 (June 1981): 252.

"Prejudice and Tolerance in Ireland." Book review. *The Annals of the*

American Academy of Political and Social Science. Vol. 456 (July 1981): 179–81.

"Attitudes in the Republic of Ireland Relevant to the Northern Ireland Problem." Book review. *American Committee on Irish Studies Newsletter*. Vol. 11 (October 1981): 3.

"Venezuela . . . Reason for the Calm." *Christian Science Monitor* (October 7, 1981): 23.

with Elizabeth Briant Lee. "Titillating, But—." *In These Times* (October 21–27, 1981): 13.

with Elizabeth Briant Lee. "Two Clinicians Tandem in Social Action." *Clinical Sociology*. Vol. 4: 10 (Fall 1981): 3–4.

"Reflessioni sul Terrorismo nell 'Irlanda del Nord." *La Critica Sociologica* 59 (Autumno 1981): 6–19.

"The Rehumanization of the Social Sciences." *Kerala Sociologist* (India). Vol. 9 (December 1981): 39–51.

with Elizabeth Briant Lee. "Propaganda Techniques." Ian Robertson. *Sociology. 2nd ed.* (New York: Worth Publishers, 1981): 580.

with Elizabeth Briant Lee. "Varieties of Techniques." Maxine Hairston. *A Contemporary Rhetoric* (Boston: Houghton Mifflin Co., 1982): 382.

Communication. *The Crisis* (January 1982): 18.

"A Response to Manners' 'Carrying Capacity and the Politics of Overpopulation.'" *Anthropology and Humanism Quarterly*. Vol. 7: 1 (March 1982): 22–23.

"Enticing Ideas That Often Distort Social Thought." *Humanity and Society*. Vol. 6: 2 (May 1982): 103–21.

"Comment on Maslow, Humanity and Society, August 1981." *Humanity & Society*. Vol. 6: 2 (May 1982): 183.

"The Long Struggle to Make Sociology Useful." *Public Relations Journal*. Vol. 38: 7 (July 1982): 8–11.

"Corporate Power and Urban Crisis in Detroit." Book review. *Clinical Sociology Review*. Vol. 1 (1982): 139–40.

"On Symptoms . . . and Causes." Book review. *Irish Literary Supplement* (Fall 1982): 40.

"Leabhair: The North." Book review. *ACIS (American Committee on Irish Studies) Newsletter*. Vol. 13 (September 1982): 10.

"Furthering Mitford's Analysis." *The Nation*. Vol. 235: 18 (November 27, 1982): 2.

"Good News!" *UU World* (December 15, 1982): 5.

"Political Criminality." Book review. *The Annals of the American Academy of Political and Social Science*. Vol. 464 (November 1982): 232–33.

"Darwinism and Cocaine." *World Press Review*. Vol. 30: 3 (March 1983): 4.

"Passing the Time with Style." Book review. *Irish Literary Supplement*. Vol. 2: 1 (1983): 33.

"History of British Empirical Sociology." Book review. *Humanity and Society*. Vol. 7: 2 (May 1983): 209–11.

"Abraham Went Out." Book review. *Humanity and Society*. Vol. 7: 2 (May 1983): 211–12.

"Minorities and the Military." Book review. *The Annals of the American Academy of Political and Social Science*. Vol. 467 (May 1983): 240–41.

"Terrorism's Social-Historical Contexts in Northern Ireland." *Research in Social Movements, Conflicts and Change*. Vol. 5 (1983): 99–131.

"Breaking Bread." Book review. *The Churchman*. Vol. 197: 5 (June–July 1983): 17.

"Some Things Remembered." Book review. *The Churchman*. Vol. 197: 6 (August–September 1983): 18.

Chairperson. "Committee on Permanent Organization Report." *SSSP Newsletter*. Vol. 14: 3 (1983): 6.

Terrorism in Northern Ireland (Bayside, N.Y.: General Hall, Inc., 1983). 2 editions: paperback and hard cover.

Chairperson, Permanent Organization Committee, SSSP. "Report: Public Affairs Liaison Proposal." *SSSP Newsletter*. Vol. 14: 3 (1983): 22.

"Britain's 'Revival.'" *World Press*. Vol. 30: 10 (October 1983): 2.

"In Praise of Bagdikian." *In These Times.* Vol. 7: 40 (October 26–November 1, 1983): 10.

"Guilt and Gratitude." Book review. *The Annals of the American Academy of Political and Social Science.* Vol. 470 (November 1983): 200–01.

"Riumanizzare le science sociali." *La Critica Sociologica.* Vol. 66 (April–June 1983): 10–18.

with Elizabeth Briant Lee. "Clarence Marsh Case (1874–1946)." *The Humanist Sociologist.* Vol. 9: 1 (January 1984): 7–8.

"Why Is Ireland's War the 'Longest War'?" Book review. *The Churchman.* Vol. 198: 3 (March 1984): 17.

"The Media Monopoly." Book review. *Contemporary Sociology.* Vol. 13: 2 (March 1984): 173–75.

"Rouge." *In These Times* (March 21–27, 1984): 15.

"The Politics of Utopia." Book review. *The Annals of the American Academy of Political and Social Science.* Vol. 473 (May 1984): 226–27.

"50 Years in the Sociological Enterprise." Book review. *Humanity and Society.* Vol. 8: 4 (May 1984): 215–16.

"State Terrorism." Book review. *The Churchman.* Vol. 198: 5 (June–July 1984): 18.

"A Better World: The Great Schism." Book review. *The Annals of the American Academy of Political and Social Science.* Vol. 474 (July 1984): 180–81.

"English Propaganda." *In These Times.* Vol. 8: 31 (August 8–21, 1984): 15.

"More Than the Troubles." Book review. *The Churchman.* Vol. 198: 6 (August–September 1984): 18.

"Lively Art," *The Quill.* Vol. 72: 8 (September 1984): 6.

"Mosley's Men." Book review. *The Churchman.* Vol. 197: 7 (October 1984): 18.

"Overcoming Barriers to Clinical Sociology." *Clinical Sociology Review.* Vol. 2 (1984): 42–50.

"The Other Side of the Coin." *In These Times.* Vol. 9: 1 (November 7–13, 1984): 10.

"The Uncivil Wars: Ireland Today." Book review. *The Churchman.* Vol. 197: 8 (November 1984): 18.

with Elizabeth Briant Lee. "Propaganda: The Tricks of the Trade." G. J. DiRenzo. *Sociological Perspectives. 2nd ed.* (Lexington, Massachusetts, 1984): 376.

"Ireland: The Key to the British Revolution." Book review. *The Churchman.* Vol. 199: 1 (January 1985): 18.

"Some Haunting Social Problems." *SSSP Newsletter.* Vol. 16: 2 (Winter 1985): 2–3.

with Elizabeth Briant Lee. "A Home for the Ethical Humanist." *Friends Journal.* Vol. 31: 2 (February 1, 1985): 21.

"Interdisciplinary Approaches to Identity." Book review. *Anthropology and Humanism Quarterly.* Vol. 10: 1 (February 1985): 20–21.

with Elizabeth Briant Lee. "Two Sociologists in Search of Action." B. B. Hess, E. W. Markson, and P. J. Stein. *Sociology. 2nd ed.* (New York: Macmillan Co., 1985): 20.

"Foreword." *Cultural Politics: Radical Movements in Modern History.* Jerold M. Starr, ed. (New York: Praeger, 1985): v–ix.

"Common Sense and Middle-class Sense." Book review. *Irish Literary Supplement* (Spring 1985): 8.

"Agents of Power." Book review. *The Churchman.* Vol. 199: 4 (April 1985): 19.

"Review Article." Book review. *Humanity and Society.* Vol. 9: 2 (May 1985): 211–13.

"Spraying Is Dangerous." *Madison (N.J.) Eagle* (May 16, 1985): 2.

"The Press Enlists in Britain's Irish War." Book review. *New York Guardian* (June 5, 1985): 20.

with Elizabeth Briant Lee. "Melting Pot Discriminates." *Friends Journal.* Vol. 31: 10 (June 1/15, 1985): 19.

"White Collar Politics." Book review. *The Churchman.* Vol. 199: 5 (June–July, 1985): 19.

"What the American Bar Association Was Told in London." Irish Heritage Week: 1985 (Clifton, N.J.: Irish American Unity Conference, New Jersey Branch, 1985): 19–20.

"In Search of a Revolutionary Class." Book review. *Guardian* (October 2, 1985): 9.

with Elizabeth Briant Lee. "Some Thoughts on SSSP's Mission." *SSSP Newsletter*. Vol. 17: 1 (Fall 1985): 9–12.

"Conflict in Northern Ireland." Book review. *The Churchman*. Vol. 199: 8 (December–January 1985–86): 19.

"Nonviolent Militant Volunteerism: The Viable Alternative in Social Action." *Wisconsin Sociologist*. Vol. 22: 4 (Fall, 1985): 120–23.

with Elizabeth Briant Lee. "Propaganda Analysis in 1937–42—And Now?" *Quarterly Review of Doublespeak*. Vol. 12: 2 (January 1986): 2–4.

"Contrasting Roles of Privacy." Book review. *Anthropology and Humanism Quarterly*. Vol. 11: 1 (February 1986): 20–21.

"The Startling Facts and Thoughts of George Seldes." Book review. *The Churchman*. Vol. 200: 2 (February–March 1986): 11.

"Introduction: Sociology, Humanist and Scientific." *Readings in Humanist Sociology*. Walda Katz Fishman and C. G. Benello, eds. (Bayside, N.Y.: General Hall, 1986): 9–23.

with Elizabeth Briant Lee. "Seven Kinds of Propaganda." Maxine Hairston. *Contemporary Composition: Short Edition* (Boston: Houghton Mifflin, 1986): 384.

"What Ever Happened to 'Propaganda Analysis'?" *Humanity and Society*. Vol. 10: 1 (February 1986): 11–24.

"Ireland: A Positive Proposal." Book review. *The Churchman*. Vol. 200: 2 (February–March, 1986): 19.

"Born to Trouble: One Hundred Years of Huckleberry Finn." Book review. *The Churchman*. Vol. 200: 3 (April–May, 1986): 19.

"Framing or Measuring?" *In These Times*. Vol. 10: 25 (May 21–27, 1986): 15.

"An End to Silence." Book review. *The Churchman*. Vol. 200: 4 (June–July, 1986): 19.

"Easy Enemies." *The Progressive*. Vol. 50: 7 (July 1986): 6.

"A Left Perspective." Book review. *Irish Literary Supplement* (Fall 1986): 40.

"Ethnic Groups in Conflict." Book review. *The Annals of the American*

Academy of Political and Social Science. Vol. 493 (September 1986): 232–33.

"The Modern Crisis." Book review. *The Churchman.* Vol. 200: 6 (October 1986): 19.

"The Campus Troublemakers: Academic Women in Protest." Book review. *The Churchman.* Vol. 200: 5 (August–September 1986): 19.

"Agents of Power." Book review. *The Churchman.* Vol. 200: 8 (December 1986): 19.

Sociology for Whom? Rev. ed. (Syracuse: Syracuse University Press, 1986).

"Depression, War, SPSSI, and SSSP." *Journal of Social Issues.* Vol. 42: 4 (1986): 61–69.

with Elizabeth Briant Lee. "Propaganda Techniques." Ian Robertson. *Sociology. 3rd ed.* (New York: Worth Publishers, 1987): 551.

"In Memorium: Jerome Davis (1891–1979)." *Humanity and Society.* Vol. 11: 1 (February 1987): 131–35.

with Elizabeth Briant Lee. "Teaching Humanist Sociology: An Introduction." *The Humanist Sociology Resource Book.* Martin D. Schartz, ed. (Washington: ASA Teaching Resources Center, 1987): 1–4.

"Education: Side-Tracked by Public Relations?" *The Churchman.* Vol. 201: 2 (February 1987): 15.

"No Ivory Tower." Book review. *The Churchman.* Vol. 201: 3 (March 1987): 19.

"The Frenzy of Renown: Fame and Its History." Book review. *The Churchman.* Vol. 201: 4 (April–May 1987): 19.

"Privacy in a Public Society." Book review. *The Churchman.* Vol. 201: 4 (April–May 1987): 19.

with Elizabeth Briant Lee. "Differing Views." *Madison (N.J.) Eagle* (April 29, 1987): 2.

"Association of Humanist Sociology." *The Churchman.* Vol. 201: 5 (June–July 1987): 3.

"Less Than Honorable." *The Progressive.* Vol. 51: 7 (July 1987): 5–6.

"George Seldes: Author Synonymous With Truth." Book review. *The Churchman.* Vol. 201: 6 (August–September 1987): 11–12.

"Mass Media." Book review. *The Churchman.* Vol. 201: 6 (August–September 1987): 19.

with Elizabeth Briant Lee. "Propaganda: The Tricks of the Trade." G. J. DiRenzo. *Sociological Perspectives.* 3rd ed. (Lexington, MA: Ginn Press, 1987): 388.

with Elizabeth Briant Lee. Letter. *Fellowship.* Vol. 53: 7–8 (July–August 1987): 29.

"Crime." *In These Times* (August 19–September 1, 1987): 15.

"Tear Down the Walls." *The Progressive.* Vol. 51: 9 (September 1987): 5.

"Relevant 'Clinical' Observations." Book review. *Irish Literary Supplement.* Vol. 6: 6 (Fall 1987): 26.

"Violence in Northern Ireland." Book review. *The Churchman.* Vol. 201: 7 (October 1987): 19.

"Reader's Corner." *Friends Committee for Black Concerns News.* Vol. 1: 2 (Fall–Winter 1987): 4.

"Comparison of High Schools." *Science.* Vol. 238 (October 16, 1987): 261.

"Signal Through the Flames." Book review. *Humanity and Society.* Vol. 11: 3 (August 1987): 209–13.

"The Catholic People." Book review. *The Churchman.* Vol. 201: 8 (November 1987): 19.

Sociology for People: Toward a Caring Profession. (Syracuse University Press, 1988).

"Playing Monopoly with the 'Free' Press." *In These Times.* Vol. 12: 8 (January 13–19, 1988): 19.

"It's Not All Stuffy." *The Quill.* Vol. 76: 1 (January 1988): 31–32.

"Religion Is the Opinion of the Masses." *Psychology Today.* Vol. 22: 2 (February 1988): 7.

with Elizabeth Briant Lee. "The Continuing Values of SSSP." *SSSP Newsletter.* Vol. 19: 1 (Winter 1988): 4–5.

"Hidden Dimensions of Inequality." *Monthly Review.* Vol. 39: 9 (February 1988): 45–46.

with Elizabeth Briant Lee. "Developing a Humanist Perspective."

Studi e Ricerche: Omaggio a Franco Ferrarotti. Roberto Cipriani and M. I. Macioti, eds. (Roma, Italia: SIARES, 1988): 295–304.

"Northern Ireland's Educational Dilemma." *Studi e Ricerche: Omaggio a Franco Ferrarotti.* Roberto Cipriani and M. I. Macioti, eds. (Rama Italia' Stares, 1988): 425–32.

"The ASA's Humanism." *Humanity and Society.* Vol. 12: 1 (February 1988): 67–74.

"The Other Side of East Side." *New Jersey Reporter.* Vol. 17: 8 (March 1988): 5.

"Drug Lords." *In These Times.* Vol. 12: 20 (April 13–19, 1988): 15.

"Belfast Diary of John Conroy." Book review. *The Churchman.* Vol. 202: 3 (May–June 1988): 19.

"A Response to Dusky Lee Smith and Larry T. Reynolds . . . William Graham Sumner as an Anti-Imperialist." *Humanity and Society.* Vol. 12: 2 (May 1988): 204–06.

"Willard 'Pete' Waller (1899–1945)." *Humanity and Society.* Vol. 12: 2 (May 1988): 155–59.

"Belfast Diary: War as a Way of Life." Book review. *Fellowship.* Vol. 54: 6 (June 1988): 28.

"Dropouts React to Irrelevance." *New Jersey Reporter.* Vol. 18: 2 (June 1988): 5–6.

"Justice and Unity: Ireland's Unfinished Agenda." Book review. *The Churchman.* Vol. 202: 4 (July–August 1988): 19.

"Bloody Ireland." *Columbia Journalism Review* (July–August 1988): 80.

"Steps Taken Toward Liberating Sociologists." *Critical Sociology.* Vol. 15: 2 (1988): 47–59.

"A Useful Kind of IRE." *SSSP Newsletter.* Vol. 19: 2 (Summer 1988): 16, 18.

"Intellectual Discourse." *The Churchman.* Vol. 202: 5 (September–October 1988): 9.

"Karl Marx: Socialism as Secular Theology." Book review. *The Human Quest.* Vol. 202: 5 (September–October 1988): 24.

"Separate and Unequal Education." Book review. *Irish Literary Supplement.* Vol. 7: 2 (Fall 1988): 54.

"Effective Public Relations." Book review. *The Human Quest*. Vol. 202: 6 (November–December 1988): 19.

"Intellectual Discourse." *The Human Sociologist*. Vol. 13: 4 (Fall 1988): 6.

Letter to editor about W. G. Sumner's radicalism. *The Humanist Sociologist*. Vol. 13: 4 (Fall 1988): 5.

with Elizabeth Briant Lee. "An Influential Ghost: The Institute for Propaganda Analysis 1936–1942." *Propaganda Review* 3 (Winter 1988): 10–14.

"What About Our 'Public Relations'?" *The Humanist Sociologist*. Vol. 14: 1 (Winter 1988): 17–18.

"Human Rights and U.S. Foreign Policy." Book review. *Humanity and Society*. Vol. 12: 4 (November 1988): 400–01.

"Beyond Malice: The Media's Years of Reckoning." Book review. *The Human Quest*. Vol. 203: 1 (January–February 1989): 19.

"On the Funny Side of Life." Book review. *Anthropology and Humanism Quarterly*. Vol. 14: 1 (February 1989): 36–37.

"British Fountainhead." *The Progressive*. Vol. 53: 2 (February 1989): 5.

"A Call to Read the Original Sorokin and Sumner." *ASA Footnotes*. Vol. 17: 3 (March 1989): 6.

"The Convergence of Science and Humanistic Intervention: Practioners in the Sociological Struggles." *Sociological Practice*. Vol. 7 (1989): 65–71.

"Aborton Rights and Fetal 'Personhood." Book review. *The Humanist*. Vol. 49: 3 (May–June 1989): 41–42.

"J-School Problems Are College-Wide." *The Quill*. Vol. 77: 5 (May 1989): 4, 6.

"More on Coleman." *ASA Footnotes*. Vol. 17: 5 (May 1989): 7–8.

"Northern Ireland: A Comparative Analysis." Book review. *Contemporary Sociology*. Vol. 18: 3 (May 1989): 348–49.

Interview with Nancy M. Whitney, on tape. Oakmont Carnegie Library, Oakmont, PA (June 14, 1989). 60 minutes.

"On Bended Knee: The Press and the Reagan Presidency." Book review. *The Human Quest*. Vol. 203: 4 (July–August, 1989): 19.

"Manufacturing Consent: The Political Economy of the Mass Media." Book review. *Peace Review*. Vol. 1: 3 (Summer 1989): 44–45.

"Propaganda and Persuasion." *Propaganda Review* 5 (Summer 1989): 42.

with Elizabeth Briant Lee. "Humanist Challenges to Sociologists." *SSSP Newsletter*. Vol. 20: 2 (Summer 1989): 2–5.

"Nationalist Revolutionaries in Ireland 1838–1928." Book review. *The Annals of the American Academy of Political and Social Science*. Vol. 503 (May 1989): 162–63.

Letter. *American Sociologist*. Vol. 20: 2 (Summer 1989): 204.

"The 'Uncensored War.'" Book review. *The Human Quest*. Vol. 203: 6 (November–December 1989): 20.

"Northern Ireland Human Rights Report." Report review. *The Human Quest*. Vol. 204: 2 (March–April 1990): 19.

Communication. *The Humanist Sociologist* (Winter 1989–90): inside front cover.

with Elizabeth Briant Lee. "Humanist Challenges to Sociologists." *The Humanist Sociologist* (Winter, 1989–90): 28–30. Reprinted from *SSSP Newsletter*, 1989.

"Abraham Maslow: Humanist, Psychologist, Teacher." Book review. *The Human Quest*. Vol. 204: 1 (January–February 1990): 11.

"Social Science in Court." Book review. *The Humanist*. Vol. 50: 1 (January–February 1990): 45.

"Doublespeak." Book review. *Peace Review*. Vol. 2: 1 (Winter 1990): 56–57.

"Doublespeak." Book review. *The California Psychologist* (March 1990): 15.

"Our Terror and Theirs." Book review. *Irish Literary Supplement*. Vol. 9: 1 (Spring 1990): 30.

"American Protestants for Truth About Ireland." Report review. *The Humanist*. Vol. 50: 3 (May–June 1990): 45, 50.

"Crimes of Obedience." Book review. *The Annals of the American Academy of Political and Social Science*. Vol. 508 (March 1990): 216–17.

"Propaganda and Persuasion." Book review. *SPSSI Newsletter* 181 (April 1990): 10–11.

"Manufacturing Consent." Book review. *SPSSI Newsletter* 181 (April 1990): 10.

"The Culture of Terrorism." Book review. *The Human Quest*. Vol. 204: 3 (May–June 1990): 20.

with E. B. Lee. "Struggles toward Equality and Justice." Presentation at the Annual Meetings of the Society for the Study of Social Problems (August 1991).

"Steps Taken toward Liberating Sociologists." *Radical Sociologists and the Movement: Experiences, Lessons, and Legacies*. Martin Oppenheimer, Martin J. Murray, and Rhonda F. Levine, eds. (Philadelphia: Temple University Press, 1991): 28–42.

Index